# COMRADES COME RALLY

Manchester communists in the 1930s and 1940s

# Comrades Come Rally
Manchester communists in the 1930s and 1940s

by Michael Crowley

*Comrades Come Rally*
*Manchester communists in the 1930s and 1940s*
by Michael Crowley

First edition published by Bookmarks in 2022
© Bookmarks Publications Ltd
c/o 1 Bloomsbury Street, London WC1B 3QE
bookmarksbookshop.co.uk

ISBN 978-1-914143-53-3 paperback
ISBN 978-1-914143-54-0 Kindle
ISBN 978-1-914143-55-7 epub
ISBN 978-1-914143-56-4 pdf

Typeset by Kev Kiernan for Bookmarks Publications
Cover design by Ben Windsor
Printed by Halstan & Co, Amersham, England

# Contents

| | |
|---|---|
| Preface | 9 |
| Introduction | 23 |
| Biographical notes to 1949 | 35 |
| Chapter 1: Dirty Old Town | 43 |
| Chapter 2: Blackshirts and Anti-Blackshirts | 55 |
| Chapter 3: Beacon | 75 |
| Chapter 4: Brittle Republic | 87 |
| Chapter 5: From the Irwell to the Ebro | 95 |
| Chapter 6: Diaries and Dispatches | 117 |
| Chapter 7: San Pedro to Salford | 139 |
| Chapter 8: Aid for Spain | 153 |
| Chapter 9: Imperialist War in Theory | 169 |
| Chapter 10: Imperialist War in Practice | 183 |
| Chapter 11: Barbarossa Begins | 197 |
| Chapter 12: Production Drive | 205 |
| Chapter 13: Second Front Now | 217 |
| Chapter 14: Factory Fortresses | 233 |
| Chapter 15: Labour Landslide | 255 |
| Chapter 16: Jewish Comrades | 271 |
| Chapter 17: Culture Front | 291 |
| Chapter 18: The Remains of Those Days | 315 |
| Biographical notes post-1949 | 319 |
| Bibliography | 325 |
| Endnotes | 331 |
| Index | 357 |

**Note on text**
The grammar, spelling and phrasing of all quotes from other manuscripts and publications are as per the original.

**Note on images**
Every effort has been made to identify the source of all images used, permission sought and credited to the best of existing knowledge, and published in good faith.

**About the author**
Michael Crowley is an author and dramatist who lives in West Yorkshire. You can find out more about his work at michaelcrowley.co.uk

## Acknowledgments

I would like to acknowledge the following. The support and assistance of the staff and volunteers at the Working Class Movement Library in Salford, particularly Lindsey Cole, Alain Kahan and Lynette Cawthra. Also, the People's History Museum in Manchester and Tameside Archives. Mike Wild for information and memories of his father Sam Wild, as well as more general advice on the British Battalion of the International Brigades (IB). Hilary Jones for information on Lily Clyne and Cheetham in the 1930s. Mike Luft for his input on his father Issy Luft and Cheetham YCL. David Mason for information on his grandfather Barnet Maransky. Tony Fox for his assistance and generosity on Cheetham Young Communist League and the IB; Alex Clifford, Alan Warren and Stuart Walsh for assistance on sources regarding the IB. Judy Williams for permission to quote from Randall Swingler. Andy Croft and Richard Baxell for advice on the manuscript. Colm Bryce at Bookmarks for his input and patience, Andy Brown for his forensic suggestions and feedback. Mary Ellen for editorial assistance; Polly Walker as ever, for her relentless support.

# Preface

This book began with a series of interviews I undertook in the early 1990s as the Communist Party in Britain was concluding its 71-year existence. I was interviewing members and former members who were active in the Party during the Second World War, for a post-graduate thesis. The roots of my interest go back further, to my time as an undergraduate in the late 1970s, and a lunchtime meeting of Salford University Socialist Worker Student Organisation. The meeting's subject was the 1926 General Strike and the speaker was an elderly man called Eddie Frow, a contemporary of the strike who had joined the Communist Party in 1924. He was an engineer and though engineers were not called upon to strike, he had walked out regardless and was sacked for it: the first of many victimisations during his working life.

During the talk he recalled sharing a platform with labour movement leader Tom Mann (born 1856). I knew Mann had been an organiser of a mass movement that unionised unskilled workers in the 1880s, that he had worked alongside Eleanor Marx, and may well have met her father. I resolved to shake the hand of history and introduce myself. Eddie was immediately interested in my studies, what I was reading, in what I wanted to know. He was instantly recognisable as someone with a thirst for knowledge and a stronger appetite than most academics for passing it on. At the time I was working on an undergraduate thesis on *The Irish Immigrant and the British Labour Movement*. He said he had a few books at home that I might find useful and invited me to visit.

Eddie and Ruth Frow's house in Stretford was essentially a library in which they permitted some small space for themselves. Where there weren't bookcases there were framed posters and trade union banners on the wall. The front garden had a caravan with books in it. Eddie showed me to a table where some texts were waiting and then went out to do some shopping, leaving me alone in the house. The trust or faith he showed me demanded I took labour history seriously from that moment on. Five years later the collection was moved into Jubilee House opposite the university to become the Working Class Movement Library, Eddie and Ruth moving in with the books and archive materials to a flat upstairs. Eddie Frow embodied working class history, and though there was no one quite like him, there were others in Manchester at that time who had battled alongside him.

He introduced me to old comrades who had fought the Blackshirts, fought Franco's army and then Hitler's. Others who had performed agitprop theatre with Ewan MacColl on picket lines, or who had served as shop stewards in munitions factories. It seemed like an oversight that their stories had not already been serialised on television or radio, that such lived history was being entrusted to a cassette recorder. Many in their 70s and 80s were still politically active, and did not view themselves as former anything. Benny Rothman, born in 1911, who had led the Kinder Scout mass trespass in 1932, had been on an access to the countryside demonstration in the Forest of Bowland the week before I interviewed him. Margaret Gadian told me she'd been walking Prestwich High Street recently with an old friend and comrade Max Druck, when someone had shouted across the road, "Maxie Druck! Are you still a communist?" "What else is there to be?" replied Max.

When I finished the thesis, I put the cassettes away. Thirty years later I listened to the interviews again whilst digitising them. The people were gone, but their voices were the bones of a publication and Eddie and Ruth's inestimable library remains; the many interviews they had conducted, unpublished memoirs, diaries, trade union and Communist Party branch records and much else. There are also other archives in Greater Manchester and online as well. What follows is a history, not just about the Communist Party but about individuals in a particular city, who did not all think alike, but all during the most important two decades of the last century were drawn into the Communist Party in Britain, often because of events elsewhere.

The 1930s were a crossroads for Europe and beyond, mapped out on the streets and in the factories of Manchester. Communism presented itself to some as the only viable alternative to fascism which was fast gaining ground on the continent. Social democrats, they argued, could not be trusted to hold the line against fascism, evidenced by the Chamberlain government's attempt to appease Hitler. Whatever we have learned about the failures and crimes of communism since then should not lead us to judge, in hindsight, those many thousands of mainly working-class people who joined the Party at that time. They had lived through the Wall Street Crash and the Depression and were faced with capitalism's rough beast marching through Berlin, Vienna, Rome and Madrid. If we had been in their midst, they would have reasonably asked us, *what else is there to be?*

*Comrades Come Rally*

"We look on past ages with condescension, as a mere preparation for us... but what if we're only an after-glow of them?"
***JG Farrell - The Siege of Krishnapur***

*Comrades Come Rally*

for Jane Passalaqua

~

in memory of
Ruth and Eddie Frow

*Comrades Come Rally*

# Chronology

| | |
|---|---|
| **Aug 1920** | Communist Party of Great Britain (CPGB) formed. Membership recorded as 5,125. In 1943 it was renamed the Communist Party |
| **Oct 1929** | Wall Street Crash. Great Depression lasts from 1929 to 1933 |
| **May 1930** | CPGB membership recorded as 2,860 |
| **Apr 1931** | Spanish monarchy overthrown and Second Republic born |
| **Sep 1931** | Means Test introduced. Battle of Bexley Square, Salford |
| **Jan 1933** | Adolf Hitler becomes chancellor of Germany |
| **Mar 1933** | German Reichstag passes Enabling Act, granting chancellor power to make and enforce laws without Reichstag involvement |
| **1935** | Communist MP Willie Gallacher elected in West Fife, Scotland. Benito Mussolini invades Ethiopia. Anti-fascist Challenge Club opens in Cheetham, Manchester |
| **Feb 1936** | Popular Front, broad left-wing coalition, wins majority in Spanish parliament. CPGB membership reported as 7,000 |
| **Mar 1936** | German soldiers march into Rhineland |

*Comrades Come Rally*

| | |
|---|---|
| **Jul 1936** | General Francisco Franco broadcasts manifesto. Nationalist rebellion begins in Spain |
| **Aug 1936** | First of three Soviet show trials. Stalin's purges begin the following year |
| **Oct 1936** | First International Brigades volunteers arrive in Albacete, Spain |
| **Sep 1938** | Britain and France appease Hitler by signing Munich Pact, granting him control of Czech Sudetenland |
| **Mar 1939** | Madrid falls to Francisco Franco's forces |
| **1 Apr 1939** | Spanish Civil War ends with Nationalist victory |
| **Sep 1939** | Germany invades Poland. Britain declares war on Germany |
| **Sep 1939** | Working in concert with Hitler, Stalin orders invasion of Poland, securing share of territory |
| **Sep '39-May '40** | The 'Phoney War' |
| **Jan 1940** | CPGB membership 19,605 |
| **10 May 1940** | Hitler launches blitzkrieg against Holland and Belgium. Both countries occupied |
| **13 May 1940** | Chamberlain resigns. Churchill becomes Prime Minister |
| **26 May 1940** | Dunkirk evacuation: Operation Dynamo |
| **22 Jun 1940** | France signs armistice with Germany |
| **Dec 1940** | Heavy bombing of Manchester |
| **10 Jul-31 Oct '40** | Battle of Britain, RAF defeat Luftwaffe. Hitler postpones planned invasion of Britain |
| **22 June 1941** | Hitler attacks Russia: Operation Barbarossa |

*Chronology*

| | |
|---|---|
| **7 Dec 1941** | Attack on Pearl Harbour. US enters war |
| **Aug '42-Feb '43** | Battle of Stalingrad, two million casualties. Decisive defeat of German army |
| **Dec 1943** | CPGB membership recorded as 55,138 |
| **6 Jun 1944** | D-Day landings at Normandy |
| **Apr 1945** | Red Army reaches Berlin |
| **8 May 1945** | VE Day |
| **5 Jul 1945** | Churchill loses general election, two CPGB MPs elected |
| **Jul '45-Oct '51** | Labour government of Clement Attlee. NHS created. Bank of England, coal, electricity, cable and wireless, rail, road, gas, iron and steel industry all nationalised. National Insurance Act introduces welfare state |
| **6/9 Aug 1945** | Two nuclear weapons detonated over Japanese cities of Hiroshima and Nagasaki |
| **1946-1947** | Severe winter across Europe. Snow drifts in UK followed by flooding; fuel crisis. Famine in Berlin, public disorder in Holland |
| **Mar 1947** | President Truman declares US intention of containing Soviet expansion in Eastern Europe. Beginning of Cold War |
| **Jun 1948** | London and Liverpool dockers strike; troops used to break strike |
| **Feb 1950** | General election fought largely on issue of rationing. Conservative Party campaign on manifesto of ending rationing. Labour argued for continuation. Labour was returned, its majority reduced to five |

*Comrades Come Rally*

# Abbreviations

| | |
|---|---|
| **AEU** | Amalgamated Engineering Union |
| **CEDA** | Spanish Confederation of Autonomous Rights (alliance of right-wing parties) |
| **CNT** | Confederación Nacional del Trabajo (National Federation of Labour: anarchist trade union in Spain) |
| **CPGB** | Communist Party Great Britain. With ending of Comintern in 1943 it became Communist Party (CP) |
| **EEF** | Engineering Employers' Federation |
| **FSU** | Friends of Soviet Union |
| **JPC** | Joint Production Committee |
| **LBC** | Left Book Club |
| **MAP** | Ministry of Aircraft Production |
| **NEC** | National executive committee of Labour Party |
| **NKVD** | People's Commissariat for Internal Affairs. Soviet Union's interior ministry, responsible for security |
| **NUWM** | National Unemployed Workers Movement |
| **PCE** | Communist Party of Spain |
| **SS** | Schutzstaffel: foremost paramilitary organisation responsible for terror within Germany and German-occupied Europe |
| **TGWU** | Transport and General Workers Union |
| **UGT** | Unión General de Trabajadores (General Union of Workers, aligned with Spanish Socialist Party) |
| **WCML** | Working Class Movement Library |
| **YCL** | Young Communist League |

*Comrades Come Rally*

# Introduction

> "In their memories, this word [communism] is far more than simply a political label, a programme or a form of organization. It is a kind of constant perspective in which the notion of another possibility is embedded."
> Alain Brossat, *Revolutionary Yiddishland*

The Communist Party of Great Britain (CPGB) was founded at a 'unity conference' of 160 revolutionaries at London's Cannon Street Hotel in July 1920. For the most part, it was an amalgamation of smaller Marxist parties, chiefly the British Socialist Party and the Socialist Labour Party. Individuals in the Independent Labour Party (ILP) also joined at this time, but the organisation as a whole was not permitted to affiliate being "so entangled in reformism".[1] It must have been a difficult decision because the ILP had a membership of 35,000, whereas the CPGB began life with a membership of only 5,125. Seventy one years later, in November 1991, 213 delegates attended a conference at the TUC's Congress House, just over a mile away from where the Cannon Street Hotel once stood. The purpose of the meeting was to wind up the affairs of the Communist Party, which at that time possessed fewer members than it had when it started. Communism in Britain never succeeded in achieving the profile in national politics that it did elsewhere in Europe.

Before Mussolini outlawed it in 1926, the Italian Communist Party had 1.7 million members, and by the end of 1945, French Communist Party (PCF) membership stood at half a million. In the National Assembly elections of October 1945, the PCF became the single largest party with 26 percent of the vote and 159 seats. The 1930s and 1940s were also the British Party's years of peak recruitment; in December 1943, its membership reached 55,138. It also elected two MPs to Westminster: Willie Gallacher, representing West Fife from 1935 to 1950, and

Phil Piratin, representing Stepney from 1945-1950. It never controlled any local authorities, though it had the allegiance of small communities referred to as a 'little Moscow', in South Wales, Clydeside, the East End of London and Gateshead. The reach of the Party far exceeded its membership, for it possessed a dedicated, schooled and often talented cadre who were adept at political intervention and grassroots leadership. It was highly influential in the trade union movement from the shop floor to the head office, with the National Government soliciting its support for the production drive during the war. The Party also initiated and led many campaigns, particularly anti-fascism and anti-racism movements and it intervened in the arts. It was, at times, a force to be reckoned with.

This book traverses the heydays of British communism when it swam with the prevailing current among the British working class, admittedly with a different destination in mind. Its setting is Manchester, a source of radical thinking from the early 1800s onwards. The city was a centre for women's suffrage, the co-operative movement, the Chartists and the Anti-Corn Law League. The inaugural meeting of the Trades Union Congress was held at the city's Mechanics Institute in 1868. It was also fertile terrain for communists until the end of the Second World War, particularly in the city's Jewish quarter in the 1930s, and the engineering industry from rearmament onwards. Manchester provided hundreds of volunteers for the Spanish Republic during the civil war; in Harry Pollitt, it provided the Party's most successful General Secretary.

Thousands of its shop floor and community activists provided much of the city's leadership in working-class politics during tumultuous times. In each chapter, contemporaries describe and interpret events, their accounts retrieved from interviews, published or unpublished memoirs and other primary sources. Their names will be unfamiliar to most readers, for they were Mancunian activists rather than national figures. The reader should be mindful that in a lot of cases interviewees are recalling events that occurred 50 years prior, also that the purpose of the publication is largely to present their perspective, their memory of what happened, rather than a balanced account.

In the British Party's formative years, it was an engineer from Manchester, JT Murphy, who acted as an intermediary between Lenin and British communists. Murphy became an influential member of the Comintern, shorthand for Communist

*Introduction*

International, an organisation launched by Lenin in 1919 to coordinate communist parties across the globe to "struggle by all available means, including armed force, for the overthrow of the international bourgeoisie and the creation of an international Soviet republic..."[2] The Comintern was under the authority of the Russian Communist Party until it was closed down in 1943 by Stalin, reluctant to alienate his newfound wartime allies in the West. It was automatically assumed that since Russia had successfully conducted the world's first workers' revolution, it should direct parties elsewhere, a premise that was to come with a heavy price in the years that followed. In return, the Soviet Union helped finance its comrades overseas, Lenin providing at least £55,000 to help launch the CPGB. Soviet money also bought the Party its head offices in King Street, Covent Garden, an asset that would save the organisation from bankruptcy 50 years later. Murphy travelled to Moscow in early 1920, an illegal and arduous enterprise involving many days' journey across freezing seas between Norway and Russia. He described what the Russians expected of their foreign comrades:

> We had got to learn that a communist party was the general staff of a class marching to civil war, that it had to be disciplined, a party organised on military lines, ready for every emergency, an election, a strike, an insurrection.[3]

Becoming a communist meant becoming a combatant and having a relationship, arguably a subordinate one, with the USSR—the socialist sixth of the globe. This remained the case throughout the Party's 71 years. Throughout the 1920s and most of the 1930s, the CPGB maintained that a communist party should consist of revolutionary cadre and not be open to all workers; inactive members were expelled. This position changed when the Comintern embraced the popular front strategy in 1935: a broad alliance of the Left to stem the rise of fascism.

In 1928 the Soviet-led Comintern predicted widespread economic collapse and mass working-class revolt. Proletarian revolution would be possible, but only if all communist parties served as vanguard organisations, winning the working class away from the futility of reformism. This perspective was defined as a Third Period in capitalism, when communists should be hostile to any co-operation with social democrats who, because they asked workers to put their faith in the reform of capitalism, were considered little better than fascists. Thus, the Labour Party in Britain were described as 'social fascists', and the Communist Party's strategy, known as Third Period Stalinism, was a 'class against class' struggle. Stalin and Ernst Thälmann, the leader of the German Communist Party (KPD), developed the policy and ensured it was imposed on communist parties everywhere.

The move coincided with Stalin's crushing of the Left Opposition inside the Russian Communist Party, beginning with the removal of Trotsky and Kamenev from the central committee. It was, in fact, the British Party's key figure in Moscow, Mancunian JT Murphy, who proposed the expulsion of Trotsky from the executive of the Comintern in 1927. In 1929, Salford engineer Eddie Frow was part of a British delegation to Moscow criticised for failing to apply the Comintern line, particularly in the regions. They were instructed to do better. Ruth Frow recalls how it affected his day-to-day practice:

> It was the start of the class against class period and it was felt that the influence of the Communist International had not penetrated the lower party organisations... Eddie accepted the criticism and carried out the policy of independent leadership which often led to his being sectarian and even stupidly rude to his fellow workers. It was an attitude that in retrospect, he regarded as harmful and negative.[4]

Trade unions were the most critical arena of Party agitation. The class against class strategy resulted in the CPGB attempting to establish new, more radical unions under their control, operating in parallel to existing unions. Thus, they gave up a degree of influence to establish 'Red unions'. Ted Ainley was born in Manchester in 1903. He and his brothers, Ben and David, were involved with the Party from its earliest days, and Ben was a member of the Lancashire District Committee. He describes the impact of the class against class politics.

> The 1929 change in line gave rise to tremendous discussion. By this time branches had been formed across Lancashire; in Burnley, Oldham, Accrington, Bury, Liverpool, Barnoldswick and elsewhere. The YCL [Young Communist League] demanded a special district-wide meeting and JT Murphy was sent down. It decimated the

> Party. It was the policy of class against class. In 1930 the area of Manchester could hold an aggregate meeting at the Bird in Hand pub. There would be 20 at a Saturday night aggregate. The Party in Liverpool dropped to bits.[5]

According to Ben Ainley, JT Murphy vowed to "scour the district to secure the election of a district committee of completely united people".[6] Despite the context of mass unemployment, the class against class strategy resulted in a decline in national membership, from 9,000 in January 1927 to 2,711 in February 1931.[7]

After the rise of Adolf Hitler in Germany, the strategy was dropped as the Comintern switched to the policy of the popular front. This policy argued that as fascism was now the main danger to the workers' movement, communists needed to ally with all anti-fascist forces, including right-wing democratic parties. In Britain, to combat the threat of fascism, the CPGB allied itself with the Labour Party and even with forces to the right of Labour. The result was that national membership rose to 18,000 at the end of 1938. Numbers continued to grow until the end of the war and the election of the Attlee government. The CPGB briefly established a mass membership and the *Daily Worker* a mass circulation. Employers' organisations, the TUC and the government took notice. In Manchester, workplace groups became factory branches. By 1943, in the larger engineering factories such as Faireys and Metro-Vicks, there were hundreds of Party members, most of whom did not see themselves as revolutionaries and who would not stay as members for long.

What drew people to communism altered during the two decades, what it meant to be a Party member also, though it always entailed a degree of sacrifice. At a fundamental level, one was hardly likely to progress in a society one wanted to overthrow. Victimisation was a more likely prospect; indeed, it was an expectation of those who joined in the 1920s and 1930s, and some comrades didn't work between the General Strike and rearmament in the late 1930s. David Ainley, born in 1909, joined the Party's youth organisation, the Young Communist League (YCL), in 1923.

> As soon as the slump came, the shop stewards were blacklisted as were the active trade unionists. There were men who never worked again in the industry.[8]

A few years later, David became the Manchester area secretary of the Party, a full-time position. "As a full-timer, you were practically starving. We didn't have money for bus fare. We'd have to walk everywhere." Margaret Gadian was married to wartime Manchester full-time organiser, Sol Gadian.

> At one time, my husband was district organiser for Lancashire. He never drew the dole. He was paid the princely sum of six pound ten shillings a week. It was meant to be the average industrial wage; it was nowhere near it. It was very difficult to manage. I scarcely ever saw him at night. He did the administrative work during the day; at night he was speaking at meetings. He would travel as far as Liverpool, Burnley, all over Lancashire. We didn't have a car, didn't even have a bicycle. And you more or less had to collect your own wages. If the membership didn't pay their dues, their monthly stamp, you went without wages. We were lucky. We had friends who would bring us luxuries like fruit and cake. Otherwise, you were on a bare subsistence. We had friends who had children, just older than ours who could give us clothes.[9]

Blacklisting of communists was routine. Margaret was informed by a Manchester's Education Committee member that she wouldn't be given work as a teacher and that she was "being watched". Bessie Wild (née Berry), recalls a comrade in the Hulme branch who was a policeman. His name was Wilf Harris, and he was on duty during an unemployment demonstration in the city in October 1931. The police ordered the fire brigade to turn their hoses on the marchers.

> Suddenly all his working-class feelings welled up. He went straight across to Manchester Town Hall and handed in his notice. And he was unemployed until 1939. No one would give him a job.[10]

In industry, an employers' organisation, the Economic League, kept a record of militants that resulted in comrades such as Eddie Frow being unemployed for years.[11] Keeping communists out of work had an impact, not just on Party members; it also worked as a warning to workers who were sympathetic to their ideas. Compared to the general population, up to the Second World War at least, communists were more likely to be unemployed, a feature common across Europe.

For leading members, there was an added risk of arrest and imprisonment. In 1925, 12 principal members of the Party were arrested and charged with violating the Mutiny Act of 1797. Five went to prison for 12 months, the other seven for six months. It meant that the central leadership of the Party was behind bars during the General Strike. Two and a half thousand people were arrested during the strike, several hundred of them communists. Eddie Frow was sent to jail for leading a demonstration in Salford against the Means Test in 1931 and five Manchester comrades were imprisoned for leading the Kinder Trespass in 1932. These were days before community sentences; you were fined or jailed. David Ainley was sent to jail for the weekend for a picket line offence during a textile workers' strike whilst Evelyn Taylor was jailed for disrupting Mosley's Manchester rally at Belle Vue.

Fighting the Blackshirts risked serious injury since opponents were often equipped with knuckledusters and a cosh. The Jewish Lads' club in Cheetham, Manchester, ran a boxing club, and many of those that fought the British Union of Fascists (BUF) on the streets went on to fight in Spain for the International Brigades (IB). Around 130 men from Greater Manchester volunteered for the Comintern initiative, the majority of the volunteers being members of the Party. They went on the understanding it was highly possible that they wouldn't be returning. Thirty-eight were killed, many of the rest were wounded, some more than once.[12] It seems an incredible step to have taken. The generation that fought in Spain were children or adolescents during the First World War. Their formative years included the Easter Rising in Dublin, the Russian Revolution, the war between Red and White armies, the creation of an Irish Republic, the Spartacist revolt in Germany, the first Labour government in 1924 and the General Strike of 1926. They were looking for work during the Wall Street Crash, the Great Depression and the rise of fascism. Communists maintained that the Russian Revolution had created a new kind of civilisation, whilst fascists foretold the end of civilisation unless democracy, Bolshevism and its disciples, the Jews, were destroyed. It was not surprising that people turned to communism and that so many of them were Jewish.

Many communists demonstrated courage, but there was more than personal commitment at play. When individuals joined the Party, they became part of an international struggle with a collective memory that supported a common goal. Anthony Crosland and other commentators have compared Marxism with a form of religious faith that provided "the emotional need for a God, a religion... for something to believe in transcending the individual".[13] But becoming a revolutionary was not typically a moment of rebirth; instead, the gradual adoption of a new world view was arrived at through literature, discourses, practice and most of all, life experience. Communist tradition drew from a well that went back to the Levellers of the English Civil War and before. There was a lot of history to take in and slightly less economics. Recruits took to it readily; it was an alternative to the staple fare of popular culture, and many were already dogged readers. In interviews and memoirs, authors such as Jack London and HG Wells are repeatedly cited as influential. Frances Dean joined the YCL before the war as a teenager:

> There was nothing else to do but read. I read everything in sight. My father was Labour. He thought that if Labour got a working majority, everything would change. We used to take the *Daily Herald*.[14]

Alongside the *Daily Worker*, *Labour Monthly* and *Russia Today*, there were Party pamphlets on contemporary issues. Branch meetings were not merely for business, but included guest speakers on current topics, and there were also weekly Marxism classes for theory. Ted Ainley, who was a teacher, ran courses in the Challenge Club in Cheetham. In 1929 Ted was chosen to attend the Lenin School in Moscow for the best part of a year. The school was founded in 1926 to teach hand-picked representatives from international communist parties in the art of Bolshevism. Students learned economics and history, Marxist theory, strategy and tactics employed by the world communist movement. There was a British version at the unlikely location of Oxted in Surrey. Joe Norman, a former engineer from Salford, was a student there in 1936:

> I studied political economy, how to debate, how to plan a speech. All useful stuff. Agitation. After six months there I came back and did some political meetings around Lancashire. I became a *Daily Worker* organiser in Wigan, but I wasn't happy. I wanted to go to Spain.[15]

*Introduction*

Although Marxism can be messianic, Party objectives remained concrete: an end to the Means Test; tinned milk for Spain, the second front in Europe; a Labour government. Such demands were held in tandem with the idea, the belief, that a revolution in Britain was possible, if not inevitable. Eric Jessop was a shop steward at Fairey Aviation in Stockport:

> This fella on the next bench said to me, he'd taken out a 25-year mortgage. I laughed at him and said, 'What a waste of time, there'll be a revolution before then.'[16]

If members sacrificed social mobility, they acquired an intellectual one which was historical and international in perspective, creating a barrier between themselves and non-comrades. People tended to marry inside the Party, particularly the more active members. Margaret Gadian:

> It was impossible to be a Party organiser's wife if you weren't committed. The commitment was always difficult. I remember the victory celebrations in 1945. We lived in a very small house and the leader of the Malayan Communist Party came to stay with us. He was over for the victory celebrations and he was speaking at a meeting in Manchester. It was an eye-opener. He was very lean. A young man. He obviously lived on not much. I asked him if he was married, out of politeness. He said 'no'. He said in Malaya and the Far East parties you could only marry someone who was considered the right sort of person, another comrade, because you were always having to go underground and having to live on so little. You couldn't marry anybody. And I thought we were disciplined.[17]

Women made up a relatively small proportion of Party membership, particularly during these two decades. In October 1934, only 15 percent of the membership was female. Manchester had a better record than other areas with women making up 25 percent of the membership in March 1938, possibly helped by their presence in textile workplaces. By the end of the Second World War, the Party as a whole had caught up with Manchester, but it was a far lower figure compared to the Labour Party which between 1933 and 1945 had a female membership of over 40 percent. The CPGB concentrated on industrial work. Working women were difficult to recruit because they weren't present in large numbers. Work as a housewife was the biggest single occupation of women members between the wars, and many would have had communist husbands.[18]

Being a public communist was the first threshold every comrade was required to cross, on the streets and at work (with notable exceptions). In the 1930s, in Manchester, the *Daily Worker* was sold in Piccadilly Gardens, on Market Street, but chiefly on Oldham Street. Bessie Wild:

> We'd shout, 'The workers' only daily newspaper!' or 'The people's anti-fascist paper!' We sold from 3pm and we drove the fascists off who sold *Action*. There were times when 1,000 copies of the paper were sold on a Saturday in town.[19]

Lives were lived inside the Party's walls, the organisation's hierarchy being more vital to some than anything at work or in wider society. At the height of recruitment during the war, Manchester, one of seven areas in the Lancashire district, had 13 branches. It was led by an area committee that included George Brown, Mick Jenkins, Maurice Levine, and Audrey Ainley. Area committee members were generally not full-time posts. That committee answered to the Party full-timers on the Lancashire District Committee, which answered to the Central Committee. The decisions of the higher bodies were binding on lower bodies and, like anywhere else, new comrades were expected to serve their time before they had their say.

The chapters ahead progress chronologically towards the peaks and out the other side. The Spanish Civil War gets six chapters for it was an event that took the lives of many Manchester communists, and one that usually merits a publication in its own right. Two of the few diaries by British Battalion members in existence from that war are by Manchester volunteers: Ralph Cantor and Maurice Levine, and excerpts are included in *Diaries and Dispatches*. The Second World War is also afforded six chapters, in part to chart the Party's growing influence on the shop floor, in part to navigate its political aerobics. The Jewish contribution is inherent throughout, but the relationship between Jews and Communism is such that it is examined in its own chapter.

*Introduction*

Cultural work was also political work and the subject could supply many more chapters than the one I've provided. Although the Party in Manchester did not produce many notable cultural figures beyond Ewan MacColl, writers and Party members such as Stephen Spender, John Cornford and Randall Swingler were widely read and nationally significant and justify a mention. If we want to know how the Party grew, we should also ask why it didn't grow further and what is its legacy from those years. The rationale for the comrades included is largely down to source material: they had been interviewed by myself or someone else or had left behind memoirs. Such individuals tended to be key activists. Manchester produced many and not all could be included because too large a cast can easily become unruly for the reader.

British communists of the period are stereotyped in drama and fiction and to a degree by historians. The hotline to Moscow makes them fair game. But was the Party as monolithic as it is portrayed to be? Mike Luft, whose father Issy Luft was a leading member of the Cheetham branch, believes that regardless of the views of the area, district or central committees, the branch as a whole would have been opposed to the Party's lack of support for the war effort between 1939 and 1941. The Cheetham branch was arguably the most critical geographical branch in the city, providing the most militant anti-Blackshirt activists, numerous International Brigade volunteers, and leading area comrades such as Mick Jenkins, the Ainley brothers and Benny Rothman.

It is also true that comrades were uninterested in delving into the gulags and millions of dead from collectivisation and Stalin's purges. Sam Wild's son Mike remarked that whenever he asked his father questions about Soviet human rights violations, his father told him it was Trotskyist propaganda. Whilst Sam's generation aspired to lead a revolution, and were prepared to give their lives for it, those I met presented as relatively self-effacing. A vanguard they were, but they did not believe this made them superior to other workers. They knew leadership had to be earned. If they were guilty of anything, it was imagining that other workers would be prepared to make the kind of sacrifices they did. Most of us are not so self-sacrificing, committed or resilient.

*Comrades Come Rally*

# Biographical notes to 1949

## Ben Ainley (Abrahamson)
Ben was born in 1901 in Ancoats to immigrant parents, the eldest of seven children. His father was a walking-stick and umbrella polisher, his mother ran a newsagent's shop. He attended his grandfather's cheder (a primary school where Hebrew and Judaism are taught) in Hightown, Cheetham, and then a Jewish secondary school. He joined the CPGB in 1922 and became a teacher in 1924. Ben became secretary of the Manchester branch in 1924 and was a member of the district secretariat for 20 years. During the 1930s, he taught classes in Marxism at Cheetham Challenge Club and was a leading Left Book Club activist in Manchester.

## David Ainley
The youngest of the three brothers, born in 1907. Their father died in 1921 when David was 14. He was influenced by Ben to join the YCL in 1923 and the CPGB in 1925. He was branch secretary of the YCL in Openshaw, elected onto the YCL District Committee in 1924 aged 16, the National Executive Committee in 1925. In 1929 David attended the Lenin School in Moscow and became a full-time worker for the YCL and editor of the *Young Worker*; became Lancashire organiser of the *Daily Worker* in 1937.

## Ted Ainley
Brother of Ben and David, born in 1903, he worked in waterproof clothing and was a union activist and founding member of Manchester YCL formed in 1922. In 1923 he joined CPGB and became full-time organiser for the North East and Glasgow. In 1929, he attended the Lenin School in Moscow. Between 1933 and 1934 Ted worked in a left-wing bookshop in Manchester and then returned to the waterproof clothing industry.

## Frank Allaun
Frank was born in 1913, growing up in Didsbury. His father was a hat manufacturer. Frank attended Manchester Grammar School, then trained as a chartered accountant but went on to work in Collets left-wing bookshop. He became secretary of Manchester Anti-War Council and a trade unionist, visiting Russia in 1935, returning to join Wythenshawe branch of the CPGB. He became branch propaganda secretary and was involved in anti-fascist activity. Frank was for a time North West regional organiser of the YCL. He remained a member of the CPGB until 1944 when he joined the Labour Party.

## Clem (Clement) Beckett
Born in Oldham in 1906, Clem began riding a motorcycle aged 14. On leaving school he became a blacksmith's apprentice, joined the Blacksmiths' Union and then the YCL aged 18 in 1924. He also spent some time in the Territorial Army. He became a speedway rider known as 'Dare Devil Beckett' partly because of his speed and because he regularly rode the 'wall of death' at Belle Vue gardens. He was suspended from riding for a time for writing articles for the *Daily Worker* exposing the exploitation of riders and went on to form a trade union for riders called the Dirt-track Riders Association. He and Arnold Jeans were the first volunteers from Manchester to arrive in Spain in 1936. He was killed at the Battle of Jarama in February 1937.

## Ralph Cantor (Cantorovitch)
Born in 1916 in Cheetham to Lithuanian and Polish parents, Ralph attended Waterloo Road School and the Jewish Lads Brigade (JLB). After attending the Sheffield Youth Congress against War and Fascism in 1934, he joined the YCL. He played the cornet for JLB and then in a band at Cheetham's Challenge Club. Amongst the first to go to fight in Spain in November 1936, he was killed in July 1937 at the Battle of Brunete.

## Wilf Charles
Wilf was brought up in Moss Side, the eldest of six children, their father working as a cobbler. Wilf left school in 1929 and worked in textiles, joining the Party just prior to the outbreak of the Second World War. During the war he was secretary of the Moss Side branch and was a CPGB delegate to the first Pan African Congress held in Chorlton Town Hall in 1948.

## Jud Colman

Born in Cheetham in 1915 to immigrant parents, his father a wood worker, Jud was the middle of seven surviving children. He attended a cheder and the local Jewish secondary, and on leaving at 14 he entered the clothing trade and was involved in the Jewish Lads Club. He became interested in politics through work and reading, joining Cheetham YCL in 1932 or 1933. By 1936, when his mother had died and his father had left home, Jud volunteered for the International Brigade. He became a member of the CPGB after the Second World War.

## Frances Dean

Born in 1917, Frances joined the Labour League of Youth in 1938 but quickly gravitated towards the Young Communist League and then the Communist Party in 1941. Frances was a shop steward at Fairey Aviation, campaigning for equal pay for women workers. She was secretary of the Communist Party factory branch during the war.

## Vic Eddisford

Born in 1925, Vic obtained a trade apprenticeship at Metro-Vicks in 1940, starting in the meter department. He became a representative on the apprentice committee and joined the Party in 1943 aged 18. He formed a YCL branch in the factory becoming a full-time YCL Secretary for Lancashire and Cheshire District in 1949.

## Eddie Frow

Edmund Frow was born in Lincolnshire in 1906 and joined the Party in 1924. In subsequent years he came to occupy numerous positions of responsibility, both in the CPGB and the Amalgamated Engineering Union (AEU). In the late 1920s he served as one of four district representatives on a Comintern commission called to assess the position of the British Party. On his return from Moscow, Eddie took an active part in the National Unemployed Workers Movement. In 1941 he was elected to the Divisional Committee of the AEU and then to the National Committee in 1942.

## Margaret Gadian

Margaret joined the central Manchester branch before the war. She trained as a teacher but was prevented from working as one until the Soviet Union joined the Allies against Germany. During the war her husband, Sol Gadian, was Lancashire District Organiser and a member of the District Secretariat.

## Benny Goldman

Benny was born in Strangeways, Manchester, in 1914. He worked as a carpenter and upholsterer and was a trade union activist. He joined the YCL in the early 1930s, becoming the Lancashire organiser. Benny volunteered to fight in Spain in January 1937, his mother dying in the same year. He was recruited to look out for deserters or fifth columnists in the battalion and undertake propaganda. He became a Company Political Commissar and was twice wounded. Benny was repatriated to England in November 1938 and was a member of a tank regiment during the Second World War.

## Mick Jenkins

Born in 1906 in Hightown to immigrant parents, Mick was the eldest of eight children. Mick's father was a cap maker and a socialist and his son sold caps on Manchester markets. Mick left school at 13 to work in a clothing factory, joining the YCL in 1923 and the CPGB in 1925. He acted as a courier for the CPGB during the General Strike, and worked among the miners in the Lancashire coalfields. By the late 1920s Mick was holding meetings of the Cheetham branch of the YCL from his parents' parlour, their house becoming known as the 'Bolshevik House'. In 1929 Mick visited the Soviet Union for seven months as part of the International Group of youth attending the Lenin School. On returning to Manchester in March 1930 he became Lancashire organiser of the YCL and a member of the District Secretariat. He was active in anti-fascist campaigns and in the building of the International Brigade. During the war he led the Communist Party branch at Fairey Aviation, arguably the most successful factory branch in the country.

## Eric Jessop

Eric was in the Cheetham branch, joining the Party in 1932. He was also at one point a member of the National Committee of the YCL. At the beginning of the war Eric was a firefighter but was dismissed along with several others for attempting to unionise the workforce. He then went to Fairey Aviation and became a shop steward and a key member of the factory branch.

## Maurice Levine

Born in 1907 in Cheetham to Lithuanian parents, Maurice was at the younger end of eleven children. His father was a tailor's presser then a scotch draper. Maurice attended a cheder before leaving school at 14, finding work in a clothing factory. He emigrated to Australia for work in 1928-1931, joining the CPGB on his return. He was soon elected onto the local CPGB Committee. He took part in the Manchester to Preston Hunger March in 1931 and participated in the mass trespass of Kinder Scout in 1932 and anti-fascist activity the years after. He volunteered for the IB in October 1936 and served in the Second World War. After the war he went back into the clothing trade and remained active in the CPGB until 1960 when he suffered ill health. Maurice remained a lifelong Marxist.

## Albert Maskey

Born Barnett Masanskey in Vilnius, Lithuania, in 1893, he was arrested by Tsarist police and convicted for radical activities between 1907 and 1912. On release he went into exile in Germany and then London, where he joined the British Socialist Party in 1919. He then moved to Cheetham, Manchester, and ran a barber's shop used by the CPGB for meetings in the early 1920s until he lost the shop in a card game. Imprisoned in Brixton in 1924, he was thereafter harassed by the Manchester police and Special Branch. Active in the National Unemployed Workers' Movement, he went on to volunteer to fight in Spain in December 1936. He was killed at the Battle of Jarama in February 1937.

## Bernard McKenna

Bernard was born in 1916, a seventh child, the first to survive infancy. For most of his childhood his father was unemployed, his mother a cleaner. He was the first boy from his school, St Wilfrid's, Chorlton, to win a scholarship to St Gregory's Grammar School in Ardwick. At 14 he became a textile-mill clerk, joining the Labour League of Youth and then, at 17, the YCL. He went to Spain in 1937 without telling his family, trained as a signals operator and was wounded on the first day of the Battle of Brunete, July 1937. Bernard was wounded a second time on the Aragon Front and also suffered from shell shock after prolonged artillery bombardment. He recovered to continue fighting and was captured and imprisoned at San Pedro de Cardeña. He was repatriated and joined the RAF the day after war was declared on Germany. He spent six and a half years in North Africa, the Middle East and Italy. After the war he became a teacher.

## Joe Norman

Joe Norman was born in Hulme, Manchester in 1908. He served an engineering apprenticeship at Metro-Vicks, but was laid off on completion at 21. He joined the Party in the early 1930s, attending the English Lenin School in Surrey. He became chair of the Salford branch of the Unemployed Workers Movement and went to Spain in December 1936 where he was elected Party organiser for the British Battalion. He was captured and imprisoned at San Pedro de Cardeña where he was a member of the camp committee. He was an RAF volunteer reserve during the Second World War.

## Benny Rothman

Born in 1911 in Hightown, Cheetham to Romanian parents, Benny was the middle child of five children. His parents were market traders. Benny attended a cheder, then Manchester Central School but was allowed to leave early to help support his family. He began work in a garage and was then made redundant in 1931. Benny went rambling with others and was introduced to the YCL. He became active in growing the British Workers Sports Federation in the north and instrumental in organising the mass trespass of Kinder Scout on 24 April 1932. He helped establish the YCL Challenge Club and was involved in anti-fascist activities. He went into engineering and became a key shop steward at Metro-Vicks in Trafford Park.

## Hugh Scanlon

Hugh was born in Australia in 1914. He began an apprenticeship as an instrument maker at Metro-Vicks in 1927. At the age of 21 he was elected onto Urmston AEU branch committee, and at 24 he became a shop steward at Metro-Vicks. By the age of 30 he was a full-time official of the union. He joined the CPGB in 1937 and left in 1953. He was a leading member of the Metro-Vicks factory branch and in 1947 was elected to his first full-time union post, as AEU divisional organiser in Manchester.

## Victor Shammah

Victor was born in 1914 to Syrian parents from Aleppo, one of six children. The family lived in Didsbury and were orthodox

Sephardi Jews. His father was a cotton merchant who lost his investments in the Wall Street Crash and died in 1932 when Victor was 18. Victor attended Hebrew classes at a synagogue then Manchester Grammar School. He was a clerk and an avid reader and founded a YCL group which met in the family home in Burton Road, Didsbury. Victor's siblings, Esther and Vera, were also members. He volunteered for Spain where he worked as battalion secretary to the Brigade Political Commissar and helped to publish the *Volunteer for Liberty* journal. Victor was killed in action on the Aragon front in March 1938.

## Henry Suss

Henry Suss was born in Strangeways, Manchester in 1915 to Jewish émigré parents. His father, a peddler, was from Austria, his mother from Poland, and they had ten children in all. Henry spent his working life in the garment trade, joining the Cheetham branch of the Party in the 1930s. He was involved in anti-Blackshirt activity and the Aid for Spain movement. He worked with Ewan MacColl and Joan Littlewood in Theatre of Action, performing in a number of productions.

## Evelyn Taylor

Evelyn was born in 1913. She joined the Communist Party in 1931. A year later she was on the mass trespass at Kinder Scout. Evelyn worked in a number of engineering factories in Manchester. She was fired from Ferguson and Pailin for union activity but a strike by the Brass and Metal Mechanics Union secured her reinstatement. In early 1936 Evelyn went to Moscow to work for the Comintern, carrying messages and material aid to the clandestine communist parties and anti-fascist organisations of Germany, Hungary, Czechoslovakia and Italy. Returning to Manchester she married local Party organiser George Brown who was killed in action in Spain. In 1938 she married Jack Jones, future TGWU general secretary, who also served in Spain. During the war she worked in aero-engine production in Coventry and became shop steward then secretary of a union branch with 2,000 members.

## Bessie Wild (née Berry)

Born in 1911 in Moss Side to Elizabeth Berry, Bessie did not know her father. She attended Sale High School for Girls on a scholarship but was unable to attend university as she had to help bring up her cousins whose parents had died at a young age. From 1933-36 she was employed as departmental secretary to Professor HJ Fleure at Manchester University. In 1934, Fleure paid for Bessie to take a six-week trip to the USSR. She joined the Hulme branch of the CPGB on her return. In 1935 she went cycling in Germany to observe the impact of Nazism. Soon after, aged 24, she became Honorary Secretary of Manchester German Relief Committee, supporting families of Jews and socialists in prison and concentration camps, and raising funds for the 'underground railways' that brought others to safety. Bessie was active in the anti-Blackshirt and Aid for Spain movements and met Sam Wild on his return from Spain, marrying him in April 1939. From time to time, Bessie and Sam housed a number of homeless IB veterans.

## Sam Wild

Sam Wild was born in Ardwick, Manchester in 1908. He left school at 14 and joined the navy at 15. In 1932 he deserted whilst in South Africa, was arrested, and returned to Britain to be discharged. He left for Spain in December 1936 with Bert Masky, who was courting Sam's elder sister, Hilda, at the time. He was promoted to British Battalion Commander on 17 March 1938, then to Major on 17 October 1938. He was wounded on four occasions and awarded the Spanish Medal of Valour, the equivalent of Britain's Victoria Cross. He led the British Battalion home to Victoria station on 7 December 1938 and is among the most renowned volunteers from Britain, becoming a member of the Communist Party of Spain (PCE) before joining the Communist Party of Great Britain. He was forbidden from serving during the Second World War and worked as a steel erector. He became president of the International Brigades Association, raising money for wounded veterans and the families of those killed in action.

# Chapter 1

## Dirty Old Town

> "The houses remain: streets of them where the blue-grey smoke swirls down like companies of ghosts from a million squat chimneys: jungles of tiny houses cramped and huddled together, the cradles of generations of the future." Walter Greenwood, *Love on the Dole*

*Salford, Sep 1931*
Sixteen-year-old Jimmie Miller is making his way along a main road. Dawn has revealed the gloom of a low sky. A half-sky. The shadowed side streets, even the main street is quiet. The boy recalls when by this time of the morning there was a clatter, a convoy of men, spilling into the road, making their way into conversations, hurrying themselves towards another day's work. Not now. Fewer chimneys smoke at this hour. He stops at a corner, peers down the side street. The prowling runt of a dog. The gable end is cleaner than most. The Accrington red-brick has lost its colour but it's not coated with soot like some. From his jacket pocket he takes a Reckitt's blue laundry square that he hopes his mother won't miss. Then he chalks on the wall with it, letters half his height. 'All Out Against the Means Test. October 1st'. He crosses the road, looks back at his work and half-smiles. The boy moves on, scrawling on paving stones and walls along the mile and a half to Salford Town Hall. He looks up at the clock, at his bright blue hand. This is where the march will end, if people show up, that is.

He's just joined the Young Communist League. There are only nine in the Salford group but he believes there'll soon be more. He's been unemployed for months, since he was sacked from a garage for fighting, and the meetings help him get through the week. Sixteen and passing time. At the weekend he has the

*Hyndman Hall Sunday School 1913*

moors, and then there is his true passion; other lads tease him for it. Acting. He's part of a street theatre group, half a dozen unemployed friends, who call themselves the Red Megaphones. They're taking agitprop to the workers, just like in Russia. Turn over the apple cart by taking the mick. Their first performance was from the back of a coal lorry on May Day. Sketches and songs. He can sing. His mother and father are Scots and they know songs; his mother is teaching him. His mother. She chars eleven hours a day. Three other children she lost in infancy. He gets his fondness for the stage from her, his politics from his father, a blacklisted union man hobbled by asthma.

He wonders if anything will come of his daubing, if anything will come of his dream to be an actor, a playwright maybe; of making plays to turn the world upside down. He must wait. For a job, for a girl, for manhood, and that won't show up until he has a job. He walks on towards Liverpool Street, to the Labour Exchange where he will tell the men in the queue about the march. He tells himself something will come along, something is bound to begin, soon.

## Crash

Two years before to the week, a London businessman, Charles Hatry, was sent to jail. He'd been convicted of fraud and forgery and sentenced to 14 years, with two of them as hard labour. For the first month he slept on bare boards and his days were spent crushing rocks into stones. It was an experience for which Hatry was unprepared, for his home in Mayfair, near the mansion of the Princess Royal, had a swimming pool which he enjoyed each morning. He had started out as an insurance clerk but by the end of the First World War became the director of

15 companies. During the next ten years a number were scuppered under bankruptcy.

His final venture, before being swallowed by Brixton Prison, was an investment in United Steel Companies, a conglomerate of coalmining, steel and engineering. But a major financial backer pulled out and no bank would loan Hatry the money to make up the shortfall. So, he began to issue fraudulent stocks to cover the loss, until his accountant betrayed him to the Bank of England. The London Stock Exchange suspended all shares of the Hatry group, which amounted to roughly £24 million, precipitating a crash in share prices, which in turn undermined American investment overseas. The scandal and the crisis was one small cog that began turning others in an already overheated financial machine across the Atlantic.

The causes of the Wall Street Crash were numerous and long in the making. From here, the event is viewed as inevitable, as a reckoning for a decade of American excess, of speculation and easy credit. The stock market had enjoyed a nine-year run with average prices rising tenfold. A plateau was expected but it turned out to be a peak and a stream of share dealing became a torrent that the ticker tape machines couldn't keep pace with. All of a sudden people wanted out of the market, stampeding so fast for the door that by 29 October 1929, known as Black Friday, some stocks had absolutely no value whatsoever. The crisis was compounded by the fact that people had borrowed money to buy the stocks in the first place. In fact, more money had been loaned than was available in the entire US currency.

For Britain the crash meant a loss of trade and investment. Unlike America, Britain had not experienced any kind of post-war consumer boom much less a roaring twenties; the markets it had lost during the First World War were never regained and unemployment stalked the north of England before the 1930s. Between the crash and Jimmie Miller's Salford morning, exports from Britain had fallen by another 50 percent and textiles, the cog that turned Lancashire and consequently Manchester, was badly hit. In October 1931 nearly a third of the adult population of Salford was unemployed. Frank Allaun was born in Manchester in 1903. He was a member of the Communist Party from the early 1930s to the end of the war.

> I vividly remember a drab street scene in Gorton, Manchester, an important heavy engineering centre. At

45

one window I saw a 30-year-old man looking after his little son and also doing the family washing...For older men losing one's job meant virtually ending one's life; many had little chance of earning their living again.[22]

The government of the day was led by Ramsay MacDonald's Labour Party which had won the general election of 1929. MacDonald believed in balancing the books and increased unemployment meant more public spending; indeed the unemployed were one of the largest areas of government expenditure. In May 1930 Labour minister Oswald Mosley, considered by some to be a potential Labour leader, proposed a Keynesian solution to mass unemployment. He urged the government to take control of banking and exports, employ people in direct works like road building, and increase pensions to stimulate demand. MacDonald rejected Mosley's memorandum and proposed comprehensive public spending cuts instead. The Labour Party was split and Mosley left. So disparate were the two sides in MacDonald's cabinet, that he went to see the king to offer his resignation, only to be convinced that it was his duty to form a national government rather than walk away. MacDonald formed the first National Government with ministers from the Labour, Liberal and Conservative parties. The majority of the Labour Party refused to support it and expelled those who did, including their own leader, MacDonald, who continued as prime minister under the new banner of National Labour. He set about tackling the deficit and was thereafter branded a traitor by the wider labour movement.

Wage cuts were imposed across the public sector, including the armed forces. For the unemployed there were benefit cuts and the Means Test. A single man's benefit was cut by 16 percent from 18 shillings to 15 shillings and threepence. Means Test assessments were carried out by 'Public Assistance Committees' who scrutinised the finer details of people's meagre assets, earnings and outgoings. It was a degrading and hated intrusion undergone to receive subsistence level dole and as a result of committee enquiries, nationally 852,000 claimants lost benefits.[23] The unemployed though, possessed their own political organisation in the National Unemployed Workers Movement (NUWM). The Communist Party of Great Britain founded the NUWM in 1921, itself having been founded the previous year. The leading figures were Harry

McShane in Scotland and Walter Hannington in England and Wales.[24] It organised local and national demonstrations and hunger marches, challenged the decisions of local and national government on matters of relief for the unemployed. It had a mass membership organised into branches with members paying a subscription of a penny.

In Salford the local branch met weekly in Hyndman Hall, number 69 Liverpool Street. Built in 1876, it was a building with a succession of occupants that speak of political change. It bore a multi-coloured brickwork front of the kind made fashionable by John Ruskin, and it was initially a meeting place for the Crescent Conservative Club. They were replaced in 1904 by the Social Democratic Federation (SDF) who gave the building its name. The SDF was Britain's first socialist party created in 1881 by the writer Henry Hyndman.[25] Virtually all left political groups in Britain ultimately descend from it and among its early members were Tom Mann, William Morris, George Lansbury, James Connolly and Eleanor Marx.

In 1930 the building became home to Salford Workers' Arts Club: "A focal point for social, political and cultural activity in the miller's community."[26] Amongst others the three-storey building hosted Salford Workers' Film Society which attracted attendances of over 400 at screenings. Schedules included experimental cinema such as Vsevolod Pudovkin's *Storm Over Asia* (1928) and Sergei Eisenstein's *Battleship Potemkin* (1925).[27] By 1931 there were around 100 attending weekly NUWM meetings there. The main figure was unemployed toolmaker and branch chair, 25-year-old Eddie Frow.

> The large club room on the ground floor had a large fireplace with a circle of words round it saying 'Workers of the world unite, you have nothing to lose but your chains. You have a world to win!' The first floor was used as a billiard room in which there were two full sized tables. The top floor was used for a socialist Sunday school.[28]

Eddie came from a family of Lincolnshire agricultural workers. As a teenager he was an apprentice engineer in Wakefield. At 17 he began to attend Leeds Labour College; labour colleges existing as provincial extensions of Oxford's Ruskin College. The following year he joined the Communist

Party of Great Britain having already absorbed, among other texts, Lenin's *State and Revolution*, HG Wells's *A Short History of the World*, and Haeckel's *Riddle of the Universe*. In 1930, still only 24, he was sent to Moscow to attend a commission examining the work of the British Party. He would have doubtless become familiar with the conflict between Stalin and the Left Opposition. On return he found work at Fords in Trafford Park and moved to Salford. When he began to recruit the toolroom into the AEU he was sacked for it. Inevitably he found himself blacklisted by the Economic League and became a leading figure in the local NUWM and Communist Party. Eddie saw part of his work as recording and reporting upon the living conditions of the unemployed. In 1929 he and a comrade called at every house on Hankinson Street, Pendleton.

> They found abject poverty. Furniture had been pawned and orange boxes filled the gaps. Food consisted of small quantities of tea, sugar, margarine and a loaf of stale bread mostly obtained on tick from the corner shop. In one group of eight houses, they were told 14 adults and 23 children shared two closets.[29]

Poverty and housing conditions in Salford were amongst the most dire in Britain. In 1931, Manchester and District Survey Society visited 950 houses in St Matthias ward, Salford. Of the 950 houses, 129 had to share a water-closet with at least one other house. Thirty three had no sink, 67 had to use a water tap outside. Over half were deemed to be suffering from insufficient light and ventilation. "Many of the houses were rat infested." At a back-to-back one-up one-down house, a water closet was shared with six other houses.

> The tenant has concreted a large part of the cellar, this is still very damp. He also pays one shilling a week for disinfectant to put down the drains. The only tap is in the cellar... There is no sink: waste water has to be tipped into the street. The house is well kept by the tenant.[30]

Salford NUWM's response to the cuts in unemployment relief was to call a demonstration for 1 October 1931. The assembly point was the waste ground, or 'croft' next to Hyndman Hall; the intention was to march to Salford Town Hall where the council was meeting, to present a list of demands, a charter for the unemployed. It was the local authorities who administered the relief and would have to implement the cuts. Eddie Frow addressed the crowd, firing their enthusiasm and listing the demands: a rejection of all economy proposals; 20 shillings a week and an end to the Means Test; a pint of free milk for the under-fives; and a hundredweight of coal for each household during the winter. The crowd was bigger than expected. The daubing by Jimmie Miller and other members of the Red Megaphones had been augmented by whitewash slogans. A Galloway Scot banged a drum as the march made its way west in the direction of Manchester city centre. Walking alongside Jimmie Miller, ringing a playground bell, was another Red Megaphones performer, Alec Armstrong, "a perfect specimen of early manhood, well-muscled and with the strength of a young lion".[31] Perhaps panicked by the numbers, early on during its route the police threw a cordon across the road, but the demonstrators pressed through it easily. Wilf Gray was at the front.

> We went through them like a knife through soft putty. I remember my head going down as if in a rugby scrum. With the pressure from our comrades behind, we pushed them to one side quite easily.[32]

More people joined the march as it proceeded. By the time it reached Bexley Square and Salford Town Hall, the police estimated it was a thousand strong, the organisers, nearer ten times that number.

Amongst the crowd was a man occasionally writing in a notebook. He was 28 years old, from Pendleton, a mile and a half away. His father had been a barber but had died when he was nine years old. As such, he was allowed to leave school a year early at 13, to get a head start in work to help support his family. There had been a few jobs since school, the last at a pawnbrokers, but like everyone else on the demonstration, he was out of work. Most of his days were spent at Salford library, completing his education for himself. His name was Walter Greenwood and he had hopes of being a writer. He'd had a few short stories published and now a novel, his first, was beginning to take shape in his notebook and his imagination.

The march had trouble squeezing into Bexley Square. It's an insignificant square and there were buildings on three sides. The pressure of numbers hemmed people in; waiting for them were police officers in uniform and in plain clothes, batons drawn. Mounted officers appeared; they charged and the square became the site of a pitched battle. People were shocked by the first advance; doing what they could to avoid baton swings and horses' hooves. But then the fear subsided and people began to fight back. Towards the end of his life, Jimmie Miller, who had long since changed his name to Ewan MacColl, wrote about the event in his memoir, *Journeyman*.

> The first engagement was fierce but the police have tasted blood and are now lashing out at anyone in their path. But we are fighting back and the horses no longer terrify us. Here a mounted cop is pulled from his horse and there a constable is deprived of his baton.[33]

Alec Armstrong continued to ring his bell as if he were signalling the end of playtime. Eddie Frow and the rest of the deputation were seized. Instead of listing the marchers' demands to the council, Eddie was dragged off and beaten.

> I was taken into the town hall where four policemen let fly with their batons. My nose streamed blood and I had to be taken to Salford Royal Hospital. When I returned to the town hall, Major Godfrey, the chief constable, came in to see what had happened to me and I was able to tell him exactly what I thought of the brutality of the police and accuse him of having instigated it.[34]

Twelve demonstrators were put before magistrates. Eddie faced two charges of assault and elected to defend himself. The prosecution accused him of striking an officer with Armstrong's bell. Eddie told the court he had assaulted no one and then made the case for the unemployed. He was sentenced to three months hard labour. These he served in Strangeways in almost complete silence for conversation was forbidden. Like Hatry, he began his sentence sleeping on boards. He left prison undernourished and a more determined revolutionary. Eddie would remain a committed Marxist, a voracious reader and bibliophile all his life. The blows he received that day stayed with him. His wife Ruth Frow: "He occasionally had nose bleeds as well as having his 'fine features' considerably altered." Walter Greenwood's first novel, *Love on the Dole*, was published in 1933. Although it begins in the

General Strike of 1926, the narrative largely takes place in 1931 and it culminates with a demonstration by Salford's unemployed. The story's central characters are the Hardcastle family who live in a fictional part of Salford called Hanky Park, "that district opposite the parish of Pendleton". Walter Greenwood and Eddie Frow knew one another, they shared a calling, a possible escape route through books, though Walter joined the Labour Party rather than the CPGB. The novel's central character is Harry Hardcastle, an unemployed engineer who then loses even his dole through the Means Test. When we get to the demonstration there appears an agitator, stirring the crowd, leading the march.

> A finely featured young man with long hair took his place on the rostrum instantly winning the acclamation of the crowd by heaping invective upon all with whom he disassociated himself in the social scale.[35]

The chapter goes on to portray the point when the march reached the police cordon:

> The column halted: drum and bell were silenced. The organiser stepped forward desirous of an explanation, receiving scant courtesy of the inspector, who, pointing his stick down the road and staring elsewhere than at the man to whom his remarks were addressed, said: 'Keep straight on.' The organiser protested, indignantly. Larry touched him on the arm: 'We'd better do as we're told,' he said: 'It's useless arguing with these men.' The finely featured young man ignored him. With blazing eyes he asked instructions of the demonstrators. Which were they to do, obey the police or follow out their original intention of marching past the Labour Exchange? A new spirit stung the marchers; it was as though they were set on their mettle; faces could be seen assuming expressions of defiant pugnacity.[36]

Just as when Eddie Frow was seized in the square:

> Harry, jostled this way and that, dodging blows, caught a glimpse of the finely featured young man set upon by a couple of constables, knocked down savagely, and frog-marched away by three hefty policemen.[37]

*Love on the Dole* received huge attention and continues to be read world-wide today. It was adapted for stage in 1934 with runs in London, New York and Paris, though *Daily Worker* editor Sean O'Casey wrote a stinging review for the *New Statesman*.[38] There was even a musical version in 1970. It was adapted for film in 1941 after being rejected in the 1930s, deemed by the film industry in the words of playwright Ronald Gow as "too dangerous".[39] In 1949 Ewan MacColl (previously Jimmie Miller) wrote a play, *Landscape with Chimneys*, set in Salford. The play includes the song, *Dirty Old Town*, which was to become a folk standard. The lyrics reputedly describe the view at the time from Hyndman Hall, the waste ground by the gas works on Liverpool Street, the Manchester, Bolton and Bury Canal. Alec Armstrong volunteered for the International Brigades and fought for the Republic during the Spanish Civil War. He was killed in action on the first day of the Battle of Jarama, 12 February 1937, aged 28.

What became known as 'The Battle of Bexley Square' was only one, relatively small confrontation over the cuts and the Means Test in the autumn of 1931. More than twice the number demonstrated the following week in Manchester and had fire hoses turned on them. Maurice Levine was from a Lithuanian Jewish family and had joined the Party earlier in 1931. He was unemployed and, in the summer, he had been on a hunger march from Manchester to Preston. In October, the Manchester demonstration set off from Ardwick Green towards Manchester Town Hall.

> The march was dispersed by the police and a man named Chris Flanagan from Openshaw was arrested and imprisoned. There was a big gulf between the employed and the unemployed then; as the march came towards London Road fire station the firemen were called out to turn their hoses on the marchers. There was a big demonstration outside Strangeways [prison] and I remember going along.[40]

Most of those arrested served their prison sentences alongside Eddie. On the same day as Bexley Square, up to 50,000 demonstrated in Glasgow. Iron railings were torn up by the crowd and used as weapons against the police. Street battles raged until midnight. The previous month a hunger march had set off from Wales to London. Ramsay MacDonald met with NUWM leaders but flatly refused to sit down with its leader, Walter Hannington. To those he did meet he stressed the importance of the country's finances. The same night there was a huge demonstration in Hyde Park. On 12 September 1931 the government had announced to the House of Commons that it would be cutting the pay of naval ratings by a shilling a day. For many men this meant a cut in pay of 23 percent. The measure sparked a naval mutiny on 15 and 16 September at the naval base of Invergordon, on Scotland's east coast. At the time of the mutiny, ten warships of the Atlantic Fleet were moored at Invergordon. The sailors there held meetings in a canteen ashore and voted to refuse orders to set sail for manoeuvres. Instead, they drew up a manifesto which they sent to the Admiralty.

> We the loyal subjects of His Majesty the King, do hereby present to My Lords Commissioners of the Admiralty, our earnest representations to them to revise the drastic cuts in pay that have been inflicted upon the lowest men on the lower deck. It is evident to all concerned that these cuts are a forerunner of tragedy, poverty and immorality, amongst the families of the men of the lower deck. The men are quite willing to accept a cut, which they, the men, think within reason, and unless this is done, we must remain as one unit, refusing to serve under the new rates of pay.[41]

Royal Marines were brought in to suppress the strike. They refused to do so and instead joined the industrial action. Though only lasting a few days, news of the mutiny crossed the world and caused a panic on the London Stock Exchange, resulting in a run on the pound.

Walter Greenwood went on to write 11 more novels as well as plays for stage and screen and non-fiction. He became a Labour councillor for the ward of St Matthias with its notoriously poor housing referenced above. Eddie Frow, as well as remaining a trade union and political activist, became, along with his wife Ruth Frow, an avid collector of radical books and pamphlets. Together they created the Working Class Movement Library that stands today on the edge of Pendleton.

*Comrades Come Rally*

# Chapter 2

## Blackshirts and Anti-Blackshirts

> "People like Benny and my dad, were leading anti-fascists… These were people who wouldn't back off… the fascists got thoroughly beaten in the heart of the Jewish community." Mike Luft (Issy Luft's son)

After Ramsay MacDonald rejected Oswald Mosley's proposed solutions to the economic crisis, Mosley began a restless journey from prominence to notoriety, from radical reformer to would-be antisemitic fascist dictator. It would end in ignominy and imprisonment. In October 1936, Mosley's second marriage to Diana Mitford of the Guinness dynasty took place in the Berlin home of Joseph Goebbels, with Adolf Hitler as the guest of honour. Ten years before, he and his first wife, Cynthia, had been members of the Fabian Society. The Fabian Society is a Labour Party organisation dedicated to advancing socialism employing a gradualist approach. It took its name from the Roman general Fabius Gurges, who avoided fighting the Carthaginian general Hannibal head-on, but attacked his supply lines instead and became known as 'Fabius the Delayer'. In the late 1920s, the economic crisis precipitated by the crash convinced Mosley that action needed to be urgent and wholesale.

### The New Party
Having failed to convince the Labour cabinet, Mosley resigned his ministerial position and laid out his programme before the Labour Party conference in October 1930. His case was that Britain should be run as a corporate state, power centralised to an inner cabinet of five or six ministers with parliament relegated

to a sideshow. Mosley had always been an economic nationalist, opposed to globalisation and laissez-faire economics; free trade he saw as producing sweated labour and low wages. Mosley believed class conflict could be abolished in Britain by nationalising industry and establishing protectionist import controls. Whilst he remained part of respectable politics, his ideas attracted interest from individuals as disparate as Aneurin Bevan and a young Harold Macmillan. The Communist Party, though, even at this stage, recognised that Oswald Mosley held more than fascist sympathies. As he was about to leave the Labour Party, the *Daily Worker* described Mosley as an "English Hitler".

> He is trying to harness to Fascism from the growing disgust among workers and the petty bourgeoisie, with all three parties. We want to organise that disgust into working class action.[42]

In March of 1931, Mosley and six other MPs formed the New Party. The *Daily Worker* commented:

> The policy of the New Party is such a mix of fascism and demagogy that Sir Oswald has not been able to find a name to describe it: its present title is only a stop gap.[43]

On 7 March, the Party's chief theorist R Palme Dutt wrote a *Daily Worker* editorial on the New Party entitled "Mosley and the Labour Party, Hand in Hand Towards Fascism". Soon after, Cynthia Mosley and Oswald Mosley supporter John Strachey, MP launched the New Party in Manchester at the Free Trade Hall. Cheetham Young Communist League activist Benny Rothman and several comrades made their presence felt from the audience.

> We'd been out rambling that day, and a group of us went down to the Free Trade Hall, and I'd come off the moors in my rambling boots. Lady Cynthia Mosley was speaking on the same platform as John Strachey, and we really heckled the buggers, because of some of the statements they were making, because Strachey was talking like he was a socialist and we heckled them until they were driven off the platform. For the first time ever, there was police interference. As soon as the meeting was over, the police rushed in to arrest one or two people. They

made a dive for me and failed. The unfortunate police inspector fell over.[44]

Rambling at the time was a common pursuit amongst Manchester young communists, a route into the Party. Comrades organised walking groups, and there was possibly something intrinsic in the pursuit that drew some towards political struggle. Alec Armstrong from the Battle of Bexley Square was "a rambler and climber of some note", who would go off alone wild camping for days, "trapping rabbits and hares". Ewan MacColl describes the moors as possessing a "spirit of revolt", where "you felt master of your environment".[45] For Benny Rothman, rambling and rights of access were about taking the class struggle into the countryside. He was to lead a celebrated mass trespass on Kinder Scout, Derbyshire, the following year (see Chapter 16, Jewish Comrades). His remark about John Strachey "talking like he was a socialist" is significant. Strachey was a journalist and a Labour MP for Birmingham, Aston. He was sympathetic to Marxism, and by the time he had joined the New Party, he had been to the Soviet Union on two occasions. Mosley had brought his economic programme into the New Party, and the command style economy initially appealed to Strachey and others on the Left. However, by the summer of 1931, Mosley had rejected closer links with the Soviet Union and was becoming openly fascist, at which point Strachey abruptly ended the association. The following year Strachey applied to join the CPGB but was rejected. The episode reveals how initially deceptive proto-fascism was and how, to some degree, it competed with communism on the same terrain amongst those who sought an end to the destructive crises of capitalism. Strachey later became active in anti-fascist campaigns and was reunited with Benny Rothman on a platform a few years later.

> Years afterwards, I was speaking with Strachey when we was on a platform together, and he was back in the bosom of the labour movement. He said, 'I'm sure I've met you before.' I said, 'Yes, when you were in the Free Trade Hall with Cynthia Mosley.' And he didn't like it at all. He had a very sour look on his face.[46]

Elections came upon the New Party during its infancy. On 30 April 1931 it fought a by-election in Ashton Under Lyne, several miles east of Manchester. It polled 16 percent, splitting the anti-Tory vote. To provide authority for the new National Government, MacDonald called the general election he was obliged to do for 27 October 1931. The New Party won no seats, and Mosley and the other MPs who had defected all lost theirs. During the election campaign, Oswald Mosley held a public meeting in Salford's Hyndman Hall, a venue socialists and communists considered their own.

## British Union of Fascists

After his election drubbing, Mosley and several associates went to Italy to observe how Mussolini's National Fascist Party governed and operated as a political organisation. They arrived in Rome on 2 January 1932 and were joined by the writer Christopher Hobhouse, who arrived from Munich. According to Mosley biographer, Stephen Dorril, the Italians treated Mosley with a degree of deference.[47] On 7 January Mosley met Mussolini at the Palazzo Venezia and invited his visitor to stand with him during a fascist parade. From Italy Mosley travelled on to Munich to study Nazism but little is known about his time there. However, he was undoubtedly impressed by National Socialism, particularly by its economic programme, and returned to form the British Union of Fascists (BUF) in 1932. The 32 founding members attended an inaugural ceremony at the former New Party office in Great George Street, Westminster. Lord Rothermere, the proprietor of Associated Newspapers Ltd, which included the *Daily Mail*, telegrammed his support from Monte Carlo. Mosley posed for photographs alongside a black banner with the Italian fasces symbol (a bundle of sticks and an axe bound together) embroidered in silver. It was a chilling spectacle, perhaps, but fascism hadn't yet accrued the connotations it was about to. On the back of BUF membership cards was written 'To win power for Fascism and thereby establish in Great Britain the Corporate State'.

Benito Mussolini was, at that time, popular among Britain's conservatives and aristocrats. He had come to power in October 1922 through a coup d'état. When 30,000 fascist Blackshirts marched on Rome, the prime minister wanted to impose martial law, but King Victor Emmanuel overruled him and asked Mussolini to form a new government. Mussolini, like Mosley, emerged from the left of politics and came to believe in a revolutionary nationalism. Once in power he set about removing all political opposition. Italy became a one-party dictatorship with a police state, but in the eyes of his sympathisers, one that stabilised the economy and provided subsidies for impoverished farmers. For the Right in Britain, he was a dictator to be admired in comparison to the ineffective talking shop of parliamentary democracy.

Whilst Mosley admired Nazism for what he saw as the regeneration of German youth, he saw the Italian model as the way out of Britain's economic troubles. He was, though, always anxious to present his brand of fascism as uniquely British. He envisaged a mass movement above party politics, ruling in the country's interests as a whole, with a corporate and authoritarian state guiding business and protecting workers from the excesses of capitalism. Mosley published a 40,000-word summary of his ideas in *The Greater Britain*. The book sold at 2s. 6d. and 10,000 copies were quickly bought. The *Manchester Guardian* said it was "an extravagant eulogy of the Fascist State (according to Mussolini and Hitler)".[48] Mosley's vision of the corporate state was a totalitarian one: there was to be no room in Britain for those who disagreed with: "all for the State and the State for all".

The BUF actively sought to recruit ex-socialists and those the Left sought to attract. They promised slum clearance, infrastructure developments for transport, greater electricity use, and farms for 100,000 families. Mosley held rallies at the same venues as communists and socialists. Maurice Levine took part in street battles against the Blackshirts in Manchester.

> I went to a big fascist demonstration in the open at Belle Vue. Mosley spoke from the stands where people used to view the firework displays in the winter time. I remember standing next to a fellow with a very pale face. He was a fascist, putting his hand out in a salute every time Mosley said something. I could see he was a working-class bloke and I asked him why he was a fascist. He was a miner from Gresford [North Wales] and he firmly believed that Mosley had the interests of the working classes at heart. Mosley had spoken on Albert Croft at Miles Platting and I went to that meeting too. There were Young Communists heckling but there must have been a lot of people supporting Mosley... Mosley was a brilliant speaker who moulded his style on Mussolini rather than on Hitler.[49]

The BUF was a one-man show, and the showman was a man of charisma. Mosley was 35 when he launched the organisation, six feet four, aristocratic, handsome, athletic: a fencing champion and a war hero. An energetic campaigner and an impressive orator with a powerful intellect, much of the BUF's impact depended on his physical presence as much as its ideas. Between 1932 and 1936, he addressed up to 200 rallies and meetings a year. His performances were crafted and rehearsed and he developed a habit of meeting the eyes of women at the front of his audience. Three months after the BUF was formed, unemployment rose to three million and, in Germany, Hitler became chancellor. In its first 18 months, the BUF grew rapidly to achieve an estimated 40-50,000 members.

Its members were mostly younger men, though older ex-servicemen were attracted to the movement, and 25 percent of the membership were women. The involvement of former soldiers and sailors, as well as their plight, fed fascist parties across Europe. Mussolini's Blackshirts, also known as Squadristi, were an armed paramilitary organisation of war veterans. In Germany, the country most adversely affected by the Depression, ex-soldiers flocked to the Nazis. It was not merely a matter of economics. The German army was conscious it had not been defeated in the field; rather an armistice had been signed, and the Treaty of Versailles imposed upon the nation. Britain emerged from the First World War with Lloyd George promising "homes fit for heroes", but reality failed to meet expectations.[50] Mosley exploited the disillusionment and the feeling of betrayal that was keenly felt across the country. AK Chesterton was a regional journalist and a Shakespearean critic who protested against the treatment of ex-servicemen. He had spent two years on the Western Front and suffered from permanent respiratory problems resulting from a gas attack in the trenches. Like many veterans, he became an alcoholic who endured nervous breakdowns. He joined the BUF and became part of Mosley's inner circle until turning up drunk on every occasion made his participation impossible. Chesterton once wrote that constant nightmares populated by the dead made him see the world as "one vast necropolis". Mosley eventually paid for his colleague to be treated by a neurologist in Germany. Chesterton remained a committed fascist all his life.

Although dubbed the Blackshirts, not all members of the BUF wore the uniform. Like Mussolini, Mosley's uniformed members acted as paramilitary stewards, supposedly a Fascist Defence Force. Initially, they numbered around 300, were paid one pound a week and lived a semi-military life. In 1933 the BUF acquired college premises in Chelsea that could accommodate 5,000. An elite section known as I Squad wore breeches and leather boots, were paid three pounds and were trained to suppress protests from opponents. In addition to the black shirts and trousers, activists wore badges and stripes to denote their rank. The movement's emblem was initially the Italian fasces, the bundle of rods, but in 1936 this was replaced with a blue lightning flash in a circle on a red background, worn as an armband.

Many Blackshirt paramilitaries were otherwise young unemployed men, some no doubt attracted by the prospect of an income. Depression-hit towns in the north, where traditional industries had declined, were fertile territory for the BUF. In 1934, when it was estimated that the BUF had 40,000 members nationally, 5,000 of those were in Lancashire. The figure was to fall to around 1,500 by late 1935 as part of a national decline, but it was similar to Communist Party membership for the county. The decline of textiles provided a favourable environment, with unemployment ravaging cotton towns. In 1931 around 45 percent of the total textile workforce was out of work and production was running at a third below 1914 levels.[51] The BUF held meetings on how the cotton industry's troubles could be solved by economic protectionism, producing several pamphlets on the matter: *Lancashire Betrayed*; *Is Lancashire Doomed?*; *Cotton!*; *Communists and Socialists Exposed*. Lancashire also had an ailing coal industry, but the BUF failed to get an audience from a more tightly knit community and home to socialists and communists. When they tried to book a meeting in a public hall in Wigan, they were refused on the grounds there would be public disorder.[52]

## Manchester

Mosley was particularly keen to establish the BUF in Manchester. The family had a civic connection, being the titled lords of the manor until 1846, with Mosley Street running through the city centre. The BUF expanded rapidly in Greater Manchester and by 1934 had 18 branches in the city and the satellite towns such as Rochdale.[53] After London, Manchester had the most significant degree of fascist and anti-fascist conflict of any city in Britain. This was due to the efforts of the BUF and the resolve of communists, particularly Young Communist League activists from

*Mussolini (left) with Mosley in 1936*

Manchester's Jewish quarter, Cheetham. Mosley's meetings were provocative; his large-scale rallies were dramatic occasions with ambitions to imitate Nazi Party spectacles. He spoke at public meetings across the city: at Churnet Street public hall in Collyhurst, at Hulme and Cheetham town halls, often with significant police protection. He also took to the streets, regularly at Albert Croft in Miles Platting. Bessie Wild (née Berry), was a member of Hulme branch of the CPGB.

> Mosley used to concentrate on the Irish because there were no Jews in Hulme. He had meetings using the slogan 'Get back to Ireland'. But there was terrific resistance. The official line of the Labour Party was 'Ignore them, they'll go away'. We thought not. They'd give an impression of strength but we'd see coaches turning up. Clerks and people like that. We knew for a fact they brought coaches from Lancashire and Yorkshire. Plenty of money… Mosley came to speak at Hulme town hall one night. He gave his speech and there was a lot of heckling. He retired to a clubroom. The crowd decided we weren't going to let him speak. It went on until one thirty in the morning, until somebody got him out of the back door.[54]

Larger rallies took place at the Kings Hall, Belle Vue. Opened in 1910, the Kings Hall was a converted tea room, enlarged in

1928 and reconstructed as a saucer-like arena capable of seating 7,000 people. The BUF's first rally at Belle Vue was in February 1933, a ticket-only event. Anti-fascists in the city decided to hold a simultaneous, alternative meeting at Manchester's Free Trade Hall.

No doubt it was thought that the scale of the opposition inside the Kings Hall from Blackshirt stewards would be overwhelming. Benny Rothman, though, was not convinced of this strategy and decided he would show his opposition at Mosley's rally. He didn't have a ticket but met a like-minded comrade outside who had been refused entry because he was known to the BUF. He gave Benny his ticket and a bag of anti-fascist leaflets.

> The stewards ushered me up the stairs onto the balcony. Below was a sea of faces… I was seated on the end seat of my row and very soon I got into conversation with a tall young steward who seemed to be in charge of that section of the hall. When he saw me in overalls, he told me that he came from Birmingham and that he too worked in engineering. I told him that he was backing an enemy of the trade unions when he informed me that he was a member of the AEU. Shortly afterwards there came a rolling of drums and a blare of trumpets, and preceded by a small army of strong-arm stewards, and followed by another group of stewards with the drum and the trumpet, accompaniment rising to a crescendo, Mosley bounded into the hall and onto the platform to a spot mounted with microphones and of course decorated with a huge Union Jack. Sections of his supporters stood up and became hysterical in their clapping and cheering as Mosley, resplendent in his tailor-made black uniform, melodramatically raised his arm to call for silence. Gradually silence was restored, and Mosley started to speak in a dramatic voice and manner. He had hardly started when an interruption came from a spot in the balcony opposite me. It was a woman's voice which I recognised right away as belonging to Evelyn Taylor.

Evelyn had joined the Party in 1931 and had taken part in the mass trespass on Kinder Scout alongside Benny. Blackshirt women attempted to evict her, but she fought back until a group of male stewards dragged her away. Maurice Levine from Cheetham was also in the hall. "She was on the balcony. I was there. She was thrown out brutally. They didn't differentiate between the sexes."[55] As Mosley began to shout down the microphone to evict other hecklers, Benny decided it was time to act.

> I leaned over the rails and asked the Stockport boys to keep the stewards off me for as long as possible and then stood up on my seat. I took the leaflets from under my overalls and scattered them in a semi-circle in front of me. All the time, I was shouting for the stewards to keep their hands off Evelyn. That of course, only lasted for a few seconds. Blackshirt stewards in the region were literally fighting to get their hands on me, and their feet too. I was knocked to the ground, where I curled up in a tight ball, protecting myself from the blows and kicks. Two or three stewards picked me up off the ground, dragged me to the top of the stairs of the balcony and then pitched me over.[56]

Benny was fortunate, his fall was broken by a steward below him. Maurice Levine recalls how his comrade Wilf Winnock took a bad beating for heckling that evening.

> Wilfie, we called him. He was at the meeting at the Kings Hall, holds about seven thousand. He got up to ask a question. Must have been provocative, you were immediately pounced upon. They carried truncheons. They'd haul you out of your seat, then in the corridor, you ran the gauntlet. He was badly injured and he was a boxer, used to box for the YMCA.[57]

On March 12 1933, Mosley held a meeting at the Free Trade Hall in the city centre. This time anti-fascists did not organise a rival meeting but decided as a body to attend, among them again, Benny Rothman and Evelyn Taylor. Despite the presence of numerous Blackshirt stewards, proceedings had to be abandoned when demonstrators repeatedly heckled, sang the *Internationale* and *The Red Flag*, drowning out Mosley's speech. It was, according to *The Blackshirt*, the first occasion in Britain when anti-fascists had broken up a BUF meeting addressed by

Mosley. Under the heading "The Truth About the Manchester Meeting", Mosley criticised the police for not throwing out the demonstrators and laid responsibility on an inadvertent coalition of the Communist Party and the National Government.

> The meeting at the Free Trade Hall, Manchester, on March 12, marks a new phase in the fascist struggle. For the first time in Britain, the Old Gang Government used police in a manner which created disorder at a fascist meeting. Fascism makes no complaint of any kind against the rank and file of the police. They have to act on instructions given from above. We indict not the police, but the National Government which can command the police.[58]

A *Daily Worker* correspondent travelled up from London to attend and found himself on what he described as a "troop train" of Blackshirts who were to attend the meeting.

> In conversation with one of the fascists I was informed the total number of these uniformed thugs, whose expenses were being paid by Mosley, was about 200.

Of the meeting's premature end, the correspondent wrote: "Mosley gave it up and went off the platform, saying, 'If you won't listen to me, I will go.'"[59] Perhaps Mosley remembered Evelyn from the Kings Hall rally, for he went to the trouble of taking out a private prosecution against her for leading the Free Trade Hall protest. The court fined Evelyn £25; she refused to pay and was sent to prison. It was impossible not to see the BUF in association with the rise of fascism on the continent. Hitler had been made chancellor on 30 January 1933. The *Manchester Guardian*'s report on Mosley's first rally at Belle Vue the following month appeared alongside an article headlined "Growing reports of Nazi terror". Mosley was defined by whom he imitated.

> If the study of demagogic arts can help a man, Sir Oswald Mosley should be irresistible. No pose of Mussolini or Hitler, no trick of floodlighting or the microphone has been missed. So far as outward trappings go, the flattery of imitation has been sincere and zealous.[60]

When Hitler was sworn in as Chancellor, the *Daily Mail*

reported it as "one of the most historic days in the latter-day history of Europe". Stephen Dorril argues that Hitler's appointment fuelled antisemitism in Britain.

> Antisemitic feelings, however, ran high in BUF branches in Hull and Leeds, where walls were plastered with posters. In Manchester, Jews were threatened with violence, shops were painted with the slogan 'Perish the Jews' and a synagogue had swastikas chalked on its walls.[61]

By 1934 Mosley's politics had become vehemently antisemitic. The *Manchester Guardian*'s report on a BUF Belle Vue rally held on 29 September was headlined "Sir Oswald Mosley's Bitter Outbursts against the Jews". Mosley is reported as describing his political opponents as:

> The sweepings of the continental ghetto financed by Jewish financiers...alien gangs brought from the ghettos to Britain by Jewish money.

At one point, he exclaimed: "Look at the mobilisation of Jews from Cheetham Hill Road. Behind those foreign Yiddish faces is foreign Yiddish gold." He developed a refrain of Jews as an enemy within who conspired to betray Britain.

> Are those people who stabbed our men in the back when they were fighting in the trenches in the last war in a British quarrel, going to lead us to war with Germany in a Jewish quarrel?[62]

Manchester chief constable John Maxwell banned marches on the day of the rally, but anti-fascists demonstrated regardless. John Strachey, who two years prior was a leading member of Mosley's New Party, was secretary of the National Antifascist Coordinating Committee and complained to the Home Office about the ban. At a Free Trade Hall meeting on 25 November, Mosley spoke of the "force of international Jewish finance" destroying the cotton industry in Lancashire.

The BUF also engaged in an aggressive, violent campaign on the streets. They held weekly street meetings across Manchester at Stevenson Square, Miles Platting and Platt Fields. The *Manchester Evening News* began to report attacks on Jewish youth, whilst the

BUF set up a headquarters on Northumberland Street just north of Cheetham, renting two large houses. Hilda Cohen grew up in a Jewish family on Northumberland Street and remembers the occasion.

> On the day of the official opening, I went along to witness the event. It was obvious that quite a number of other people like me had come along to witness the event. Like me, they stood on the periphery, watching the supporters as they strode up the drive and mounted a guard on either side of the steps while he performed the opening ceremony. There was an air of disquietude.[63]

Blackshirts would sell their paper outside a local cinema and walk through the area in numbers, confronted by Benny, Maurice and others. Maurice Levine:

> Blackshirts would walk through Strangeways which was a Jewish area. We'd tangle with them. They had boxers with them. Moran, he was heavily scarred. I got near him, he took a swipe at me, I took a swipe at him. They were provocative. They did it almost every night... A favourite café of theirs was Walter's on Great Ducie Street, near Victoria Station. They would walk through Strangeways along Bury New Road to Northumberland Street to provoke the Jewish population. There would often be scuffles with Strangeways' inhabitants, who were very sensitive to the menace of fascism in their midst.[64]

A routine chant was "The Yids...the Yids...We're going to get rid of the Yids". A common insult yelled at locals was "Sheeny", a 19th-century London slur. Verbal encounters often became physical. A notable increase in incidents towards the end of 1934 prompted Chief Constable Maxwell to send a report to the Home Office. He complained that fascists in uniform had a policy of provoking Jews and that since the Belle Vue rally and the Free Trade Hall meeting of September and November, there were routinely four or five incidents of public disorder every week, mainly in the Cheetham area. Significantly, in October 1936, Manchester became the first council in Britain to ban the wearing of political uniforms at public meetings officially.[65]

## Cheetham YCL

The organisation that galvanised opposition to the Blackshirts in Cheetham and elsewhere in Manchester was the Cheetham branch of the Young Communist League. The YCL, the Communist Party's youth organisation, had its own meetings, organisers, paper and regional and national committees. In the 1930s there doesn't seem to have been a fixed age when members automatically progressed to becoming members of the Party, hence there were YCL members well into their twenties. Some never made the transition and ultimately drifted away. Because of its activist nature, turnover was an issue that the Party lived with. Cheetham was the largest YCL branch in the country outside London, East London, to be specific, where the composition was also largely Jewish.[66] Their parents primarily worked in the local sweated trades as pressers, cabinet makers, cap makers, and waterproof garment makers or worked as market traders or in one of the travelling trades. This kind of employment had long working hours, minimal wages and poor working conditions as workshops competed for trade. Work was also seasonal with slack seasons during which workers had minimal or no work at all.

Maurice Levine began to attend classes on Marxism in the 1920s whilst still in his teens. The classes were run by George Staunton, a founder member of the Communist Party of Great Britain and originally a member of the British Socialist Party. After spending a couple of years working and seeking work in Australia, Maurice returned to Cheetham in 1931 and joined the Party.

> I joined Cheetham Communist Party. It was a strong organisation, but the Young Communist League was stronger still. They had a social club in Cheetham, the majority of the members were Jewish. It had about 200 members in this club called the Challenge Club. Challenge was the name of the weekly YCL paper. From that club came the mass trespass... There were not such large numbers in other parts of Manchester.[67]

Cheetham YCL's strategy was clear, and it was consistent: defend the community, drive the fascists off the streets. In 1935 the Blackshirts tried and failed to hold a street meeting in Cheetham at the waste ground known as Marshall Croft. Issy Luft was a Cheetham YCL member who became secretary of the

*Members of Cheetham YCL, early 1938. Second from right, Benny Rothman. Third from right, Issy Luft. Then Percy Davidson and Maurice Levine. Two women crouched to Issy's right are Lily Clyne and Bella Clyne. Centre top in mackintosh, Monty Rosenfield. To his right in glasses, Ralph Cantor. Fifth from left in cap, Phil Jackson. To his right, Jud Coleman (pic courtesy WCML)*

Crumpsall Communist Party branch and a principal organiser of the Aid for Spain movement in Manchester. His son Mike, who is also the maternal grandson of George Staunton, recalls his father's combativeness and the story of the day.

> People like Benny [Rothman] and my dad were leading anti-fascists. It wasn't just the political campaigning. It was on the streets. These were people who wouldn't back off. The fascists tried to demonstrate through Hightown and have a meeting in Marshall Croft. There was a big fight there and the fascists got thoroughly beaten, in the heart of the Jewish community. It was seen as a direct provocation. And the fascists were dealt with so harshly that the police would not offer them police protection for marches into Jewish areas. It got completely out of control as far as the police were concerned.[68]

Mike Luft believes that the YCL's periphery in the Challenge Club was at least as large as the YCL membership, meaning there were 400-500 organised anti-fascists in a relatively small area of the city. Operating out of premises on Herbert Street, they organised rambles, possessed a band led by Ollie and Ralph Cantor that played at Sunday night dances, and showed films that included classics of the Soviet cinema. There were tutorials on political economy and historical materialism led by Ben Ainley, speakers' classes that prepared people for the soapbox in Stevenson Square. For a period in the mid-1930s, the YCL dominated political life in Cheetham. Learning to box was also a useful skill to acquire in the circumstances. Maurice Levine boxed for the Jewish Lads Brigade and competed for their team at a national level all the way to the Albert Hall in London.

The BUF managed to hold two meetings in Cheetham Town Hall in February and April 1936, permitted by the chief constable despite a petition by 3,500 and thousands demonstrating on the day. When the BUF tried to march into the area down Cheetham Hill Road they were fought off. Blackshirts out of uniform were also used as strike-breakers in 1934 at a factory in Openshaw. The employer had hired labour that no one recognised and by their accents were thought not to be local. The Party sent Maurice Levine to the factory to find out who they were.

> There was a big strike in a wire works in east Manchester called Richard Johnson and Nephew. They'd brought in American consultants to speed up production and there was a strike. Blacklegs were brought in. I was asked to go to the factory and follow the blacklegs. They got on a bus, I discreetly sat behind them, and they finally arrived in Higher Broughton at the barracks of the Blackshirts in Manchester. Northumberland Street. Young unemployed men brought in from other parts of the country.[69]

Nationally the Communist Party of Great Britain grew during the Mosley years, albeit from a small base. In February 1931 national membership was recorded as 2,711; in February 1936, 7,000. It grew in Manchester and in the Cheetham area possibly because of anti-fascist activity. Chief Constable Maxwell's report to the Home Office at the time testified how the BUF invigorated the local Communist Party.

> ...until the advent of the Fascists the Communist element in the city was negligible and was losing ground. The feeling aroused by the Fascists has revived the Communist Party in Manchester... Moreover, the Fascists in Manchester appear to have adopted a policy of deliberate provocation of the Jews.[70]

Communists in Cheetham already had a strong organisation before the Blackshirts arrived. There existed a politically educated, committed and well-organised group of activists, most of whom were Jewish. They were the children of Eastern European émigrés who had fled the Russian Empire, and many of those had been members of the Jewish Socialist Bund. Their children had, in turn, grown up experiencing the casual antisemitism of the 1920s and 1930s in Manchester. Maurice Levine had ambitions of becoming an engineer but knew little would come of it because it was a given that engineering companies did not accept Jews. Benny Rothman, who worked in a garage in the early 1930s and went on to work in Metro-Vicks in Trafford Park, was a much remarked upon exception.

In their youth, before the Blackshirts arrived, Benny, Maurice and others had to tackle gangs of non-Jewish youth who came into the area to intimidate and fight. The Blackshirts were a significant progression from this, but it was not a phenomenon that a group of combative young men and women in a close-knit community couldn't overcome. Joining the YCL or the Party was logical, partly because there was no political alternative. Maurice Levine:

> The Communist Party was in such marked contrast to the Labour Party. At that time, you have the National Government. The defection of MacDonald and others. And one was influenced by the Russian Revolution.[71]

BUF membership declined as the organisation became increasingly antisemitic, associated with thuggery and the Nazis. On 7 June 1934, Mosley held a rally at Olympia in London; the violence of his stewards towards hecklers appalled others in the audience and provided negative publicity. The event also coincided with Hitler's Röhm purge, "The Night of the Long Knives", when the SS murdered at least 100 political opponents from its own Brownshirts' ranks.[72] By the end of 1935, membership was down to around 8,000. On 4 October 1936, Mosley attempted to march through the East End and was turned back at Cable Street. As in Manchester, the communists were pivotal in organising the resistance on the ground. But it should be said that there was a degree of reticence by the Party's leadership regarding physical conflict with the Blackshirts. International communism had recently embarked on the strategy of the popular front—seeking to build bridges and common cause with social democrats, in Britain attempting affiliation to the Labour Party. General Secretary Harry Pollitt did not want to alienate those he hoped to form a government with one day.

> It will be fatal for us if the CP's opposition to Mosley is looked upon in the working class as in the nature of a brawl and not a real political struggle.[73]

The district leadership in Lancashire applied no pressure to dissuade comrades from driving the Blackshirts from the streets of Manchester. Bar a couple of councillors in Suffolk and Sussex, the BUF failed electorally. This was apparently a shock to Mosley who surrounded himself with those who idolised him. Ultimately the BUF ran counter to British political culture. This from the front page of the first issue of *The Blackshirt*:

> If the state is allowed to drift to a violent struggle, such things as dictatorship, the imprisonment of opponents, censorship, the suppression of speech and other acts, the iron hand, inevitably arise as factors in the struggle for power and in the maintenance of order after that struggle.[74]

In January 1937, the government passed the Public Order Act. The Act forbade the wearing of political uniforms, the use of stewards at open-air meetings, and the use of insulting words in public speeches. The police had the authority to ban marches if they threatened the peace. Viewed by many MPs as a necessary piece of legislation, it was denounced in the *Daily Worker*. Mosley as an individual continued to draw attention. After the Munich Agreement of 1938 granting Hitler carte blanche to invade Czechoslovakia, he praised the Munich agreement in a speech at Manchester and insisted that Hitler could be trusted to keep it. In April 1939, he toured northern England to spread the message that Britain had nothing to fear from Germany. Two months before the outbreak of war in July 1939, he held a 'Britain First' rally at Earls Court with a reported attendance of 30,000—one of the biggest indoor political rallies ever held in Britain. His message was that Britain could avoid the coming conflict, forge a peace with Hitler by allowing him to wage war to the east, as outlined in *Mein Kampf*. This was not an unpopular opinion amongst a section of the public or many in the political class as the "Great War invaded the mind of mankind".[75]

In May 1940, MI5 agents uncovered correspondence between Mosley and a Scottish Unionist MP, Archibald Maule Ramsay, that outlined plans to unify fascist, antisemitic and peace groups in Britain. Mosley, Maule, Mosley's wife Diana and 1,600 others, mostly members of the BUF, were interned in prison without trial. Mosley's sister-in-law, Unity Mitford, was so distressed at the thought of war between the two countries she loved she went to an English Garden in Munich and shot herself. However, the bullet lodged in her brain without killing her. Incapable of caring for herself, Hitler sent her back to England. Oswald and Diana were allowed to live together for most of the war in a house in the grounds of Holloway prison. In November 1943, Home Secretary Herbert Morrison ordered their release.

The Blackshirts were all but defeated by the end of 1936, but for young communists in Manchester and elsewhere, the threat of fascism continued, intensified, *on that arid square… that tableland scored by rivers.*[76] It had to be fought there as well. It seems an extraordinary impulse to make one's way into another nation's war fought in another language.

But having spent the last four years of your youth exchanging blows with antisemitic fascists on your own streets, and possessing a faith in the destiny of working people of all countries, when the call came from your Party, the question was asked as a matter of casual conversation, in the Challenge Club, in the room above the barber's shop after a meeting, in sweated workshops, in the queue at the Labour Exchange: *Are you going? Are you going to Spain?*

*Comrades Come Rally*

# Chapter 3

## Beacon

> "The sun slowly disappeared and the darkness of another troubled night descended upon this bloodstained land.... It is hard to appreciate such beauty against such a cancer of fascism which is spreading all around us..." Diary entry of IB volunteer Maurice Levine, 30 Dec 1936

Few people in Britain today are familiar with the Spanish Civil War. It has fallen below the horizon now, behind the enormity of the Second World War. The figure of General Franco populates the roster of 20th century dictators, but the names of the battles and the nature of the atrocities escape most people. There are, however, two chapters from the three-year-long war that still attract the attention of some. One is the bombing of Guernica,[77] the other is the International Brigades' story—the thousands of volunteers that made their way to Spain to fight for the beleaguered Republic against Franco's forces. The former is preserved in Picasso's epic painting *Guernica* (1937), the latter examined, particularly of late, by some forensic histories, and captured in memoir.[78] There is also some fiction, and two notable films: *For Whom the Bell Tolls* (1943) and *Land and Freedom* (1995).

Internationally between 32,000 and 35,000 men from 53 countries served in the ranks of the International Brigades (IB), a Soviet initiative to recruit and organise foreign fighters. Another 5,000 served outside the IB, mostly with the anarchist militias organised by the anarchist-led trade union CNT (Confederación Nacional del Trabajo) or, as in the case of George Orwell, the socialist militias organised by the POUM—the Workers Party of Marxist Unification, branded Trotskyist by the Communist

Party of Spain. 2,550 men went to fight from Britain; women served as medical staff. Of the 2,550, some 540 were killed and the majority of the rest were wounded.

The IB was politically as well as militarily significant. While the vast majority of volunteers were working-class men, the presence in their midst of writers and intellectuals was welcome publicity at the time. Their literature has back-lit the volunteers' place in history, particularly labour movement history. The poet John Cornford and the more established Christopher Caudwell were both killed in action. Arthur Koestler worked as an English language journalist whilst spying for the Comintern. He was captured by Franco's forces and sentenced to death but then exchanged for a high-profile nationalist prisoner. André Malraux was a French novelist who served in the Republican air force, whilst American novelist Ernest Hemingway reported for the North American Newspaper Agency. The author of *Cider with Rosie*, Laurie Lee, joined the IB, if only for a few months.

There were others. George Orwell, author of the best-known memoir, *Homage to Catalonia*, fought for the POUM. It is significant because he witnessed what historian Anthony Beevor terms the "civil war within the civil war": the conflict between the Soviet-led forces and anarchist militias in Catalonia.[79] There were street clashes, executions, and a propaganda offensive. In his memoir and letters of the time, one can see how the events created in Orwell a view of Stalinism that was to inspire *Animal Farm* and *Nineteen Eighty-Four*. The Party was sceptical of recruiting bohemians to the IB for they could prove poor soldiers. The poet Stephen Spender's lover, Tony Hyndman, enlisted but then deserted. He was arrested and imprisoned by Republican forces and then ignominiously repatriated after Spender wrote to Party general secretary Harry Pollitt. Simone Weil, the French philosopher, joined the Durruti Column, a 6,000-strong anarchist militia. Her poor eyesight resulted in comrades refusing to allow her to join the front line for fear she would shoot them. Sent behind the lines, she knocked over a pot of boiling water, badly scalding herself and had to return home.

Roughly 80 percent of the British IB volunteers were manual workers or unemployed, escaping the lethargy of the dole.[80] Nearly 75 percent were Communist Party or YCL members. The first two volunteers to arrive from Manchester were remarkable individuals: speedway rider Clem Beckett[81] and a Russian émigré whose anglicised name was Arnold Jeans. Jeans is recorded as

*Clem Beckett
(courtesy Gallery
Oldham, Oldham MBC)*

arriving in September 1936, Beckett in November. Beckett was a speedway rider who became known as 'Dare Devil Beckett' for his incomparable speed and because he regularly rode the 'wall of death' at Belle Vue gardens. He joined Oldham YCL aged 18 in 1924. The most well-known rider of his generation, he took part in displays across Europe. He was suspended from riding for a time for writing articles for the *Daily Worker*, exposing the exploitation of riders, and went on to form a trade union for riders called the Dirt-track Riders Association. In Spain he formed an unlikely friendship with the writer Christopher Caudwell.[82] They were both killed on 12 February 1937 at the Battle of Jarama, manning a machine gun post together. Maurice Levine:

> Clem Beckett was a tough working-class type. He'd toured the continent and Russia with his fairground attraction. When he first came [to Spain] he was put on servicing vehicles but he said he had come to Spain to fight. He left it and teamed with Christopher Caudwell, and well, they both lost their lives. [Beckett] was a

machine gunner in the territorial army. They were fighting on February 12th at Jarama.[83]

Arnold Jeans came from a Russian family and was fluent in several languages. He ran a left-wing film unit called Plato Films and earned his keep as a private tutor to the wealthy Bowes-Lyon family.[84] Arnold was 33 when he went to Spain. Not surprisingly he was an interpreter and put in charge of the initial group of around 20 English volunteers which included Maurice Levine. Maurice:

> People in the Party in Manchester thought he was an agent or something like that, because he spoke with a foreign accent and he came from White Russians who had fought against the Reds in the civil war. His father was a professor, they had settled in Riga and he had come to England. He was in command of that little unit of 22 or 20 men. He was a fine fellow. A great leader of men.[85]

Another member of that group was Winston Churchill's nephew, Esmond Romilly.[86] Romilly had already declared himself a communist, and then abandoned it for democratic socialism by the time he cycled across France and boarded a boat for Valencia. He wrote about his experience in Spain in a memoir entitled *Boadilla* first published in 1937.

> If there was one who deserves the appellation of hero, it must have been Arnold Jeans—a man whose death passed quite unnoticed in England; a Latvian or Russian by birth (no one was ever quite certain which), it was he who held our whole group together and was its leader in the difficult work of rear-guard organisation as well as at the front.[87]

Arnold was killed at Boadilla del Monte in December 1936. He and the other early arrivals fought alongside Germans in the Thaelmann Battalion, largely made up of those fleeing Nazi persecution. A battalion is typically around 700-strong and it was some time before there was a sufficient number of British volunteers to form their own. Continual losses meant that numbers had to be supplemented by Spaniards. A disproportionate number of volunteers from across the world were Jewish; particularly in the case of Poland and the United States. So much so that Yiddish came to be spoken across the different nationalities. It was also the same in Britain's case, and in Manchester's with the Cheetham area providing a number of young men. Twenty-year-old Ralph Cantor (originally Cantorovitch), cornet player and band leader at Cheetham Challenge Club, arrived in November 1936 to be part of Jeans' number one company, the XIVth International Brigade. He had a Spanish language textbook sent from home and so improved his command of Spanish he became an interpreter to the general staff. He kept a diary and was a prolific author of letters back home.

> The fascist planes bomb food queues which line the big buildings and consequently great damage has been done to life and property, but notwithstanding their efforts to demoralise the people these ultimately serve to spur them on.[88]

Ralph's diary entries describe a variety of responsibilities: carrying food five kilometres at night; stretcher bearing; interpreting for English speaking patients at the hospital; questioning German prisoners. He was next to his friend and comrade from Cheetham, Jud Coleman, at the Battle of Brunete in July 1937 when he was shot in the neck. He was carried to lower ground but died soon after. Amongst the non-Party volunteers were fellow travellers who were to join the organisation during or after the war. Sam Wild was born in Ardwick, Manchester in 1908. When he was two years old his mother died in a workhouse infirmary and was buried in a communal unmarked grave. His father went to fight in the First World War and Sam was brought up by Irish relatives. Growing up he saw himself "as more Irish than English" and chose to box under the name of McGrail, his mother's maiden name. "I was always conscious I was living with someone, reluctant aunties. I wasn't welcome. I was an obligation."[89]

Sam left school at 14 and joined the Royal Navy at 15. In 1932 he deserted whilst in South Africa, was arrested, and returned to Britain to be discharged. He left for Spain in December 1936 with Bert Masky, a Party member who was in a relationship with Sam's elder sister, Hilda. Sam's daughter, Dolores Long, wrote of the friendship between Bert and Sam.

> Bert and my dad became friends and when the Spanish

*Sam Wild, Spain Sep 1938*

Civil War broke out, Bert decided to go to Spain. He was much more politically aware at that time than my father and he explained what Spain was all about and why democracy was at stake, and that what was happening in Spain could be happening in the whole of Europe. He persuaded my father to go with him, so my father went out to Spain with just a kind of gut feeling that there was something wrong with the world.[90]

Sam may well have been involved with Cheetham YCL's Challenge Club, fighting the Blackshirts, though not a member of either the YCL or the Party. He was to become the final commander of the British Battalion in Spain, surviving the conflict after being wounded on four occasions. He is among the most renowned volunteers from Britain, becoming a member of the Communist Party of Spain (PCE) before returning home to join the Communist Party of Great Britain. He was interviewed several times about his experience in later life.

In the main, it was working-class people... Romantics also went there and people who were unemployed. There were academics, trade unionists of every description. You'd have a miner sleeping in a dugout and a poet or a philosopher... Two of Churchill's nephews went to Spain.[91]

There were also those who expressed no steadfast political allegiances before or after the conflict. George Fletcher from Moss Side was described by volunteer Jack Jones as "very much a military man, I don't think he had a political idea in his head".[92] George was in the Lancashire Fusiliers for 15 years and served in France. He had temporary command of the British Battalion in Spain for three weeks after the death of Battalion Commander Harold Fry, and he later served as Sam Wild's adjutant. Sam and George had joint weddings on their return from Spain and were to remain life-long friends. There's no evidence that George was involved in anti-fascist activity. He and others *balanced all, brought all to mind* and in some cases personal reasons accompanied the sense of duty that led them to fight. Between a quarter to a third of the Communist Party in Manchester fought for the International Brigade[93]; others like Benny Rothman and Hugh Scanlon were turned down. Regardless of their politics or ours, the reasons given or guessed at, their actions can justifiably be said to be daring in the least.

Many of the volunteers were ill-suited to soldiering partly because they were physically unfit. It was the hungry 1930s, and the more impoverished workers and the unemployed were malnourished. Unlike Sam, many had never handled a weapon before. Benny Goldman was an upholsterer from north Manchester and a local organiser for the Young Communist League. As a member of the Jewish community, he'd also fought the Blackshirts. He left for Spain without telling his family. "The first time I fired a rifle was at the Battle of Jarama. I fired it at someone to kill them."[94] The Party distorted the numbers who volunteered for propaganda purposes and also for their military significance, but it is difficult to exaggerate their courage. Many in Britain felt there was too much complacency concerning the rapid rise of fascism in Europe. Bessie Wild:

> People imagine that the newspapers were full of anti-Hitler stuff. They weren't. Large numbers of people would defend Hitler. 'He had built the autobahn' they'd say. There wasn't an awareness. The *Manchester Guardian* was good that way. There wasn't a consistent drive to make people aware. They suppressed it.[95]

Through the IB volunteers and the Aid for Spain movement at home, the Communist Party in Britain enhanced its reputation and support. Membership of the Party more than doubled during the conflict.[96] This followed a period of stagnation during the early 1930s.

Ken Loach described the struggle against Franco as a "beacon" in history. Long after the Second World War, particularly from the 1970s onwards, the volunteers' story was increasingly mythologised on the left of British politics and beyond. They were unintentionally heroic individuals whose lives were otherwise commonplace and who, in their youth, threw themselves into the blast furnace of European history. People name-drop IB volunteers to this day. They were a rare breed, and many of those that returned from Spain then went on to fight Hitler, if the armed forces would take them. Benny Goldman was initially refused because of his political record; however, on the second time of his asking, he was accepted into a tank regiment.

> I applied to join the British Army and was refused.
>
> *Did they know you'd been in Spain?*
>
> Oh yes. After I'd been home a few months, they came to the house to check up on me. When I was in the army—and this is funny—I received a letter asking for the cost of my repatriation [from Spain] which was four pounds and would I send it to them.[97]

As well as combatants, there was also medical staff, which included women who served as nurses. Labour MP Ellen Wilkinson, who was among the first female MPs from Manchester and a founder member of the CPGB, set up the Spanish Medical Aid Committee and the National Joint Committee for Spanish Relief. Manchester nurse Madge Addy arrived in Spain in 1937 and became the head nurse in an old monastery in Uclés in Castile. Madge wrote detailed reports for the *Daily Worker* about the work on the hospital's "Manchester Ward".

> Please ask Manchester to do its utmost to send money so that you can buy stuff necessary. Don't send anything for me, devote every penny to the hospital.[98]

Patients died from malnutrition, and there was only one syringe at the hospital. Republican soldiers were brought in wounded having fought in their bare feet. Lilian Urmston, a nurse from Staybridge, worked in a cave hospital at the battle of the Ebro. She crossed the River Ebro to evacuate the wounded in October 1938.

> Just as dawn was breaking, we were crossing the newly-repaired pontoon bridges. We had just reached the other side, and our ambulances were toiling along the hastily prepared road, when we heard the familiar cry of 'Aviación!' Ambulances were pulled up at the side of the road, under the shelter of the cliffs—and we lay in ditches, tense with expectation and apprehension.[99]

Beacons burn brightly from a distance; from close quarters defending the Republic was a bitter struggle with heavy losses suffered by International Brigade volunteers from across the world. Maurice Levine:

> We were always outgunned. The enemy had greater resources. We were always hungry, badly clothed. That experience is something which has never left us.[100]

The IB volunteers' experience is annotated in three chapters through excerpts from interviews with Manchester veterans, primarily Sam Wild, Benny Goldman, Bernard McKenna, Maurice Levine and Joe Norman, all of whom were members of the CPGB. All five were wounded, Sam on four occasions, Benny and Maurice twice. There are also excerpts from Maurice Levine's and Ralph Cantor's diaries. During their first major battle, the Battle of Jarama in February 1937, the British Battalion's position became known as Suicide Hill. If some volunteers had half-expected never to return from Spain when they left Britain, Jarama confirmed this as a probability. Benny Goldman said that he was warned by a Party official before he left Manchester.

> You knew that the odds were that you would get killed or severely wounded. I was very politically minded. It was a charged climate, moving towards war. It was not like today. Today we are not politically conscious.[101]

That Franco's coup was not immediately successful, that the Republic could not easily defeat the Nationalists, mainly due to

German and Italian military support, guaranteed a prolonged conflict. The IB helped to detain German and Italian forces, just as they managed to stall their advance at Jarama. Indeed, the Valencia Road, which was the key objective in the Battle of Jarama, was held by Republican forces until the end of the war. Joe Norman was born in Hulme, Manchester in 1908. An engineer at Metro-Vicks, he was laid off when he completed his apprenticeship at 21. He became chair of the Salford branch of the Unemployed Workers Movement and went to Spain in December 1936. He was interviewed for the Imperial War Museum in 1977.

> We delayed the outcome of the Spanish Civil War for three years. If Hitler, the fascists had come instead of being stuck in Spain, we might be a subject nation today. That's how I see it.[102]

Elsewhere social democracy was failing to tackle fascism. In France, Leon Blum's Popular Front government, which had initially sold arms to the Republic at the outbreak of the war, closed its border with Spain to all commerce weeks later. American oil companies backed the Nationalists, General Motors supplied them with trucks. In Britain, a Conservative-dominated national government led by Stanley Baldwin, also refused to take a stand.

> We English hate fascism, but we loathe bolshevism as much. So, if there is somewhere where fascists and Bolsheviks can kill each other off, so much the better.[103]

The majority of the IB volunteers would have left school at 14 whilst Stanley Baldwin was educated at Harrow and Cambridge. Somehow the volunteers had a clearer understanding of the nature of fascism, and their endeavours helped to drag the truth of it into the light: that no appeasement would be possible. Whilst undoubtedly there was a strong current of anti-militarism in Britain at the time, it is also the case that by the end of 1936, organised solidarity with the Spanish Republic had spread throughout the country. That the Labour Party supported Baldwin's non-intervention policy for the first year of the war only strengthened the position of the CPGB, in Britain and in Spain also, where the only meaningful international assistance came from the Soviet Union. The IB has always posed a problem for the official Labour movement in Britain because it can claim no credit for its creation. Before we look at volunteers' experience, partly through their own words, we should examine the nature of the conflict they entered and the historical reasons for it.

*Comrades Come Rally*

# Chapter 4

## Brittle Republic

> "Nationalisation of the land. Dissolution of all religious orders, with seizure of their property. Dissolution of the army, to be replaced by a democratic militia. Dissolution of the Civil Guard." Programme of Spanish Socialist Workers Party, Jan 1934

The outbreak of the civil war in Spain in July 1936 was foreshadowed: in October 1934 'Spanish Civil War' was the headline of the *Daily Worker*. It referred to the violent suppression of a miners' strike in Asturias, northern Spain. The strike had been called in response to a coalition of right-wing parties winning the national election the previous year, and the entry into government of a confederation of right-wing parties known as CEDA, (Spanish Confederation of Autonomous Rights). CEDA was largely the party of the catholic middle classes and small holders in the north of Spain. The strike in Asturias followed an uprising in Catalonia and smaller incidents elsewhere across Spain, and it was essentially an insurrection; a prelude of what was to come. General Francisco Franco controlled the movement of troops that crushed the miners' rebellion; it would be him that would lead the coup two years later. The miners and their supporters armed themselves and occupied small towns in the region. In the town of Turón, armed miners arrived at a seminary and murdered 34 priests, six young seminarists aged between 18 and 21, as well as several businessmen and civil guards.[104] Convents and churches were burned throughout the region. The suppression of the uprising was equally, if not more, savage; the eventual death toll reached almost 2,000 with 30,000-40,000 miners taken prisoner.

The Second Republic was new, established after King Alfonso fled in 1931. Prior to this, Spain had been a monarchy with the brief interregnum of the First Republic between February 1873 and December 1874. Many on the left regarded the Second Republic as theirs and the 1933 election of a conservative government as illegitimate. The army, the church, and many large landowners, however, viewed the Republic as a stepping stone to communism. Those unconditionally committed to the new democracy were thin on the ground on either side. 1930s Spain had a history of political and religious violence, a dangerously polarised society in which the centre repeatedly failed to hold. The advancement of women's rights during the Second Republic was an incitement to nationalist parties. Women could not vote in Spain until 1933. Few women dared to stand for the Cortes (parliament). Of the 1,004 deputies elected to the parliament in 1931, 1933 and 1936, only ten were women, including Dolores Ibárruri, who became better known as 'la Pasionaria' (the passionflower). The Republican government of 1936 was the first to appoint a female minister: Federica Montseny. Montseny became minister for health, introducing a programme of sex education for women and working to eradicate prostitution.

Spain had entered the 20th century with an average life expectancy of around 35,[105] with two-thirds of the population working on the land. On the surface, it was a monarchy, but beneath King Alfonso XIII's reign, an increasingly splintered nation began to unfold. Of all regions, Catalonia had a history independent of Spain with its own small empire in the late Middle Ages.[106] In the War of Spanish Succession (1701-1714) it had even sided with England against Philip of Anjou. Catalonia had never rested easy inside a centralised state run from Madrid, and in the upheaval of 1934, a Catalan state was proclaimed once again, lasting less than 24 hours on that occasion. Nineteenth-century industrial development had not brought democracy any closer, but served to make Spain more socially divided. In the 1930s Barcelona had a growing working class whilst in the south, two percent of all landowners owned two-thirds of all the land on which 750,000 labourers scratched a living. Spain was on the road to capitalist development, but different regions were at various stages, and none was significantly advanced. By the time the Second Republic was born in 1931 and the king fled the country, Spain could just as accurately be viewed as several separate regions as much as one country. In the past the monarchy, the army, and the church had all failed to unify Spain; the new Republic was also to fail.

## Anarchism

A testament to the peculiarity of Spain was the resilience of anarchism as a political tradition. Elsewhere in Europe anarchism declined and disappeared after the First World War; in Spain it grew. It existed not as a detached ideology but as something rooted in communities, towns and villages, combining liberal individualism with communitarianism. As a political outlook and activism, it had a significant impact on the fate of both the Republic and the war, and it is worth examining this curious singularity.

Anarchism came to Spain before socialism did. In 1868 the central figure of European anarchism, Russia's Mikhail Bakunin, sent Giuseppe Fanelli to Spain.[107] Fanelli had fought in the 1848 rebellion in Italy, and later became a decisive figure in the development of the First International in Spain, which was essentially anarchist in outlook. The First International was a grouping of Marxist organisations across Europe and the wider world; it emerged from the International Working Men's Association formed in London in 1864. Bakunin joined the Association, and at the fifth congress of 1872, he challenged Marx on the attitude revolutionaries should take to the state. Marx believed that the state could facilitate socialism whilst Bakunin believed federations of self-governing workplaces and communes should replace it. Marx won the day in the Association, and Bakunin was expelled. The attitude towards the state amongst a small group of intellectual revolutionaries in the 19th century might seem a trivial irrelevance to all but labour historians, but it is helpful in understanding the Spanish Republic of the 1930s.

Whilst socialism struggled to establish roots in Spain, anti-state politics attracted support. Both the Catholic Church and the Castilian state were highly centralist and oppressive, whilst anarchism offered independence and a contrasting morality in free will and mutual aid. Socialists had a reliance on state intervention to deliver change and were viewed as overly bureaucratic, whereas Bakunin believed in the "spontaneous creativity of the masses".[108] Furthermore, Spain was largely an agricultural society; socialists orientated themselves towards the working class, viewing agricultural workers as inherently reactionary. By 1872 there were nearly 50,000 Bakuninists in Spain, support being highest in Andalusia and Catalonia: the most backward agrarian region and the most advanced industrial region.[109] In 1910 anarchist groups and larger organisations came together to form the CNT, Confederación Nacional del Trabajo (National Federation of Labour); a trade union organisation best described as anarcho-syndicalist in nature in that it believed then, as it does today, in creating a revolution through a general strike and the replacement of the state with communes. Trade unions emerged in Spain as politically rather than industrially demarcated; the UGT, Unión General de Trabajadores (General Union of Workers), is a union aligned to the Spanish Socialist Party. By 1920 the CNT had 700,000 members and the UGT 160,000.[110]

Class conflict in Spain in the early 20th century was violent, routinely so. As the CNT grew stronger, employers adopted the practice of *pistolerismo*—hiring armed thugs to intimidate and murder activists. But anarchism had always had two faces of its own, one that was legal and open and another that was clandestine and violent. Peter Kropotkin, a Russian writer, influenced by Bakunin, advised: "We need two organisations, one above board, broad-reaching, working in the open, and the other secret and active."[111] For a period in the late 19th century the violent tendency inside anarchism came to the forefront, "placing chemistry at the centre of the revolution". It was a current that emerged not just in Spain. Famously and tragically in Chicago during the May Day demonstration of 1886, an alleged anarchist bomb killed seven policemen and four demonstrators. The courtroom speech of one of those sentenced for the crime is evocative of the depth of remote idealism within anarchist thinking at the time.

> Anarchy is Greek and means, verbatim, without rulership; not being ruled. According to our vocabulary anarchy is a state of society in which the only form of government is reason. [112]

In Spain during this period, there was a series of bomb attacks and assassinations, most notably, the attack on the Corpus Christi procession in Barcelona in 1896, and the murder of the Spanish prime minister the following year. There was also a notorious bomb outrage at a production of the opera *William Tell* in 1893. It is during this period that the image of the anarchist as a cloaked figure, brandishing a pistol and a bomb is established. During the civil war, particularly the first year, anarchist militias were responsible for the murder of many civilians, particularly the clergy in what can only be described as a policy of terror.

Anarchism was only one connection between Spain and Russia during this period. There were broader social and political parallels. Both countries had little experience of democracy, were largely agrarian economically with small but volatile working classes, and both were ruled from an authoritarian centre. Lenin viewed Spain as a country ripe for revolution, and indeed the Russian Revolution of 1917 sparked three years of extreme militancy in Spain that became known as the *trienio Bolchevisata*, the Bolshevik years (1918-1920). The propertied classes in Spain lived in fear of Bolshevism for decades after; at one point it was rumoured that Lenin had arrived in Barcelona to lead the Spanish revolution. Fear, it seems, always drove the authorities to look for authoritarian solutions and a military dictatorship installed itself in 1923.

There were high expectations of the Republic when it came to pass in April 1931. Most Spaniards were Republicans and pleased to see the back of the monarchy and the dictatorship. The anarchist trade union CNT expected its long-awaited freedom to organise but, while the socialist trade union the UGT was brought into government, the CNT was excluded. In response, the union initiated several widely supported strikes against the Republican government, in particular a miners' strike in Barcelona in early 1932, plus another at the end of December 1933 that resulted in the death of 75 strikers and 11 civil guards. No sooner was the Republic born than the CNT proclaimed that the new authority was no different from the old and confronted it. When strikes for better working conditions were met with firearms by the authorities, the CNT's rhetoric was of a "socialist dictatorship spilling proletarian blood".[113] Before long, they were calling for a social revolution to overthrow the Republic. The increasing violent repression of revolts by the civil guard and the army led the Socialist Party (PSOE) to follow their example. The party's leader, Largo Caballero, who was closely associated with the miners' rising, was imprisoned, emerging in 1935 more of a Bolshevik than when he was sentenced. He went on record as saying that the revolution in Spain could only be achieved through violence, and was dubbed the 'Spanish Lenin'.

## Coup d'état

The spur for the outbreak of civil war was the election of a popular front government in February 1936. The Popular Front Alliance was an electoral coalition, a pact of various left-wing parties that narrowly won the election against the National Front, an alliance of right-wing parties. After the result, 250,000 uniformed socialists and communists marched through Madrid in celebration; elsewhere people marched to prisons demanding the release of those imprisoned during the uprising of 1934. The Left behaved triumphantly but didn't have the majority to warrant it and talk of a coup began soon after the election; there had already been a failed military coup in 1932, a year into the Republic, led by General José Sanjurjo in response to reforms of the army. Its centre was Madrid and it was easily suppressed within 24 hours. In 1936 the expectation of violence created it; in the spring and summer political murders increased with communists and socialists fighting Falangists. Paramilitary groups on the left and right began to arm and drill. Even deputies to the Cortes carried firearms they had to surrender before sessions.

The military rising on 17 July 1936 was intended to be a swift matter. The intention was not a civil war but an exchange of power from the Cortes to military rule. This coup was intended to mass its forces and seize power from outside Madrid. General Franco obtained the support of around half of the Spanish Peninsula Army and the 30,000 strong Army of Africa—Spain's most professional and hardened soldiers, based in Morocco. Hitler personally ordered the Luftwaffe to fly the army to the mainland. On 11 July an aircraft set off from Croydon, England, on its way to the Canary Islands. It had been chartered by a right-wing English publisher, Douglas Jerrold, and it was to take Franco to his army in Morocco. It took a few days for the news of the coup to break through; newspapers had been forbidden from reporting on it. Much of the first fighting occurred at barracks in Madrid and Barcelona as soldiers committed themselves to the Republic or the rebels. The Republican government managed to retain half of its rifles, some tanks, and aircraft, and naval capacity was fairly evenly split, but many of the officers

*Republican poster during Spanish Civil War (left) and General Francisco Franco 1930*

from the Republican Army defected to Franco's Nationalists. The fidelity of many that remained nominally loyal was questionable. What was crucial in preventing a rapid victory for the Nationalist forces was the government's order to distribute weapons to the trade unions. Both the CNT and the UGT had called general strikes the day after the rising and opened their existing weapons caches, some buried after the rising of 1934. The quick formation and action of the workers' militias were enough to secure towns and villages, and even cities, for the Republic. In the immediate aftermath of the rising, the only city the Nationalists managed to take was Seville. Madrid, Barcelona and Valencia were secured for the Republic, with large parts of Aragon and Catalonia being controlled by anarchist militias— who were not synonymous with the Republic. The emergence of these militias indicated the nature of the future war. As the battle lines were drawn across the country, Franco's rebels unexpectedly controlled only half of the peninsula.

*Comrades Come Rally*

# Chapter 5

# From the Irwell to the Ebro

> "I'm sure you'll realise that I should never have been satisfied had I not assisted. Only my hatred of fascism brought me here." Clem Beckett to his wife, Feb 1937

Four months before Franco's rising, German troops marched into the Rhineland, a demilitarised zone established after the First World War by the Treaty of Versailles. In 1935 fascist Italy invaded Abyssinia and the year before an attempted Nazi coup in Austria was suppressed by military forces loyal to the government. In Britain, the Blackshirts were marching. Resistance to Franco in Spain was viewed as standing against the incoming tide of fascism in Europe. At the outbreak of the civil war the activity of the CPGB consisted of two strands: arms for Spain and food for Spain. It had recently put behind it the class against class politics that prevented it from entering alliances and embraced the notion of a popular front against fascism. Within a month of the rising, Germany and Italy began to provide military support for Franco's forces. In contrast, Stalin initially shied away from any direct involvement in the conflict in order to avoid alienating France and Britain, who he believed he would need in a future alliance against Germany. But he also believed it would be to Russia's advantage if Germany's involvement in Spain was protracted. In September 1936, Russia sold 50 aircraft to the Republic through Mexico and sent 20 pilots to Spain. In the same month the Comintern called for volunteers to form International Brigades (IB) to fight against Franco's forces.

### Over the frontier

Though some, like John Cornford and Felicia Browne[114] had gone before the Comintern call, and though many were not

*International Brigade at Albacete. Benny Goldman, fifth from left*

Comintern warriors, recruitment of IB members in Britain was through the Communist Party. Activity on the home front was not enough for some. Benny Goldman:

> In Britain, the fascist movement was making very rapid headway. Oswald Mosley was organising demonstrations in the major cities. You had leading socialites following the fascist movement and supporting it; the *Daily Mail* and Lord Rothermere, and whilst he did it in a backhanded manner, the King. He was fascist-minded. Yes, we went on anti-fascist demonstrations, but I felt at the time it was inadequate. What we were doing had no real meaning and the centre of the struggle was in Spain. That was the acid test.[115]

Twenty-eight-year-old Sam Wild from Ardwick, Manchester, was working as a boilermaker in the Paramount Theatre when he left for Spain at the end of 1936 with Bert Masky.

> I felt strongly against fascism. What I'd heard about it in Abyssinia, saw what Hitler was doing in Germany to the Jews and the communists, the Japanese in the Far East. I came to the conclusion that fascism was about to conquer the world, and it was about time somebody started to do something about it. I had no sense of adventure; it was a profound political feeling.[116]

Joe Norman from Hulme, Manchester was accepted on his second request:

> Although I was in the Party, I was more of a militant trade unionist, and I had a keen anti-fascist outlook. I would do anything to combat fascism in Britain or anywhere else.[117]

Maurice Levine's decision to fight was straightforward. His attempt to get into Spain was protracted.

> I was already a political animal. I was already very interested in what was taking place in Europe; in Germany and Italy in particular. Other countries in Europe—Bulgaria, Yugoslavia, Hungary - they were all semi-fascist countries. The only real democratic countries were the Scandinavian ones and England and France…You knew there were groups of people in Europe, mostly political exiles and Frenchmen, who had already gone over the border and were taking part in militias, mostly on the Aragon front.

Maurice tried to make his way to Spain in September of 1936, before the International Brigades were formed.

> I was trying to go to Spain at the time, along with Bill Benson, a spring-maker from Eccles, but we were turned down. I first approached the local office of the Communist Party with Benson in September…they did not know it was possible, or whether there was an organisation dealing with it.[118]

Having had no luck at the Manchester offices, Maurice and Benson went down to London, to the Party offices there, only to be told the same thing: there was nothing in place for volunteers as yet. They stayed a week in London waiting to hear something. At the end of the week, they went back to the offices in King Street but there was no change. Party General Secretary Harry Pollitt expressed the view that there was no point because Franco's forces would be victorious in a matter of weeks. Maurice and Bill retuned to Manchester until the second week of November when the International Brigades had been formed, and they were asked by the Party if they still wanted to go.

> I knew three others, Jewish boys who wanted to go, members of the YCL from Cheetham. There was my pal, Bill Benson, a boy from Disbury, only about 20, named Eddie Swindells. There was Ralph Cantorovitch who lost his life. There was George Westfield who lost his life, Eddie Swindells lost his life. Out of the first eight who left Manchester, five were killed.[119]

When Maurice and his five comrades returned to King Street, they were given the fare for a weekend ticket to Paris and an address of the Brigade recruiting office, but no papers. When they got to the Paris recruiting office, in the absence of papers, they were turned away. In hindsight Maurice understood their suspicion.

> They were worried about fascists infiltrating and they did. That is why André Marty appeared paranoid. The representative of the Republican government wouldn't accept us. We didn't know what to do. But in the same building were the offices of the metal workers trade union. We went to see them. They believed our story. They said leave it with us. They put us in a hotel in Paris. We met this chap every night from the union. We didn't have any money. He said one night, 'I'm going to order English tea for you as a treat.' We were bloody starving at the time. The tea came, all very delicate. After five days we were called back to the office. Two more English had come out. We were told to meet a man at Austerlitz [train station] who would give us tickets for Perpignan.[120]

André Marty was a leading member of the French Communist Party (PCF) from 1924 to 1955. During the civil war he was secretary of the Comintern and the political commissar of the International Brigades, in practice the Comintern's representative in Spain and the IB's chief organiser. He was stationed at the IB training base in Albacete and developed a reputation for executing his own men. He saw fascist infiltrators where there weren't and was given the nickname 'the butcher of Albacete'. He claimed to have executed 500 IB volunteers but such a figure is highly dubious. British sculptor and soldier Jason Gurney:

> He may have been a great chap in his day, but in Spain he was both a sinister and a ludicrous figure. He was a large, fat man with a bushy moustache and always wore a huge, black beret—looking like a caricature of an old-fashioned French petty bourgeois. There is no doubt he was quite literally mad at this time. He always spoke in a hysterical roar, he suspected everyone of treason, or worse, listened to advice from nobody, ordered executions on little or no pretext—in short, he was a real menace.[121]

Bernard McKenna was 21 when the civil war broke out, having been in the South Manchester Young Communist League for two years prior. He described the branch as having a core membership of 16-18 members. Three of his comrades, Alec Armstrong, Fred Killick and Vic Shammah went over to Spain before him and were killed.

> I saw Mick Jenkins [Manchester district organiser] and got refused because I had no military knowledge, but as things got a bit tighter, I got the okay to go.[122]

The Party made it a requirement that volunteers be at least 21 years of age and preferably unmarried, but found this difficult to enforce.

> Some people from North Manchester, under 21, were sent back when they got there. Monty Rosenfield was one—at least three or four. When numbers dropped off, the British CP wanted to keep a standing, and they relaxed their own rules.[123]

The route to Spain for volunteers usually involved an interview at the Party headquarters in London, the purchase of a ten-shilling weekend ticket to Paris, which required no passport, then reporting to the PCF office in Paris, followed by a long journey south and then a perilous or relatively straightforward passage across the Pyrenees. During the latter half of 1936, the border between France and Spain was open for volunteers to cross, but by 1937 it was closed, and volunteers were led across by guides, often at night to avoid border patrols. In January 1937 Neville Chamberlain's government enforced the Foreign Enlistment Act, which meant that British volunteers could no longer be recruited openly.

Bernard McKenna's border crossing was relatively straightforward.

> I left my family, my brother and younger sister. I didn't make much difference. I was a jack of all trades in a textile firm in Manchester. I dropped a letter from London. I met Springall [Political Commissar of the British Battalion] at King Street. Then a group of us got the night train to Paris.
>
> *And you managed to get into Spain before the French closed their border?*
>
> Yes. I was given a code to use in Paris—a sentence and a cigarette with a lionheart on it. It was like a recruitment office, like a labour exchange. I was given some money and a ticket and told to go to Austerlitz. When I got there, there were three or four hundred, less than 20 British. We went to Perpignan and then on coaches to Figueres.[124]

Benny Goldman described a more arduous journey.

> It was one of the worst experiences I've ever had.
>
> *Worse than the fighting?*
>
> It was part and parcel of it. We didn't know we were going to cross the Pyrenees. We walked from Perpignan to a mile over the frontier. It was late January, knee-deep in snow.
>
> *What were you wearing?*
>
> I was in a jacket, an open-necked shirt. In Perpignan we were in a barn, 10 or 12 of us. This guide came with four more. They spoke in French. I didn't understand what the devil was happening. Slowly and surely, it became

clear. Knee-deep in snow. There were two American comrades—and I was seriously thinking of joining them—I'd already reached the depths of despair. Three or four in the morning we were going up one mountain, down the other side, up another. On and on, it was endless. And they said they were shattered; they couldn't put one leg in front of the other and we had to leave them there.

*Did you ever see them again?*

No. We never knew what happened to them. We got into Spain just as it was getting light.[125]

## I remember him very clearly

The Party had hoped the bulk of their IB volunteers would have some military training, but it was not the case. Added to that, the training many volunteers were provided with was inadequate. Early British arrivals like Maurice Levine and his comrades came face to face with political commissar André Marty.

When we finally got to Albacete we paraded in the bullring before André Marty. There were hundreds circling the bullring, they were pouring into Spain, different nationalities. Marty stood in the centre, calling out for specialisms. Who were the machine gunners etc? We seven were almost the only ones who hadn't any experience. We were told to join the French battalion and I was given a bag of potatoes and told to peel them.[126]

Sam Wild had experience of both small arms and the Lewis machine gun from his time in the Royal Navy and was made British Battalion armourer at the Battle of Jarama in February 1937. Accounts from veterans generally describe the training received as rudimentary. The shortage of arms and ammunition for the International Brigades and the Republican Army, in general, is well documented. Unlike many, Bernard McKenna arrived to receive relatively good basic training, albeit in French.

I was lucky. I had about three months' training. Went right through the French infantry handbook, start to finish. A very demanding commander, a Czech. He obviously had military experience. A little dumpy fellow he was, reminded me of Pushkas in later life. He knew his stuff and ran the section well.

*Were you using Soviet arms?*

Mixed arms. Old French, old Swiss. We had a firing range at Albacete. I was machine-gun drilled. Hand grenades, small mortars. I was competent.

*The training, what language was it in?*

When I first got there, French was the lingua franca, spoken and written. I could read and write it, I was okay. By May [1937] the language changed to Spanish. We were incorporated into the Spanish Army.[127]

Benny Goldman's experience, when he arrived in Spain in early 1937, was very different.

The first time I saw a rifle was in Madrigueras [Albacete vicinity]. We were shown how to put a clip in the rifle. The clip didn't have bullets. We were shown how to handle the rifle. It was a Soviet rifle from after the First World War. We didn't fire it because the ammunition was scarce.[128]

Sam Wild confirmed that at most, those fighting at Jarama had received six weeks' training. He also added:

When I look back, I'm surprised there were any survivors from the early days. The first guns we got were from Austria and bore the date 1888.[129]

A typical schedule at Albacete was: rise at 5.30am, breakfast at 6.15am, fall in at 6.45am, training until noon. Resume at 2.15pm, finished at 5pm. Lights out at 10pm. In the evening there were lectures on Marxism and the nature of the Soviet Union. By the end of 1936, the British were in sufficient numbers in Madrigueras (a village 20 kilometres north of Albacete), to form a company of around 145 men. They were part of the French 'La Marseillaise', a battalion formed under the XIV Brigade.

Battalion members from Manchester, Maurice Levine, Bill Benson and others, first saw action outside the town of Lopera in Andalusia in December 1936. Shortly before the action Maurice and Bill were ordered to guard the commandant's quarters at Madrigueras. They could smell liver and onions prepared for an evening meal, and Maurice crept into the kitchen where the cook gave them some leftovers. Unfortunately, he was caught by the commandant, Gaston Delasalle, who had him imprisoned for six days. He was then taken to the front having never fired a rifle.

> Six or ten of us were detailed to carry a machine gun, a First World War machine gun. I was allocated to a French team. I lay next to the gunner as he set up the Maxim. All evening I had been repeating in French the number of my unit in case I got lost. "Troisième Pièce, Compagnie Mitrailleuse." In front I could see flashes of fire as the enemy opened up.[130]

The following day he and his comrades were ordered away from the hill they had been occupying, back to their own company as the language barrier was too problematic. Maurice was sent to a field hospital to care for the wounded of what became known as the Battle of Lopera which began on 27 December 1936. The objective was to take the Nationalist-held town. The XIV Brigade had around 3,000 men, but no artillery or air support. There followed an air bombardment without opposition. Two of the British fatalities that day were central committee member and historian Ralph Fox from Halifax, and the poet John Cornford from Cambridge; in the same company as Maurice.

> I remember this very clearly. Someone called out that Ralph Fox had been left on the hill wounded and this young man John Cornford, who had a bandage around his head because he had been wounded at University City in the December fighting, immediately cleared off to help this man. I wrote to Cornford's brother and told him what I knew.[131]

Maurice believes that the white bandage around Cornford's head gave him away to enemy soldiers. Before that day Maurice had not seen a corpse before. Initially it was a shock, "I got a bit of a wind up." It was something to which he would get accustomed.

> A man from Oldham called Rawson who had fought in World War One, a communist leader in Oldham. I remember him lying with his back against an olive tree. He was so pale, he'd been out of work four of five years, probably suffering from malnutrition. He got killed in action the following day. I remember him very clearly.[132]

The XIV Brigade lost 300 men in the Battle of Lopera with hundreds more wounded. The commander of the Brigade's French battalion, Gaston Delasalle, the officer who had Maurice imprisoned, was accused of incompetence, cowardice, and of being a spy by André Marty. He was court-martialled and executed by firing squad in early January 1937. His guard prior to execution was Maurice Levine.

As new arrivals came, the British were to form their own battalion in early 1937 consisting of four companies: three infantry and one machine-gun. The number one company was later named in honour of Labour leader Clement Attlee. That battalion came under the command of the XV International Brigade: a nationally mixed, mainly English-speaking brigade that included American, British, Canadian, Irish, Bulgarian, Greek, Serbian, French and Belgian volunteers. In units, a brigade comprises roughly 4,500 soldiers (IB brigades were generally smaller in number), a battalion up to 700 and a company 175.

## Two through my arm, two through my body

The XV Brigade, also known as the Abraham Lincoln Brigade, first took on the enemy at the Battle of Jarama in February 1937, the first major battle of the civil war. In November 1936 the seat of the Republican government had been moved to Valencia in case Madrid fell to the Nationalists. The Battle of Jarama was a Nationalist offensive to capture the road between Madrid and Valencia and displace Republican forces to the south of Madrid.

The Nationalist forces comprised 25,000 troops, including an elite force of Moroccan Legionnaires as well as German armour. Republican numbers were roughly the same but they were soon pushed back to the Jarama River, 25km south east of Madrid and within shelling range of the arterial road. Republican defences massed on the low hills east of the Jarama. On 11 February Nationalist troops crossed the river below and began advancing up the rocky slopes, through clutches of olive trees, towards them. It was at this point the British Battalion was sent into action. Benny Goldman and the other volunteers undergoing training in Madrigueras were ordered on to lorries to be taken to the front.

> When Franco first raised the rebellion, he made very rapid progress, they were very well armed and they had trained troops from Germany, the Condor Legion. They swept across Spain with the object of seizing the Jarama Bridge… four or five miles from the Madrid Valencia road linking Madrid, Valencia, and Barcelona. If they had seized that bridge the war would have been over. The Republican government put in two of its best divisions and the whole of the International Brigades. I was ready to go. In those days you were fired up with a lot of enthusiasm for the fight against fascism. You were quite prepared to fight and die.

Fifty-five years after the battle, Benny recalled his first experience of action.

> We got there. I was behind an olive tree. I'd dug a little hole behind it. An explosion took place. I don't know if it was a mortar or a grenade. Blood started pouring off my chin. I knew then that I'd been wounded in the head. If you're wounded in the head the odds are, you're going to die and I didn't want to die. So, I galloped back…they slapped a bandage on my head. I was put on a stretcher; we were still under fire. A piece of shrapnel had been imbedded in my cheek. Eight days later I was back at the front. I was in the front for two months. One minute you're talking with someone, joking or arguing with someone, the next minute you're burying them.[133]

IB casualties at the Jarama were notoriously high. They were up against fierce Moorish troops, outnumbered and outgunned. Maurice Levine says the Moors had a reputation for cruelty.

> We knew the enemy was in front of us. There were all sorts of stories about the Moors. They mutilated you.

You believed it. They took away your manhood etc. All these horror stories.[134]

Some brigaders were naïve in combat, providing targets by standing on the skyline. International Brigade historian Richard Baxell:

> The battalion was then subjected to a three-hour artillery and machine-gun barrage, before being attacked by 'at least three battalions' of experienced Moroccan infantry. For many of the British volunteers, this was their first experience of action, and they faced the battle-hardened, elite regulars of Franco's Army of Africa. The Moroccan troops were highly skilled soldiers, in their element when advancing across the open terrain of the Jarama valley.[135]

On a single day, 12 February 1937, the British Battalion suffered 275 casualties out of 600. Among the Mancunians killed at Jarama on that day were: Clem Becket, Mandall Montague, Alec Armstrong, Norman Wilkinson, and Arthur Porter—who had arrived in Spain the week before.

Bert Maskey was killed at Jarama on 14 February, Fred Newbury died of wounds on 20 February, Frank Whitehead was killed on 24 February. Eddie Swindells was killed on a date unrecorded. WR Kenny from Manchester is recorded as "dying of wounds sustained at Jarama". Robert Ward is recorded as "died in Colmenar hospital from wounds sustained at Jarama, 14 June 1937."[136]

Due to losses at Jarama and elsewhere the accusation developed that the Republican Army used the IB as shock troops: soldiers that would lead the advance and expect to take higher than average casualties. Shock troops are classically elite, highly trained units, as the Moors were for the Nationalists, but the opposite was the case with the IB and some charged the Republican Army with being careless with the lives of foreign fighters. They were to stay in their trenches until 17 June by which time almost all of the officers had been killed or captured and the battalion of 600 men reduced to around 400.

Sam Wild was one of those wounded on 12 February on the Pingarrón hills. He was leading a group that remained to cover the withdrawal of his comrades, creeping through an olive grove. Sam received four bullet wounds in him: two in the arm and two in the left side. He was in hospital until 7 May when he returned to the front.

> You had to take the fighting in your stride. We were put in a position on a hill confronted by Germans and Moors and suffered casualties. Two through my arm and two through my body. A lad led me out—when he got a bullet in his leg. All four went through me.[137]

Casualties were such that one of the hillocks became nicknamed 'Suicide Hill'. Maurice Levine was also wounded at Jarama.

> I was at the Battle of Jarama for a few days. At that time, I was in number one company. I was made a political commissar. I was really a welfare officer. I was wounded at Jarama, went back after eight to ten days. Until we left in the middle of June.[138]

The International Brigades halted the fascist advance but at a heavy cost. Maurice Levine:

> During that time—12 February to the middle of June, four months, that part of Madrid area was never taken. From the original five or six hundred there were very few left. People had come since. But few were left from the original force.[139]

The Madrid Valencia Road was held for the Republic for much of the rest of the war.

## An army like no other
Some of those that survived the first day at Jarama had to be forced into action at gunpoint the next day. Historian Richard Baxell:

> During the night a number of stragglers were discovered at the cookhouse by George Aitken, who had replaced Dave Springhall as battalion political commissar. Aitken attempted to cajole them back to the line but, as he freely admits, some volunteers were pressed back to the

front under the threat of his gun. Another group of men were found hiding in wine vaults in a farmhouse behind the lines. They were also marched back to the front. Coerced or not, the volunteers would be desperately needed on the frontline over the next two days.[140]

Joe Norman recalled there being some desertions:

After Jarama discipline began to slip, that was why the Party sent more members into the battalion. There was no leave, and we'd taken such a hammering. The morale began to slip. No enthusiasm. No one refused an order, but no enthusiasm. A number of desertions. Some got away like any other army.[141]

Fred Copeman, who was wounded in the head and the hand and was to become Battalion Commander, also recalled: "Groups of men, led by some of the finest members of the battalion, were leaving the line without permission."[142]

Many of the deserters returned after a few days, perhaps having stiffened their resolve. This apparently, was not unusual. Jud Colman, a Manchester textile worker and a member of the YCL, is listed as a deserter after the Battle of Brunete at the end of July 1937. He returned and fought in the Battle of Teruel at the end of the year.[143] One or two made it as far as Barcelona and went to the British consulate. Those that were caught, with a few exceptions, were generally not shot, although it was discussed. Punishment for desertion usually involved digging latrines for the guardhouse. Apart from any moral considerations, shooting deserters from a volunteer force wasn't practical as they needed more volunteers to join. In some instances, brigaders were executed. During the summer of 1938 Maurice Ryan, an Irish corporal in the Machine Gun Company, was charged with firing on his own comrades whilst drunk at the Battle of the Ebro. An order came from brigade headquarters for him to be executed by the British Battalion. Sam Wild, who had been made Battalion Commander in March 1938, did not convene a firing squad but took Ryan to one side, informed him of the decision, and then asked him to walk in front of him and his adjutant George Fletcher. Ryan was shot in the back of the head. Eugene Downing was a comrade of Ryan's:

Vino was his downfall. During the Ebro battle he turned

*Sam Wild, bottom right, in hospital after Jarama*

his gun on his own comrades while roaring drunk. Eventually, he was executed. All this was well known to those of us in Mataro Hospital as new causalities arrived during the battle. I heard additional details from Prendergast in London during WW2. Sam Wild had given him the details. Sam and George Fletcher had taken Ryan for a walk and informed him of the decision that had been taken. He responded calmly: "You wouldn't do that Sam would you?" But he was wrong. He was shot in the back of the head.[144]

Since Downing wasn't present when Sam Wild executed Ryan, how would he have known Ryan's final words? Sam's son, Mike Wild, believes it is because Downing was in hospital at the same time as George Fletcher. Fletcher was described by comrade John Dunlop as "being in tears over that".[145] Mike Wild told me that his father always referred to the incident by saying "orders is orders", but that the event probably remained on his conscience. Wild was also known as a commander who would not have asked his men to carry out an order that he wouldn't carry out himself.[146] As well as the regular military hierarchy, the International Brigades also had Communist Party organisers and political commissars. Joe Norman was elected Party organiser for the British Battalion.

I was elected Party organiser to explain our objectives in the Spanish struggle and to collect Party dues. That kept us together. There is no doubt about it, with a political understanding we were able to explain why we were doing this. A political commissar was a different kettle of fish. He was really a personnel officer. Anything that went wrong in action he reported to the top brass. Mind you, we never knew what was said when they met.[147]

As far back as the English Civil War, Cromwell's New Model Army had a form of commissar in their religious ministers, whilst the IB version was adopted from the Red Army. Initially, the IB elected their military officers. Partly because of his military experience, Sam Wild was elected as a military commander of a British company at Albacete.

You had to be the first to attack and the last to retreat. Officers were elected by the men in the early days… Because of political cohesion, there was a spirit in that army like no other.[148]

He himself, having served in the armed forces, was not in favour of electing officers. In addition, to begin with, there was no saluting in the IB; as Joe Norman put it, we used to approach our officers and say, "Alright!" When the Brigades were incorporated to the Republican Army in January 1937, a greater level of discipline and hierarchy was introduced, which Joe thought was for the best. The casualty rate of volunteers prompted talk of cannon fodder in the British press. The *Daily Mail* even suggested that volunteers were not aware they were travelling to Spain to fight in a war. Under a headline "Britons lured to Spain" appeared photos of British prisoners captured at Jarama. The article read:

Here are the first pictures exclusive to the *Daily Mail* of some of the 35 misguided and helpless British prisoners who were captured by General Franco's forces on the Jarama front. They were sent to Spain by communists with promises of work at £6 a week. The first most of them knew of their real fate was when they were given arms and drafted onto the Reds' front line.[149]

Sam Wild was wounded on three other occasions after

Jarama: in the thigh at the Battle of Brunete in July 1937, in March 1938 and then in August 1938 at the Battle of the Ebro. Despite the latter injury in the hand, he refused to leave the front and was awarded the Spanish Medal of Valour, the equivalent of Britain's Victoria Cross. The citation read: "His untiring energy and efficiency gave an example of bravery to the whole Battalion."[150] Whilst recovering from his wounds, Sam returned to England to raise support for the Aid for Spain campaign. He was met by Special Branch at Newhaven on 1 October 1937, who described him in their report as:

> A seaman, born at Manchester on 19th August 1908, height 5'8", medium build; hair dark brown, eyes brown, complexion sallow, clean-shaven, proceeding to 34 Stockton Street, Moss Side.[151]

Sam was the third and final British Battalion commander and promoted to major in October 1938. Garry McCartney, a railway worker from Glasgow, who served in a machine gun company under Sam, said of him: "Sam was a great person and the battalion would have done anything that Sam asked them to do."[152] On one occasion Joe Norman recalls he and Sam fought their way out of capture with their fists.

> Me and Sam Wild, Bob Walker and the Welsh commissar Dobson—he got killed on the Ebro at the finish—we were retreating from the Aragon front. We walked along the mountains and down into the fields grubbing for anything that was growing. Ten days of doing that. We were going along a viaduct to see where the enemy was, then all of a sudden, we were surrounded. Dobson he was a big lad, he hit this officer under the chin, I clocked another one with my water bottle, Sam he let go and Dobson he put the boot in another one and we started off. I jumped over the side of the viaduct, got caught up in barbed wire and found Sam at the other end. Walker and Dobson, we didn't see for three days.[153]

Joe believed that one of the reasons the IB suffered high casualties was that there were Franco supporters in the leadership of the Republican Army deliberately ordering foreign fighters into the firing line.

Some of them were in the pay of Franco all the time. Sometimes men were sent into action and we didn't really know why, impossible positions. We know now the fascists were [involved] up high—and they were telling us what to do to make sure we got hammered. My company at Teruel lost 13 men, we were left in an olive grove at night, that's how I got captured.[154]

Alex Clifford, author of *The People's Army in the Spanish Civil War*,[155] responded to this assertion by commenting:

Paranoia about Fifth Column traitors was rife during the civil war, but the reality was that Republican military defeats were the result of the poor training, equipment logistics and leadership of the People's Army, and the superiority of the enemy on these counts. For the most part, International Brigaders were under the senior command of Soviet Red Army officers at divisional level, and Spanish Communists at corps level and neither demographic was liable to be in the pay of Franco.[156]

Upon capture Joe Norman was sent to San Pedro de Cardeña prison camp, as was Bernard McKenna.

Bernard first went into action at the Battle of Brunete in July 1937, 15 miles west of Madrid, a Republican offensive to drive the Nationalists away from the capital. It was the Republicans however, who were driven back, suffering many casualties.

Three hundred went in, and 80 came out. It was a half-hearted offensive. We made big advances. If we had brought the troops, it would have been all right. I don't know if it was stupidity or what.

Maurice Levine said of Brunete:

I saw him [Battalion Commander Copeman] weeping after the Brunete offensive. I estimate 86 lost at Brunete and a hell of a lot wounded. The Battalion was never the same after that. It was never the same. I saw Copeman weeping: he was a hugely emotional man. He was a tough guy. Boxed in the navy. A really tough guy... People didn't come back from leave. The Scottish Medical Aid Committee were putting people on freighters. There was an organisation helping people desert: British Intelligence.[157]

As well as general soldiering, 22-year-old Bernard McKenna was a signals operator. His job was to lay telephone lines across the front. It was a dangerous responsibility and an exhausting one. "The trouble was, while everyone else was sleeping at night, you had to go out and mend the lines."

> I was wounded on the first day. A slight wound, I was shot in the foot. I was walking along carrying a telephone. I got back a few days before the end. A right bloody mess.

After Brunete, Bernard fought on the Aragon front near Zaragoza. Zaragoza was known as the second city of anarchism.

> It was their town. But by some foolishness they allowed the fascists to take it at the beginning of the war, against all the odds. Then they tried to take it back, but by inept military tactics—no really organised forces.

Combat apart, daily soldiering for the International Brigades was tough. Bernard again:

> I went mad with thirst. I used to set off with a water bottle but we were going from dawn to four o'clock. The Nationalists were better armed, much better trained than us. Most of the European International Brigaders had some military training, but not us.[158]

In his article *Myths of the International Brigades*, Richard Baxell says "almost 50 percent of the British and Irish volunteers had some form of training before their time in Spain." He goes on to say that "in no way did this make them a match for Franco's elite Moroccan soldiers and Foreign Legion".[159] Bernard and others were aware that the odds were increasingly uneven.

*Did you discuss the fact that you would lose the war?*

> We didn't say that, no. I had the feeling, later on, we wouldn't be winning. I think we accepted from the start

that we wouldn't win the war, that we wouldn't get out. But you accepted that. You were there to do a job. That was it.[160]

Benny Goldman was more fatalistic.

You developed a mentality that is perhaps difficult to understand. You knew you were never going to get out of Spain alive. Everyone I think realised they were going to get killed. You were there in the firing line. The door was closed. You were in Spain and in the army.[161]

This seems a realistic assumption to have made. Certainly, by August of 1937, the war was going badly for the Republican Army, and the IB had been in the front line at Jarama, Brunete, and along the Aragon front. Most of the volunteers didn't have passports and if they did desert it was very difficult to get out of the country. In March 1937 General Franco ordered that any captured foreign fighters should be executed. A year later the order was withdrawn under pressure from Mussolini, so that IB prisoners could be swapped for Italian soldiers held by the Republican Army. Bernard McKenna:

Normally in the earlier course of the war when they caught International brigaders, they shot them. We were rebels against the rebels. In retaliation, when we took a group of prisoners, we separated all the officers out, including those that tried to dodge, took the infantry off to a camp and shot the officers. Very grim—we got used to it.[162]

The Battle of the Ebro between July and November 1938 was the largest and longest battle of the civil war. Hugely costly for the Republican Army, it was the last battle that the IB were involved in. Owing to prior casualties the British Battalion had to be heavily fortified by Spanish recruits. Sam Wild:

In each battalion there were Spaniards and by this time a general recruitment had taken place in Catalonia. Many of the youth joined. There were 400 Spaniards in the battalion and 300 British lads. We had quite an influx of young Catalonians.[163]

It was a decisive victory for Franco's forces. Between 10,000 and 15,000 Republican soldiers were killed and nearly 20,000 captured and more than 90 members of the British Battalion were killed during the battle. The back of the Republican Army was broken. Even after the establishment of prisoner exchanges, some IB volunteers were shot upon capture. The future of those that were imprisoned was uncertain.

*Comrades Come Rally*

# Chapter 6

## Diaries and Dispatches

> "1 March 1937. Only four left from the first English boys at the front." Diary of Ralph Cantor

Whilst many survivors wrote memoirs about their experiences in Spain, Maurice Levine's and Ralph Cantor's are among the few surviving diaries from British Battalion members of the International Brigade. Cantor and Levine went out to Spain at the same time; they were part of the same small group of British volunteers. Hence their diaries cover the same events, in particular the Battle of Lopera and the trial and execution of Colonel Delasalle. Cantor's is in the form of pencil notes in a pocket diary; Maurice Levine's consists of typed-up prose, around 4,000 words copied from a lost notebook he wrote in at the time.[164] They are both, in their own way, unique records. Cantor was killed at the Battle of Brunete in July 1937, whilst Maurice survived the war, and alongside his own diary are his remarks on Cantor's.

What we have in Cantor's case are entries from the front line scribbled down at the approximate time, an almost immediate response to events. There are no crossing-outs or second drafts; we are close to his thoughts. In Levine's case, though he has typed up his notebook at a later date, possibly back in England, the prose is urgent and present tense, often broken, remarking on several occasions that he "cannot read own notes". The text reads as Maurice writing to himself in the knowledge that he might not see the war out. In the end it was utilised as a source for his short publication, *Cheetham to Cordova*.

## Ralph Cantor

Though a 1937 pocket diary, he uses the November and December pages for entries during 1936, hence one can assume the days of the week were different. He records leaving Manchester on 22 November, arriving in Dunkirk and then Paris on 24 November.

### *25 November (1936)*
*Visited Louvre, Moulin Rouge.*

### *27 November*
*Perpignan to Figueres. Slept at Figueres Castello Fortress.*

The expansive castle at Figueres hosted foreign fighters when they first entered Spain. It was also the location of the final meeting on Spanish soil of the Republican parliament before the fortress fell to Franco.

### *1 December*
*Barcelona. Marched behind band. Marvellous town. That night to Valencia and Albacete.*

### *4 December*
*Attached to French machine gun squad—but rescued by timely arrival of Ralph Fox and others.*

In the notes section at the rear of the diary, Cantor records the names of the Mancunians and when they arrived.

### *November 1936*
*Ralph Cantor, Julius Colman, George Westfield, Eddie Swindells, Bill Benson, Maurice Levine*

### *5 December 1936*
*Fred Killick, Fred Bloor, Walter Greenhalgh, Hugh Barker, Michael Brown*

### *No date given*
*? Garrett, Edward Slam, Alec Armstrong, Bert Maskey, Lance Morgan, Bob Goodman, Vic Shammah, Pat Kennedy, Bob Ward, George Brown, Jim Kenny, Sydney Silver, Cyril Bowman, Benny Goldman, Alec Porter, Tommy Tanning, Clem Beckett.*

The first action that Ralph saw was at the Battle of Lopera on 27-29 December 1936. He was under the command of Gaston Delasalle, a man whose leadership Cantor had doubts about prior to the battle.

### *15 December*
*Lasalle our commandant takes us on 25-mile route march across ploughed fields. Feet all blistered. Old men all done in.*

The XIV International Brigade (3,000 men) led by General Walter launched the attack to regain Lopera from the Nationalists. At that time there were too few British to form a battalion, barely enough to form a company. The Brigade had little training, no telephone communications, nor any air or artillery support. The Nationalists had a shock brigade of Andalusian troops (2,000 men) and 2,000 Moroccan regulars and Spanish cavalry. In what Anthony Beevor describes as a debacle,[165] the XIV Brigade was decimated by machine gun fire, mortars and artillery. After 36 hours the attack was called off. International Brigade casualties were one in ten dead (300) and 600 wounded. Losses at Lopera, in Cantor's opinion, were down to an inept if not treacherous command.

### *27 December*
*Moving in convoy to front. Air raid. Several killed with machine gunners. News that Cornford killed. Carrying ammo all night. Lasalle orders us up the hill into the fascist machine gun fire.*

### *28 December*
*Saw Ralph Fox for the last time at 7am. Found killed by a stray bullet at 9pm. By French?*

### *29 December*
*Deliberately kept without water despite heat. Little food.*

### *30 December*
*Meeting of lads objecting to spate of lies coming from Commander and political commissar. Learn that Lasalle commanded brancardiers to desert their stretchers.*

Brancardiers translates as stretcher bearers. It could be the case that Ralph Cantor made entries in hindsight, days after the event, even after Delasalle was executed for treachery, but that is not the feel of the document. What are the lies that he is referring to here? It's two days after Fox was killed, Ralph believes by friendly fire and a note on the International Brigade Memorial Trust website says of Ralph Fox: "Various rumours surround his death, including a story that he was killed by British volunteers and the CP covered up the fact."[166]

The lies could also refer to the case of Delasalle who was executed for being an enemy agent. Although it might be true that Marty saw infiltrators where they didn't exist, could he have been correct in Delasalle's case?

### *Sunday 3 January 1937*
*Trial of our commandant Delasalle. Proved to be receiving money from Italians. Nathan chief witness. Verdict and sentence and execution within minutes.*

Walter Greenhalgh from Miles Platting, Manchester, who also fought at Lopera, is less convinced. He believes that Delasalle was made a scapegoat for a more general incompetence. "We much preferred to believe that there was treachery rather than incompetence."[167] Anthony Beevor finds probable cause in André Marty's propensity to execute his own men. He quotes the Soviet writer Ilya Ehrenburg who described Marty as "like a mentally sick man".[168] Nathan refers to George Nathan, a First World War veteran from Hackney who briefly replaced Delasalle as commander of the largely French Battalion, before becoming Chief of Staff of the XV Brigade on 26 January 1937. During the Irish War of Independence, Nathan had served as a paramilitary for the British Army, which he was candid about. In response, Irish volunteers voted by 26 to 11 to leave the British Battalion and join the American Lincoln Battalion. Nathan was openly gay, and historian Cecil Eby argues that as such he was prevented from joining the Communist Party. The Bolshevik government of 1917 had decriminalised homosexuality; a measure reversed later by Stalin who made homosexuality a crime punishable by up to five years imprisonment with hard labour. Some Marxists at the time labelled being gay as a fascist perversion. Like Cantor, Nathan was killed at Brunete in July 1937.

At the end of the battle, the gallant English major... was

*Diaries and Dispatches*

*Ralph Cantor's diary, courtesy WCML*

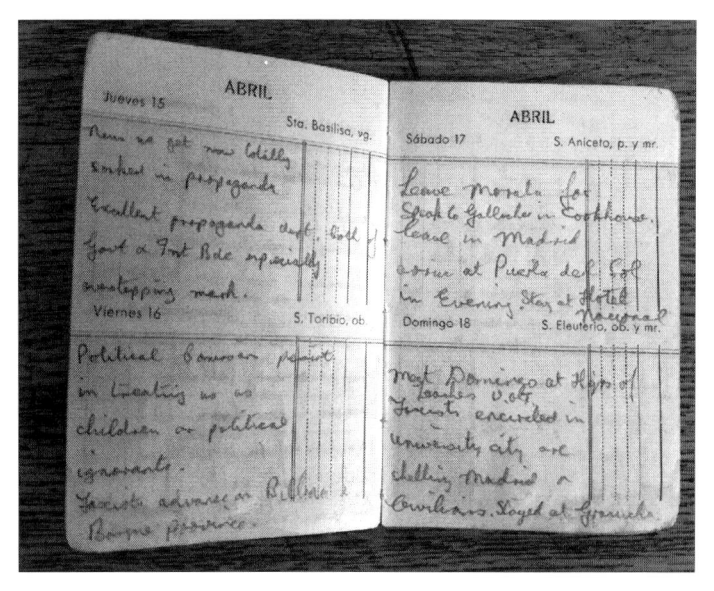

killed... In his last moments, he ordered those around to sing him out of life. At nightfall he was buried in a rough coffin beneath the olive trees near the River Guadarrama... 'Gal' and Jock Cunningham, two tough men who had been jealous of Nathan, stood listening [to the funeral oration] with tears running down their cheeks.[169]

Maurice Levine believed that Nathan's ability as an officer was not recognised by the British. When Maurice refers to 'they', one assumes he means the CPGB. Copeman refers to Fred Copeman who became a British Battalion Commander.

They didn't want people elected and they didn't want Nathan. But the French knew of his character and he went to command a French battalion. He was a military man. Copeman couldn't compare to Nathan.[170]

In February 1937 Ralph Cantor saw action alongside the rest of the British at Jarama. Unlike many others he survived.

### *Saturday 13 February*
*First day of action. Fiercest battle.*

### *Sunday 14 February*
*Heavy air raid today.*

### *Monday 15 February*
*Benson and Swindells killed.*

### *Wednesday 17 February*
*Americans arrive. Are 450 strong. As I write 60 planes come over and bomb shattering the ground.*

### *Tuesday 23 February*
*Ambulance driver (Yank) shot while evading patrol. Move body to mortuary.*

A series of entries throughout the diary concern Ralph's dissatisfaction with political commissars and other complaints.

### *Saturday 10 April*
*Political commissariat makes grave errors, or shows*

*favouritism in sending comrades to England and other decisions. Much grumbling.*

### Thursday 15 April
*News we get now totally soaked in propaganda dept. Both the government and the International Brigade, especially overstepping the mark...*

### Friday 16 April
*Political commissars persist in treating us as children or political ignorants. Fascist advance on Bilbao.*

### Saturday 24 April
*Political commissariat of battalion and brigade definite failures due to inexperience, wrong approach and wrong line. English battalion commissars succeed in provoking discontent in some decisions. Political commissars also badly chosen.*

### Monday 26 April
*Political commissars all along have fed us on lies. Political commissars are the most disliked men in the brigade. Spirit of the men, notwithstanding, is excellent.*

It should be said that there is evidence that scepticism of political commissars was widespread and volunteers were apt to call them "comic stars".[171] Years later Maurice Levine wrote a response to Cantor's diary, after it came into the possession of Eddie and Ruth Frow.

> It is evident from his diary that Cantor was occupied most of his time behind the actual front. His criticisms of the Political Commissars stem from factors only hinted at. The breeding ground and source was the lengthy stay (four months) at the Jarama front. The Political Commissars had to explain why they stayed such a lengthy period with all the discomforts and strain, living in dug-outs, monotonous food, lack of comforts and being infested with body lice.[172]

With the exception of two short rest periods, the British Battalion remained at Jarama until 17 June. After 73 days in the front line, the Brigade was finally withdrawn, allowing some of the British to take a few days rest in nearby Madrid. Cantor's expressions of disaffection are interesting. They cut into the mythology surrounding the IB that fogs the history.

> ### *Sunday 2 May 1937*
> *Disturbing feature of the war is the distinctions which are too acute for justification. Sergeant receives more than double a volunteer. An officer more than four times as much, higher officers much more. Also acute distinction in food and accommodation. Separate doors for officers in one case.*

Inequality in pay would be down to the Republican Army and though Cheetham volunteer Benny Goldman remarked in interview that "money had no meaning", it clearly did. Sam Wild commented on the issue in interview.

> I was paid too much. I got a wage of about 1,000 pesetas a month. Which was too much for my requirements. The men were paid ten pesetas a week.
>
> *What did you spend it on?*
>
> Cognac, coffee, girls if you wanted them because prostitutes were still allowed in Barcelona. I've known myself sitting outside a bar in Barcelona when men from the battalion passed and stopped. "Hello Sam, are you enjoying yourself? Could you spare me 20 pesetas?" And that was the difference to other armies. In the villages people gave you wine and would never accept any money from you.[173]

Maurice Levine and Ralph Cantor grew up near one another, a matter of streets away. They were two of 16 volunteers from Cheetham who went to Spain. Six returned.

> I lived close to the Helman/Cantor family during the 20s and 30s. They were in some way unusual in that area of Cheetham between Strangeways and Hightown. Most of the parents were immigrants from Lithuania and Poland. The children had biblical first names

like Abraham, Isaac, David, Lazarus, Joseph, Maurice (Moses), Rachel, Sarah etc. The Helman/Cantor family had names entirely different, Lancelot, Oliver, Horace, Carmen etc. They were a socialist family with the mother I believe the source of their thinking. I remember the surprising thing for that neighbourhood and the time—the 1920s—the mother going out to work. This was most unusual. The Jewish families of the period were large and mother had enough to do to cope with ever increasing additions to the family.

Ralph was 20 years of age, of average height and first attended Waterloo Road Board School (Elementary) and later Manchester Central High School. He was alert and intelligent and had a knowledge of French.[174]

Cantor taught himself Spanish taking with him a phrase book and writing home to request a book on Spanish grammar. He acted as a translator for English patients and interviewed German prisoners. He wrote a great deal: letters, postcards, poetry, an article for the American *Daily Worker*. He had aspirations of not just writing a memoir, but of becoming a writer. Issy and Norah were Cheetham comrades from the Helman family, Norah being Ralph's half-sister.

Ralph Cantor
Socorro Rojo Internacional
Plaza del Altozano 161
Albacete
1-5-37
Dear Norah (Chucky), Issy, Edgar & Paul

I received your letter of the 16th two days ago, but am only able to answer it now, as we have just come out on rest. I wrote you a card when we were all joined together again, and Sydney is now coming into line and is certainly very brave. By the way, in connection with the book idea, "No Hay" which is Spanish for "not likely". Every Tom, Dick & Harry waited for this Spain issue to commence writing their book which naturally, each considers an epic. However as you know, my letters are more or less empty & abstract but I have a mine of information in my diary also I have spoken to many prominent Spaniards. I think "Victor Gollancz", "Martin Lawrence" & etc will be overwhelmed very shortly with requests for publishing these epic books. I have already read some of the books on "Spain" and it is amazing how some people will rush into print & obtain good publishing houses to sponsor their books which I have found to be misinformed and untrue. Of course I suppose it's the "Box Office" value that does it. At present, these books are just propaganda for one side or the other, but later I expect (perhaps in a year or 18 months time) there will be a number of really good objective books. I feel annoyed too at some of the journalists, some of whom are sent from as far as America, and are prepared to accept what they call "Tales of heroism" leadership etc. from any official behind the line. The American women journalists clamour for "sob column" material, and both the men & the women are just as portrayed on the screen. Frank Pitcairn is an exception. He has visited us in the front line. He goes into the "University City" and the "Casa del Campo" regularly for news. He is the most admired reporter here.[175]

He repeatedly notes the presence of Stephen Spender and is serious about his own poetry. Spender he describes as having an air of embarrassment about him, "hard to imagine him speaking with Gallacher". One of Cantor's poems was accepted by the American left-wing magazine *The New Masses*.

***14-4-37***
Dear Norah, Issy, etc,

The American journalists over here are very numerous and two of them took copies for publication in the United States. I have sent one copy home but in case it doesn't arrive, I am sending you another copy. This poem took me only about an hour to write and I chose a simple rhythm. However in order to test my capabilities in this direction I wrote a parody about an eccentric figure we have here. In this case I chose a more complicated rhyme and rhythm and it took me about an hour again to write 90 lines. Anyway it went over well and it was passed round the general staff. When I come home, am going to try my hand when I will have plenty of time to spare.

On Saturday 6 March 1937, Cantor and others were withdrawn from the front to be addressed by Harry Pollitt at Morata de Tajuna on the outskirts of Madrid. Cantor made notes in his diary from the speech remarking that Spender, Hemingway, Willie Gallacher, Professor JBS Haldane and the journalist Henry Brailsford were also present.

> Pollitt's speech at Morata de Tajuna. "In thirty years of speaking never before have I spoken under such stress and emotion. Japan got away with it. Italy have got away with it. It will not happen in Spain. The English stopped the fascists from entering Madrid"...pledge of Home Front struggle. Came by air on Spanish passport. Big arms consignment—trickling through of volunteers— read report in News Chronicle and Mail demanding the suppression of the Communist Party and arrest of its leaders. Also said this is the first time since Garibaldi there has been an international column. Pollitt spoke about the similarities of Madrid and Petrograd.

The notes are the basis of an article Cantor wrote for the US *Daily Worker*. Cantor reads as idealistic, disappointed with less than professional conduct, repelled by propaganda. Perhaps he feels it unnecessary, something only the enemy would stoop to.

### Wednesday 31 March
*Some disgusting characters sent out from various countries. No selection. Trotskyists, drunkards, thieves, hypocrites. Glasgow, Manchester, London and France worse culprits.*

### Thursday 1 April
*Battalion has a bad name (unmerited). Probably started by Tapsell, Vidal, Deck. Copeman has faith in men.*

Maurice Levine refuted the second statement. Ralph Cantor was killed in action at the Battle of Brunete in July 1937, aged 21. His comrade from Cheetham, Jud Colman, was next to him when he died. Jud wrote to Norah and Issy with the news.

Same address
Tuesday July 13

Dear Norah & Issy

I have never been a good letter writer and I find it difficult to express myself in the news that I want to tell you. Ralph has gone from us. I was with him to the last, believe me he never suffered in the slightest it was all over in a few seconds. Later on I will tell you if it is possible, I will tell you exactly what happened, all I can say is he died a true and good anti-fascist fighter. I am ok though naturally terribly shaken, the shock was so great I am now in the rear resting, I will probably do some work behind the lines, I will write again of course and let you know exactly what happened.

I cannot write about the offensive of course as anything might happen. France I notice is at last adopting a more favourable attitude to Spain. The crisis seems to be drawing near. I expect you will see Mr Cantor and break the news to him and also to Lance and Babs (I do not know her other name). Tell Mr Cantor how sorry I am but as you all know such things must happen in war. I cannot find any more words except that this fight will go on, we have great struggles in front of us and I know we will be victorious, we have lost a lot of comrades but I assure you they will be avenged, we will not rest until the fascists are completely destroyed and Europe made a place where the word war is no longer understood.

Best of health and luck
Sincerely Yours
Jud

I have addressed this letter to 142 Waterloo Road as I have lost my diary with all my addresses in it.

At some point, Eddie Frow wrote down a verse by Ralph and left it in his file at the Working Class Movement Library.

*But we who fight to live today*

*Are not drops in the ocean*

*We are the men who change the world*

*The crux of future motion.*

**Ralph Cantor, Spain**

## Maurice Levine

Maurice Levine wrote a great deal, about Spain, about his early life, about the Party. There are two hefty bundles of notes, sketches, memoirs and unfinished manuscripts at the Working Class Movement Library. Only 54 pages made it into print as *Cheetham to Cordova*, a highly engaging pamphlet published in 1984. His eventful life spanned the 20th century and at times he writes quite detailed, vivid prose about his upbringing, the Depression, his experiences in Australia and Spain. Amongst the many pages are eight A4 sheets, typed up from a notebook he must have kept in Spain.

The diary entries end in January 1937 but one feels certain that the notebook, wherever it is, contains more. What we have begins:

> Jeans, Birch, and Tich Adderley are dead, Lesser and Scott are missing. We advanced towards the pueblo, (our objective was the monastery like building) in two lines, the first line was about twenty to thirty yards ahead of the rear one...Someone was yelling to keep our heads down...Someone else was shouting, "Adelante,", "Abajo", "Alto ahí". We suddenly found ourselves in the middle of some nasty cross fire, which turned out to be from a group of Thaelmann comrades and some Fascists who had occupied a small fort-like construction. We received orders to attack, retire, then advance on what had been our left flank then to retire and reform and attack the woods on our right flank, who after firing back at us, cursed us in fluent and unmistaken English, it turned out to be Romilly, Scott, and a few of the

German comrades. Whoever it was that issued those orders, they should have been shot.[176]

There is no date on this first page, because presumably there are other earlier lost pages. The following entry is headed Saturday 19 December and it is probable that the entry above refers to the defence of Madrid. The writing doesn't bear the coolness of hindsight, it feels like it was written soon after events.

Maurice was initially a political commissar but news of his basic medical training got out and on 24 December 1936, he was put in charge of the field hospital.

Christmas Day... It is not a bit like Christmas where we are, I am in a rambling stone-built house... It is 11.40pm and I have only now had time to sit down... I think that I shall fall asleep if I sit for long... It's been a very hectic day... We, or rather the Company were ordered into action just before midday... We are attacking in the direction of Lopera and have been under heavy shell fire... The camilleros, or stretcher bearers, have behaved magnificently, they have risked their lives time after time to bring in their wounded comrades...The British joined with us late this afternoon, they deployed their troops a few hundred yards from where I had (on Nikki's advice) set up my forward first aid post... I have about two dozen Spanish comrades who are acting as stretcher bearers and helping out with the first aid arrangements... We have managed to "commandeer" two camions to use as ambulances to convey the wounded from the post to the temporary hospital that I am now in... I am hoping that HQ will send down a qualified doctor for some of the wounds are beyond my ability to do much for, except dress and give an injection of morphine.... We are trying to evacuate most of the wounded back to Andújar where they can be moved to bigger hospitals... This building is overflowing with wounded... I managed to "organise" some blankets and have tried to make the wounded comfortable the best way that we can. There are no beds, the nearest thing to a bed is in the large "wine" room, so called because it was a storage room for wooden wine (or olive) barrels...

The comrades have managed to place lengths of wood across several of the smaller barrels and have made straw or grass filled mattresses out of any material that they could lay their hands upon. I followed the British Company (it was not a Battalion as rumoured) as they went into action this afternoon, they arrived about 4.00pm and were on the M.M. Company's left flank, on the British left flank was the French Companies... The British Company was commanded by an ex-British Guards officer, Captain George Nathan, I met Bernard Knox, Jock Cunningham and John Cornford once again. We had little time or chance to talk. I have made up my mind to try and get attached to their company.

Maurice did get attached to the first British company of which Cantor was also a part.

Tuesday 29 December. Cornford was killed early this morning, he was shot in the head, I think that the white bandage he wore was the cause. (His badge of courage as he often referred to it). The political commissar Ralph Fox was also killed by a machine gun burst, his companions Nathan Segal and Geordie Johnson died in my clearing station about 3 hours ago. They both regained consciousness for a short time and were able to tell me something of what had been happening. I could only give them injections and I feel so inadequate to deal with these comrades. I have very little in the way of field dressings, drugs or surgical equipment, and I have no means of sterilising anything. I have been promised supplies, but each time I send the runner it's always "Mañana".

Of Delasalle's trial and execution, Maurice writes:

His execution was within a matter of minutes after being sentenced. He behaved with a certain amount of self-restraint until he was placed against the wall.... He cursed Marty in no uncertain manner, calling him a maniac, a homicidal, neurotic, and accusing him of being responsible for the deaths of hundreds of innocent members of the International Brigade.

As well as the diary, like Cantor, Maurice wrote numerous letters home. One particular letter from Maurice Levine is illustrative of what it meant to be a member of the Party at this time. For more experienced comrades, it was beyond having a relationship with the Party, it became one's persona. The letter is to Manchester District Secretary, Mick Jenkins, from Spain, 25 September 1937.

Dear Mick

It was only a fortnight ago that I read your letter which you wrote to Ralph Cantor and which he received just prior to the July offensive on the centre front. Ralph told me about it as we were resting a couple of days before the action commenced. I suppose you know all of the history of that action, so it will be futile of me to go over the general details. Of the more personal happenings you will know by now that I was hit. Once more my rabbit's foot did its duty.

I was having a little battle of my own with four or five fascists. They were only 20 yards away and we were all standing up. I managed to get two and then they got me. The twilight helped the bad shooting; by all the rules I should be organising the unemployed in heaven but I've the luck of a Jew.

During the close fighting—I should really say the hand to hand fighting—I got a fleeting glance of George then I was wounded. [The following two lines of the letter censored] This was on the night of July 6th when the British Battalion played the most important part in the taking of Villanueva de la Cañada. I watched [censored] reactions that day. It was the first time that [censored] was really in action. You know that I'm sparse in my praise of people. I can say that [censored] fought and died like the very best of his class that have fallen in the revolutionary struggle. When I reflect that fighters for freedom like [two lines censored] and the others from the M/c district who have fallen here in the Battle against fascism were attracted to the Communist Party as their party it is a sure guarantee that our Party will continue to attract the very best of the working class and those of the middle class for the fight against reaction, for progress and a Socialist Britain.

I shall shortly be returning to M/c. The Party and the YCL I have been told have made big strides forward since I left last November. I shall be looking forward to seeing a party that has a firm standing in M/c politics. Are you running a candidate in the November elections for the Cheetham ward? I don't think the day is very far off when the Party will represent one of these wards in the council chamber. I feel quite keen to know and feel the influence and progress the party has made since my absence. However, I shall have to leave my enquiries of the development of the revolutionary movement in M/c until my return.

A week ago I received a letter from Mr O'Neill. He states that my card will be made up to date on my return which means of course that I shall return (to) full union membership rights.

Remember me to the comrades
Salud! and revolutionary greetings.
Maurice

Twelve months prior to writing the letter, Maurice was working in a Macintosh factory in Cheetham. He was among the first British volunteers in Spain. His sense of duty, of responsibility, pervades the letter. It bears the tone of a British Army officer in correspondence to a superior during the Second World War. By all accounts, Maurice Levine was a courageous soldier. He was wounded twice. On the first occasion in April 1937, George Brown wrote to Mick Jenkins a few days later.

Maurice got wounded a few days ago. He volunteered for a patrol to go over towards the enemy lines on recognisance, and was unfortunate to get a bullet through the arm though not serious. He will be back with us in a few days. I think Maurice is one of the most courageous men in our battalion which has already displayed its supreme courage to the world and I may say with all fairness that our comrades from the Manchester and Salford area are second to none.[177]

It was George Brown that Maurice was referring to in the censored sections of the third paragraph of his letter.

Maurice was ten years older than Ralph Cantor. He had been to Australia to look for work before he'd gone to Spain. His commitment, his Marxism and confidence in the future of socialism, was greater than most others. For such comrades the Party was the embryo of a new society within the womb of the old and life was subordinate to destiny. The CPGB was unlike any other party in Britain; not only in where its loyalties lay but in the scale of its ambitions. Members' allegiance and discipline was incomparable to other political parties, as was the authority its leadership aspired to.

*(left) Maurice Levine, Spain, middle-right*

## General secretary Harry Pollitt
Harry Pollitt was not a cult figure but he was hugely respected, revered by some, in a way that the theorist Palme Dutt was not; Pollitt's leadership style was charismatic and paternal rather than polemical.[178] Dorothy Arnold wrote to Pollitt from Spain to inform him she was getting married.

> Albacete 19th April [1937]
>
> Dear Comrade Pollitt
>
> This letter is to confess that I am disobeying your order not to get married to a foreigner. Well, you can blame it on to our countrymen, who have the same chance but fail to take it! I hope at any rate it won't mean a complete goodbye to work in England. I also hope to do some creative work one of these fine days—which after all is necessary. Thus, do I salve any conscience you see! I hope I shall be forgiven. Salutations com[m]unistas. (It's a Frenchman)
>
> Dorothy J Arnold[179]

The letter suggests the two were acquainted. Whilst there may be an element of tongue in cheek banter regarding Pollitt's "order" there was also possibly a serious underlying issue. Under the 1914 British Nationality and Status of Aliens Act, "the wife of an alien shall be deemed to be an alien".[180] A British woman who married a foreign national became a foreign national herself. It wasn't until 1948 that UK women were granted a right to their own nationality regardless of their marital status. Bert Maskey's wife lost her British nationality when she married a Russian national. Pollitt had likely warned Dorothy not to marry a foreigner because she might not be able to return to the UK. Nevertheless, the General Secretary considered his province to be a wide one.

Pollitt's most onerous responsibility was informing relatives of the death or capture of a volunteer. He wrote letters of condolences to the families and also received requests for information from relatives, as well as correspondence from the British Battalion. The Pollitt Papers at the People's History Museum in Manchester is a sizable file. The lack of accurate and timely information on the fate of volunteers was a recurring problem and a cause of distress for families. Often families were informed or misinformed of a son's death from a comrade home on leave. Labour Party member Frank Whitehead from Wythenshawe, Manchester, was killed at Jarama on 24 February 1937, but the news came to the family unofficially, some weeks later by word of mouth from local Communist Party members. The family wrote to Pollitt complaining bitterly.

> You state you have no responsibility but this is not true. As the organisation who sends these men out you are responsible, it is your duty to tell relations whatever news you get. Mrs Whitehead, who is too ill to write, desires a death certificate and full information on where and when Frank met his death. She also wants her son's body returned to England. Unless we get satisfaction, we shall have no hesitation in exposing the damnable inefficiency of the British Communist Party to the capitalist press. We are aware that Frank was not influenced by the Communist Party to go to Spain. But you paid his fare and must face up to your responsibilities.[181]

Information back to Britain could be poor for a number of reasons. There was a high turnover of volunteers and officers. There were language barriers, the front was moving rapidly, volunteers used aliases, particularly Jewish volunteers. Bodies were not recovered, people deserted, sometimes temporarily, then returned to their unit. The Party did not have the necessary administrative infrastructure behind the lines.

Harry Pollitt often knew personally the men and the families he was writing to. Evelyn Taylor, who had been active in fighting Mosley's Blackshirts, married George Brown shortly before he left for Spain and wrote to Pollitt on news of her husband's death.

> I was told last night and felt I had to write to you although I don't know quite what to say. It doesn't seem to be true that he is dead. I was so sure he would come back. You know as well as I do what a fine lad he was and I am not blaming you or the party. He went willingly. He told me he should have gone before but

wanted to stay to see me. Those last few weeks we had together were the sweetest of all. We had only started our life together. In the few months that I lived with him we came together as one person…Please Harry let me know what happened.[182]

In such circumstances Pollitt would write to the Battalion Commander, and there might be no way of knowing exactly what happened. Bodies were often unrecovered, or left in unmarked graves. Pollitt was looked upon as the ultimate authority for the British volunteers in the IB. He granted or refused permission to go, to receive leave, and he had to inform mothers and wives of the death of those he sent. It bore heavily upon him.

*Comrades Come Rally*

# Chapter 7

## San Pedro to Salford

> "Every day or so a prisoner, by chance or for some imaginary offence, was taken out and beaten unconscious by eight or ten guards." Bill Alexander, British Volunteers for Liberty

### San Pedro de Cardeña

Both Bernard McKenna and Joe Norman described San Pedro as a concentration camp. Cecil Eby, in his book on American IB volunteers, *Between the Bullet and the Lie*, describes the living conditions as "like a preview of Dachau or Buchenwald".[183] The descriptions raise a point of definition: was San Pedro a concentration camp or a prisoner of war camp? A concentration camp is defined by the Oxford Language dictionary as:

> …a place in which large numbers of people, especially political prisoners or members of persecuted minorities, are deliberately imprisoned in a relatively small area with inadequate facilities, sometimes to provide forced labour or to await mass execution.

The vast majority of prisoners at San Pedro were soldiers, mostly International Brigaders. Lincolnshire volunteer Walter Gregory in his memoir, *The Shallow Grave*, mentions a number of Portuguese labourers also being imprisoned there, and Bernard McKenna remarked in interview that Spanish civilians were also incarcerated. But its primary purpose it seems was to hold soldiers not civilians. The conditions and treatment described by inmates, though, rank it as a concentration camp.

Each floor of the building seemed to have been knocked into one large room with perhaps one hundred or [so] men confined within it. There was no furniture, no chairs, no beds, just bare boards upon which we slept, and no blankets. The food was a wet concoction served to us each morning.[184]

According to Gregory, prisoners died of disease and others were taken away by the Gestapo for summary execution. The camp was situated at a monastery built in 1711, ten miles from the city of Burgos, which was the base of General Franco's Nationalist government during the war. In recent years mass graves holding thousands of bodies have been found in the region, with some exhumed for identification. Dreadful as captivity was, the International Brigade prisoners at San Pedro may have been more fortunate than the Spanish prisoners, for IB prisoners could be traded for their Italian counterparts. However, German and Italian IB members were singled out for particular cruelty.

Like Joe Norman, Bernard McKenna was captured during a retreat.

> On the fourth day, I was moving between limestone cliffs and a motorcycle unit came round the corner and I was buggered. I was taken back to Gandesa, a cell underneath the ground. Joined by some Americans. The following morning, I was handed over to the Italians and taken to Burgos.
>
> *The camp?*
> An old converted monastery. About 2,000 Spaniards. It was holding about five or six hundred internationals at the time.
>
> *Were all the Spaniards soldiers?*
> Soldiers and civilians, I don't think it mattered to them. They were separate from us, so we didn't come into contact. Kept us in a special wing, lots of troops and guards.
>
> *How were you treated?*
> Badly. In all respects. Thin blanket, bag of straw, lice, poor food, beatings, no medical attention.[185]

When Joe Norman was first captured, he was also taken

to the town of Gandesa. There, he encountered a *Daily Express* reporter at the scene.

> We heard the tide of battle rolling further away. We felt very lonely. We passed back down the road, with hands on heads, back to Gandesa. We had had nothing to eat for two days; we were tired, hungry, miserable and forlorn. We did not feel any better after we had been sneered at by a *Daily Express* reporter. We sat on the ground in the town square when he came up and started asking questions, to which he did not care for the answers. He stood jeering and sneering at us for some time, and then he left with the remark, "You'll all be shot." Nobody bothered to bid him farewell.[186]

Violence by guards was endemic at San Pedro and the food and conditions were barely enough to keep a person alive.

The camp was also the principal setting for the Bureau for Psychological Research activities, directed by the chief of Psychiatric Services of Franco's army, Antonio Vallejo Nágera. His project was to analyse the political enemy's psychology and personality; prisoners were ordered to complete written tests and questionnaires. Joe became a member of the camp committee—a Communist Party initiative to maintain morale and discipline. The English-speaking committee was roughly ten strong.

> From memory, me, Tony Gilbert, Major Frank Ryan—an Irish lad, Gary McCartney I think, an American, a Canadian, and I'm not sure; I think a Chinaman was on. That's as far as my memory goes.[187]

Prisoners organised lectures, "courses on mathematics, politics, the economy—we had all kinds of people amongst us, university lecturers there".[188] Chess pieces were made from soap, and there was a short-lived newspaper, *Jaily News*, and even an international choir. The committee resolved disputes between prisoners and organised a queue for food rather than a scramble. Bernard McKenna said: "We used to dream of food, almost fight over food." Joe recalled how the organisation of prisoners by the camp committee saved lives.

> We got the rumour that the Republican Army had broken

through at Saragossa. Naturally, all the lads said, "let's make a break for it." We, the committee, discussed this, and we said: "No, this is a deliberate rumour put out by the fascists—they want you to break out, they want the excuse to mow you down." It was true enough. They hadn't broken through, but we had a job holding them.[189]

Being a member of the camp committee drew the attention of the guards, and the Gestapo, who Joe assumed was in overall control of the camp. He recalled a second occasion when talk of escape and a force of habit nearly led to summary execution.

The Gestapo had heard we were planning a breakout. And the Gestapo sent for me. Me. And they said if they heard anymore, they'd start shooting a few of us. And when they said "Dismiss" I gave the Republican salute. You should have seen their faces. One of them pulled a revolver. I thought "Oh Christ, this is it."[190]

The committee was twice subject to what they believed was to be their execution by firing squad.

Twice at 3am in the morning, they brought us out into the yard to face a firing squad. I thought, "Bloody hell, what a way to die—by a firing squad." They put us up against a wall, twice. Waiting for an officer to come and give the order. Why he didn't come, I don't know.[191]

Prisoners died at San Pedro from disease and beatings. Joe described the food as "8oz of bread a day and one meal—hot water with pepper on top and a piece of fish". The sanitary conditions were appalling, and most prisoners were infested with lice during their captivity. Many prisoners, including Joe Norman, were kept below street level in what was effectively a dungeon. At one point the drains became blocked and the space became flooded, the water in the cellar thick with excrement and dirt.

Volunteers were called for to dive down under the water and unblock the drains. Norman was one of the three to go down. They unblocked the drains but the other two men caught typhoid and died.[192]

Joe maintains that prisoners were murdered.

> They saw many of our lads off without trial, without warning... we lost many of our lads stabbed with bayonets when they were going out to the toilet.[193]

There was also the well-documented case of Jimmy Rutherford. Jimmy was first captured at Jarama and repatriated but returned to fight in Spain. His initial repatriation condition was that he would not return and his captors had warned him that if he did return as a foreign fighter and were to be re-captured, he would be executed. Recaptured on the Aragon front, and sent to San Pedro, Jimmy tried to hide his identity by using the name Jimmy Smalls. Other prisoners attempted to shield Jimmy from the Spanish officers, Joe offering to take his place in the fingerprint queue.

> He was only a youngster. I said, "My God, you're in a hard spot here now." He said, "I am. If they find out who I am, I've had it." Someone must have smelt a rat. There was this German Gestapo officer there, in charge of the camp. They took him away the same night. That was the worst thing. You couldn't do anything about it.[194]

Jimmy Rutherford was executed on 24 May 1938 for being in contravention of his repatriation agreement. In light of this, the Party forbad any repatriated comrades from returning to Spain. On 21 September 1938, Juan Negrín, President of the Government of the Republic, announced in Geneva, before the General Assembly of the League of Nations, the immediate and unconditional withdrawal of all non-Spanish combatants in the Republican Army, hoping the Francoist side would do the same. The hope was not realised. On 28 October, one month after their retirement from the front, the International Brigades paraded in Barcelona to more than 250,000 people. La Pasionaria addressed the departing troops:

> From all peoples, from all races, you came to us like brothers, like sons of immortal Spain; and in the hardest days of the war, when the capital of the Spanish Republic was threatened, it was you, gallant comrades of the International Brigades, who helped save the city

with your fighting enthusiasm, your heroism and your spirit of sacrifice. And Jarama, Guadalajara, Brunete and Belchite, Levante and the Ebro in immortal verses sing of the courage, the sacrifice, the daring, the discipline of the men of the International Brigades.[195]

They arrived in London on 7 December 1938 and were met by a sizeable crowd, addressed by the then leader of the Labour Party, Clement Attlee.

In January 1939, the majority of the British prisoners were released from San Pedro in readiness for their exchange for Italians held by the Republic. All but a small number were released in February and April 1939. They were first taken by train to San Sebastian and Ondarreta prison. After a month they were escorted across the border into France where they were given new clothes provided by the British government and a hot meal. Then onto Calais. Two prisoners were not released: Tom Jones from Wales had to wait until March 1940; the Irish leader Frank Ryan was taken instead to Germany, where he eventually died in June 1944.

## Different country, same struggle

At the outbreak of the Second World War, Joe Norman joined the RAF Volunteer Reserves, whilst Bernard McKenna joined the RAF as a wireless operator. "War broke out on the Sunday, I joined on

*Remains of prisoners exhumed at San Pedro, October 2019 (courtesy Eli Brauner)*

the Monday. I was still an anti-fascist, and it was an anti-fascist war."[196] Until the entry of the Soviet Union in June 1941, the Communist Party classed the war as an imperialist war that the Left shouldn't support. This must have jarred with International Brigade veterans; certainly, Bernard was not prepared to adhere to the Party line. "I took no notice of the bloody CP, and I was still a Party member." Maurice Levine joined the parachute regiment and took part in the Normandy landings.

Despite his considerable military experience, Sam Wild was not allowed to join the army, the Home Guard, the naval reserve, or even serve as an air raid warden. The police informed him personally that he'd been blocked from any service.

> They wouldn't even let me in the Home Guards. They said I was an "undesirable". I wrote a protest to the Chief Constable of Manchester who was in charge of all that business and he said, "I will make the decisions. I've decided you're not suitable and that's that." I couldn't even get in the demolition squads, although I was a qualified building worker.[197]

Indeed, Sam was subject to considerable security service surveillance over a number of years.

On his return from Spain, Sam threw himself into the Aid for Spain movement. A former battalion commander who was promoted to the rank of Major, and a recipient of the Medalla Militar, Spain's highest military award in recognition of battlefield bravery, he was among the most prominent British veterans and spoke at meetings across the country. After being wounded at the Battle of Brunete, Sam had returned to England to address several rallies in October and November 1937. By the Second World War, he was a renowned communist. He was made president of the International Brigade Association (IBA) which campaigned and raised money for IB veterans and their dependants. The security service surveillance file on Sam runs for 92 pages, beginning when he first left the port of Dover for Dunkirk on New Year's Day 1937. On the penultimate page of the file is a photostat of a letter by Fred Copeman, dated 4 March 1937, to a Mrs Duncan in New Cross, south-east London. Copeman had been wounded in the arm and head at Jarama the month before.

> I have a chum who was a sailor I knew in the navy. He

isn't in the Party but he is a great fighter, his name is appropriate, it's Sam Wild. He has been wounded in the chest and is very bad. I don't think he will live. If I believed it would do any good, I'd pray for him. Sam was the last man to leave the ridge when the artillery found it. Sam it was who went back through hell to look for me, as he thought I'd been left behind, he got it then, two through the lungs. When I asked him in the hospital how he was, he said he had two through the chest, that they missed his heart because it was in his mouth. He was one of our best Lewis gunners. Maybe I am getting melancholy.[198]

At the bottom of the letter there is a handwritten note in biro. "Does this imply that Wild took part in the Invergordon mutiny?" Sam Wild was in the navy at the time of the mutiny, but in answer to the security officer's question, he was serving elsewhere. However, word spread right across the navy and Sam would have heard of the events and been in solidarity in spirit.

The security file on Sam includes copies of internal Party documents and letters between himself and General Secretary Harry Pollitt. It also includes photographs of envelopes; it is apparent that his mail was intercepted, but also evidence that the Party in Manchester may have been infiltrated. In one report, Special Branch officers are referred to as being "in constant contact with NUWM (National Unemployed Workers Movement) ringleaders". Remarkable as it seems, the report below suggests that there may have been an informant inside the International Brigade Association.

On the 15th instant three persons visited Liverpool from Wigan, as delegates from the provisional Release Frank Ryan Committee, which they explained had been set up in Wigan three weeks earlier, following a meeting there which was addressed by Councillor JP Mannion and Sam Wild. The result of the meeting between the Wigan delegates and the Liverpool men was that a provisional committee known as the East Lancashire Frank Ryan Release Committee was formed, which included the three Wigan men, together with five others.[199]

It is not far-fetched to assume that the source was someone

well known to Sam. At different times, two different sources are quoted in reports: "Sloane" and "CC". CC probably refers to chief constable and there are memos from Special Branch or CID operatives via the chief constable to the intelligence services. Sloane is perhaps the name of an agent. This is from a report from 4 October 1940:

> Our agent was at the same time advised that he should avoid contact with a certain Salamon, a Jew from Palestine who the IBA regard as a Trotskyist. It appears therefore that the conflict between Stalinists and Trotskyists, which was noticed in Spain, has been carried over to this country. According to our records, Salamon belongs to a Trotskyist group in Liverpool but lives in Manchester.[200]

The files suggest that Sam Wild was of national significance to the security services: a colonel writes to the chief constable of Blackburn that more can be found on him on page nine of *Civil Security Review*. In hindsight, the comprehensive interest in Sam Wild seems excessive. But as president of the International Brigade Association and an active communist, Sam was more than just a figurehead. Prominent among hundreds of returned IB veterans with considerable military experience, he was an active revolutionary who had connections to the Soviet Union, and to comrades elsewhere through the Comintern.

> We should have no interest in the IBA were it not for the fact that there are definite indications that this organisation has the intention to found certain cells in our army. We have been informed that the IBA intends to establish bases in all the armies on British soil, with the idea that these should take over military control in the event of a general revolution.[201]

The excerpt above is a report written on 4 October 1940, less than a month after Hitler had planned to invade Britain. The Soviet Union had not yet entered the war and was considering joining the Axis forces. The Communist Party did not officially support their own country at this stage because for them their country was the Soviet Union. The following is from a report on Sam's speech to West Salford CPGB branch on 30 June 1940.

Wild related some of his experiences of the International Brigade and described the methods to deal with tanks and aerial attack... He said that France had made a big mistake when communists and members of the IB were put into concentration camps. These people should have been allowed to remain at large in order that they could continue to fight against fascism. He also stated that all factory workers in this country should be armed under the supervision of responsible persons, to resist any invasion which might be attempted.[202]

Invasion was an immediate threat. The evacuation of Dunkirk had taken place a week before the meeting, followed by France's surrender on 21 June. Mussolini's Italy had joined the war on 10 June. And here was a revolutionary soldier advocating the arming of workers. In such a context, Sam Wild was viewed as an enemy within. Mike Wild, Sam's son, recalled that after the war, the Party paid for a telephone in the house so that comrades could use it for Party business. Even when the phone wasn't in use, it would regularly make a clicking sound, as if someone was at the other end of the line.

Sam, like many veterans, struggled to get work. Employers were wary about having them in the workforce and Major Sam Wild would have been at the top of the list. The Party did provide some financial support for him for a while, but he was denied the full-time Party role he sought, possibly because of his unwavering anti-authoritarianism. His son Mike explained that his father often told him that the people he most identified with in Spain were the anarchists. Strange as it may seem to say of a war, Sam missed his days in Spain.

> I'd become so attached to Spain and the Spanish people; I became sad. I felt guilty leaving the Spanish people at that time... coming back to a country that had behaved infamously... They were the happiest days I've spent, the most fruitful days I've spent. After, I never did anything that was worthwhile. In Spain I made a contribution for a correct cause.[203]

After the Second World War Sam worked in construction as a steel erector. He became a shop steward in the Construction Engineering Union and stood as a Communist Party candidate for the local council election in Collyhurst, Manchester. Mike Wild:

> My dad was a very good shop steward. When he was working on Barton Bridge, it collapsed into the Manchester Ship Canal in the early 1950s. He led the campaign to condemn the firms and support the relatives of young erectors who had died. He was blacklisted by employers and he got ill and suffered unemployment and probably what would be called now PTSD. He led the IB veterans to the end of his life in 1983, and was a loving grandfather and supported Bessie in arranging the 1976 reunion of the IB veterans at Loughborough, and the recording sessions. He went on several visits to Spain and was honoured by visits to other countries where IB veterans were still active in politics. He was awarded a medal on his 70th birthday in East Germany.[204]

Mike Wild explained that he and his brothers often heard his father shouting in his sleep and that however early he got up, he would find his father in his chair by the coal fire. As a child himself, Sam had lived with a father who had fought through the First World War and probably suffered trauma as a result. Many of those who fought for the International Brigade in Spain would likely have suffered from trauma at the time, as well as post war. A First World War veteran who fought in the IB compared the Battle of Jarama to the Somme.[205] And it should not be forgotten that Sam had executed Maurice Ryan.[206]

Sam's outstanding bravery, and his fearlessness in Spain, was remarked upon by his contemporaries. Red Army officers referred to him as "the English Lion". Joe Norman said of him: "Sam Wild, he had all the guts in the world." He remained president of the IBA to the end of his life, reading the eulogies at veterans' funerals whenever he could. The last eulogy he read was during Easter 1983. He caught a cold that day which developed into pneumonia, and he died a few days later, aged 74. At his funeral they played Paul Robeson, and his coffin was draped with an IB banner. The mourners sang *Jarama Valley* and *England Arise*. Mike Wild:

> Sadly, he died before the current recognition of the

International Brigaders came about, but he knew he was loved and respected and unveiled the memorial in Manchester Town Hall and has a posthumous plaque on the family council house in Longsight from the then Greater Manchester Council. His funeral in Sheffield and a memorial in Manchester were very well attended and he was recognised as a modest, brave and inspiring leader in Spain and later in the labour movement. I don't think he was bitter or disillusioned and once said it took time for the true facts of history to be recognised by society. It is true he never found an official and paid role in the movement but looked back with pride and left it for history to be his judge.[207]

In 1981 Sam received a letter from Dolores Ibárruri, otherwise known as "La Passionaria". Ibárruri was a prominent Republican and communist during the civil war, a commanding orator best known for her slogan ¡No Pasarán! ("They shall not pass!"), issued during the Battle for Madrid in November 1936. Sam named his first daughter after Dolores. La Pasionaria spent 41 years in exile, returning to Madrid in 1977. She died in 1989.

To Comrade Sam Wild,

My dear comrade and friend Sam. It is with profound emotion that I join the so deserved homage given to you by the International Brigade Association. We have not forgotten and will never forget what your heroic participation meant to our national-revolutionary war and your permanent solidarity to our people. A tender and fraternal hug from Dolores Ibárruri.

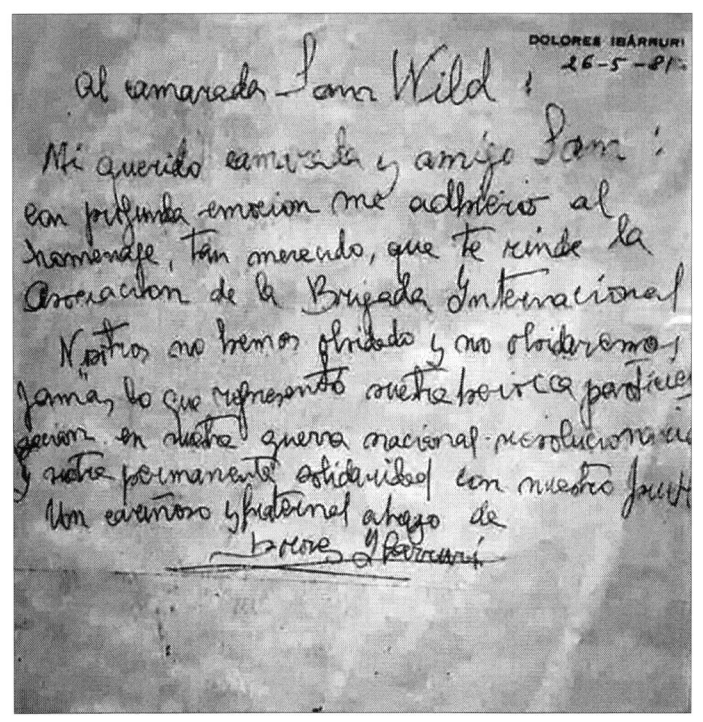

*Letter to Sam Wild from Dolores Ibárruri (aka La Passionaria), a prominent communist activist during the civil war who coined the slogan ¡No Pasarán!*

*Comrades Come Rally*

# Chapter 8

## Aid for Spain

> "They came home in 1938 but we still carried on. We had a convoy that went round the country collecting for widows and the wounded." Bessie Wild, Aid for Spain activist, member Hulme CPGB

In his 1986 book *The Signal Was Spain*, Jim Fyrth describes the Aid for Spain movement as, "the most widespread and representative mass movement in Britain since the mid-19th century days of Chartism and the Anti-Corn Law League".[208] This is a considerable claim, particularly when one considers that during the first half of its existence, the movement lacked the support of any major political party. During the three years of the civil war, a variety of voluntary organisations across the country sent food, clothes, vehicles and medical personnel to the beleaguered Republic.

A total of around 2 million pounds was raised in cash; food ships were organised, ambulances constructed, refugees accommodated and cared for, all without material support from the government. The funds were raised at dances, concerts, rallies and meetings, jumble sales, and simply by going door to door or workbench to workbench. The cause was embraced by political activists across the spectrum but mostly by the Left and by religious groups and pacifists opposed to war. But at the centre of the movement, of this broad alliance against fascism, was the Communist Party who were not just prepared to work with individuals and groups with differing politics, but undertook the task with wholehearted conviction. It was a new departure for the Party which was emerging from a period of insularity.

The Labour Party found responding to the Spanish Civil War problematic. Communists wanted the National Government to provide arms for Spain, it sent volunteers to fight and medical staff to assist the Republican Army; they were opposed to non-intervention and saw such a policy as aiding fascism. The Labour Party's initial position was that non-intervention was the preferable policy because it would reduce the risk of the war spreading to other European states; any free trade in arms would only lead to escalation. However, not everyone in the Labour Party supported this policy. Leading left-winger and deputy leader Stafford Cripps was an outspoken opponent of non-intervention. Arthur Greenwood was jeered when he moved the motion of non-intervention at the 1936 Party conference.

Attlee's Labour Party did go on to reverse their decision in 1937, after it became apparent that the international non-intervention treaty initiated by France's Popular Front government was being flouted by Germany, Italy and the Soviet Union. As Nazi Germany's foreign minister Joachim von Ribbentrop wrote of the Non-Intervention Committee in his memoirs:

> It would have been better to call this the Intervention Committee, for the whole activity of its members consisted in explaining or concealing the participation of their countries in Spain.[209]

The fast-growing Aid for Spain movement placed the Labour Party leadership under pressure, as historian Tom Buchanan explains:

> Firstly, active solidarity with the Spanish Republic became widespread in Britain, involving all classes to some degree. Unlike the summer of 1936 when concerned individuals had left the matter to their political party or trade union, by the end of the year, organised solidarity with Spain, independent of the official labour movement had spread throughout Britain.[210]

At the outset, there was a great deal of support for the movement from Manchester and Salford. One exemplary local voluntary group was the North Manchester Medical Aid Committee. It was founded on the initiative of Issy Luft, veteran of clashes with the Blackshirts in the Cheetham area of the city. During an interview, Mike Luft, his son, remarked:

> My father was secretary of the Crumpsall branch of the Communist Party but he was also a delegate to the organisation that organised material support for the Spanish Republic. He was very active in campaigning around Cheetham Hill. It stemmed organically from the Party's anti-fascist work. The Party had very good credentials defending the Jewish community in Cheetham. In terms of getting material support, it wasn't just trade unions and the official organs of the labour movement. It was just ordinary people on the streets, they went round with handcarts around working class Jewish communities.[211]

The North Manchester Medical Aid Committee included people from a variety of political parties and no party at all. The chair of the committee was Labour Party member GP Nathan Malimson and they met at his surgery. It was a productive organisation and among much else, it raised sufficient funds to send three ambulances. It was this committee that supported the work of nurse Madge Addy.

Born in Rusholme, Manchester, in 1904, Madge was a hairdresser who became a registered nurse. She arrived in Spain in 1937 to care for the International Brigade at Uclés Monastery in Castile, becoming head nurse there. Her work was regularly reported on in the *Daily Worker* and beyond, in particular her practice of conducting blood transfusions from herself to patients.

> Saving life by giving her own blood is just a casual affair to Nurse Madge Addy, of Manchester, whom I met at the office of the Spanish Medical Aid Committee in London yesterday. She had just returned from Madrid and was extremely reluctant to discuss her experiences. However, I found that she had been giving one transfusion a month to a wounded Spanish soldier, and has been responsible for saving quite a number of lives. She has just come from a hospital, containing 800 patients, where the staff have been trained by an English nursing unit, which had to start its duties by

teaching the girl probationers to read and write. 'But if staffing was difficult, food and medical supplies difficulties were a thousand times greater', she said. 'We have seven doctors who work like Trojans, but what can all their efforts amount to without the necessary materials?'[212]

In a letter to the *Daily Worker* dated 16 March 1939, she wrote:

It is heart-breaking to watch men die because you cannot get nourishment to keep their strength up. We have only a small quantity of anaesthetic left and so many operations are performed without anything at all.

Madge Addy did not return with the International Brigade at the end of 1938 but remained as the only British nurse in Spain. At the end of the civil war in April 1939, she was imprisoned, but later released at the request of the British Embassy. During the Second World War, she was recruited by Special Operations Executive (SOE) and sent to occupied France. SOE was a secret organisation that conducted espionage, sabotage, and reconnaissance and gave aid to resistance movements. Madge was sent to Marseille to help organise the first British escape route for pilots and airmen from France to Spain. It is unclear whether she was ever a communist, but through the strategy of the popular front, Madge and others collaborated with Party activists. She would periodically return to Britain to speak at rallies to raise money and supplies, sharing platforms with leading communists.

Aid for Spain changed the fortunes of the Party and it altered the lives of individuals involved. It was a training ground for activists and with the leadership of the Labour Party absent, people went from collecting money or clothes to becoming committed communists for years to come. Hugh Scanlon was born in 1913. He left Stretford elementary school when he was 14 years old to become an apprentice instrument maker. At age 21 Scanlon became a shop steward at Metropolitan-Vickers (Metro-Vicks), joining the Party two years later in 1936. By the Second World War he was union convenor, a full-time AEU district official by 1947 and union president in 1968. Cabinet papers released to the National Archives reveal that in June

## Aid for Spain

1968, Prime Minister Harold Wilson considered resigning in the face of trade union militancy, in particular the growing number of unofficial strikes. It was Scanlon, along with the Transport and General Workers Union leader Jack Jones, an International Brigade veteran from Liverpool, who provided a way out for Wilson by insisting the TUC resolve the issue of unofficial disputes. After Scanlon retired it emerged that MI5 had prevented him from holding board positions on nationalised industries and that in the early 1970s the Wilson government ran a propaganda campaign against him. It was for him that Harold Wilson coined the phrase "Get your tanks off my lawn". I interviewed the then Lord Scanlon at his home in 1992.

> Things began to change in the late 1930s in two directions. Politically the Left was beginning to be strengthened, industrially we were overcoming the disaster of the General Strike and the Depression that followed. I joined the Party because of Spain, in 1937.

*Did you think about going?*

> Yes, and they asked me not to. The Party said we were involved in converting motorbike sidecars into ambulances; Benny Rothman was involved in that. We did it at someone's house and a centre with a good garage. You also went collecting for milk for Spain. It had its humanitarian appeal for many people. The Party certainly grew in strength.[213]

As far as the Party was concerned, Aid for Spain was not an entirely separate campaign to that of the International Brigades, but rather a separate front. In Barcelona in December 1938, when Sam Wild addressed volunteers about to return to Britain he said: "We will now carry our struggle on to other fronts."[214] Many IB volunteers were active in Aid for Spain before and after they had fought, and the Party connected the two parts of the struggle. Towards the end of May 1937, a memorial meeting was organised for the 11 Manchester brigaders who had been killed at the Battle of Jarama. On the platform alongside leading local communists were the actress Dame Sybil Thorndike and Manchester Unitarian minister and pacifist, Stanley Mossop. In July 1937 around 1,500 marched from Ardwick Green in memory of George Brown, killed at the Battle of Brunete on 7 July. At a second memorial meeting at the co-operative hall in Downing Street, Ardwick on 25 July, chaired by the local communist engineer, Edmund Frow, the platform included the president of the Manchester and Salford Trades Council, a representative of the Transport and General Workers' Union and a Labour city councillor with a letter from the Manchester Borough Labour Party approving his attendance.

The Manchester and District Medical Aid Committee toured an ambulance bound for Spain around the cotton towns of south east Lancashire to encourage the production of others and by the end of September 1937, the same committee had sent five fully equipped ambulances off to the front. At the other end of the equipment scale, in Moss Side, more than 30 women were engaged in making bandages for the Republican Army.[215] Tinned milk, other non-perishables, and clothing were regularly taken by food-ships. By the end of 1939, 29 had been sent from Britain, and by August 1937 three had sailed from Salford docks. Of course, these had to be paid for and Manchester's Food-ships for Spain campaign had offices on Deansgate, with Winifred Horrocks as secretary.

Demonstrations for the food-ships were regular events in Manchester; six depots were set up in the city for receiving supplies, including the Young Communist League's Challenge Club in Cheetham Hill. The local YCL took a lead in bringing together other youth organisations under an umbrella of Youth Food-ships for Spain. The secretary of the largest local branch, Monty Cohen, organised a youth rally at the co-operative hall at which they showed the film *The Defence of Madrid*.[216] The food-ships and other aid provided to the Republic was not merely a political gesture or strategy, it made a material difference. Historian Bill Williams:

> ...by 1939 the Spanish Republic had received from British voluntary organisations and private donors a total of £2m in cash, 29 food-ships, and ambulances, as well as hundreds of volunteer relief workers, military personnel and medical staff.[217]

Whilst many like Hugh Scanlon were politically radicalised and drawn into the Party through Aid for Spain, others were already experienced activists by then. Bessie Wild was a contemporary of Scanlon, born in Moss Side in 1911. She was educated at Sale Grammar School and described her younger self as "uninterested in politics". At 23 she went on an organised trip to the Soviet Union which appears to have been a turning point.

> I was so very impressed with what I'd seen in the Soviet Union. I had no background in the labour movement. I came back and joined the Party. I joined Hulme branch. There was a cross section of humanity. A good many unemployed and skilled workers.[218]

Bessie put her better than average education to political use and became secretary of the Relief of Victims of German Fascism and then shortly after Franco's attempted coup, received a letter to attend a conference in Paris opposed to the policy of non-intervention.

> It was the beginning of something very big. There was a march outside headed by an old communard. It was clear there was going to be big resistance politically. There was tremendous support locally. Bury got a little group going for bandages. In Stretford, Doctor Robinson, stalwart of the Labour Party, he did tremendous work on ambulances for Spain. In food-ships for Spain the co-op came into action. We had bumpers [collection points] in the shop. I remember going round Anson estate. Hardly anyone had liquid milk in those days among the working class. They were all on tinned milk…[219]

The communard referred to was a veteran of the Paris Commune of 1871, when soldiers of the National Guard seized control of the city and attempted to establish an independent government based on direct democracy. It is worth bearing in mind that during the 1930s, whilst there were many in France who had lived through the First World War, there were some who could recall the Franco-Prussian War of 1870-71.

Sam Wild married Bessie Berry on 1 April 1939, the day the Spanish Civil War ended. It was a joint wedding with veteran and friend George Fletcher marrying Joanna Kelly. The witnesses at the wedding were Harry Pollitt, Fred Copeman, and Manchester Labour MP John Jagger. Proceeds from the wedding went to the Aid for Spain movement.

## Art for Spain
Henry Suss was in the Cheetham branch and a member of Theatre Union, formed in 1936, the same year Henry joined the Party. For Henry, theatrical work was political work.

> Ewan MacColl and Joan Littlewood started Theatre Union. We produced living newspapers during the Spanish Civil War and work by Spanish playwrights… mainly at the Free Trade Hall. And there was a socialist church in Hyde. We used to do the Bolton co-operative society and we used to go to union branches, and at most demonstrations, we used to do sketches. We always attended the annual event for access to the mountains—mass trespass. Ewan MacColl was acting and writing. He did write some songs too. I knew him very well. From Salford. He was a member of the Party. He was kicked out now and again. He was a rebel communist. Entirely undisciplined.[220]

In 1937 Henry was cast in a production of *Lysistrata* by Aristophanes, adapted by MacColl and produced by Joan Littlewood at the Free Trade Hall, to raise money for a food-ship. In the Greek original, Lysistrata persuades the women of the warring cities to withhold sex from their husbands as a means of forcing the men to negotiate peace. MacColl renamed the play *Operation Olive Branch*. In the same year, he also wrote and produced two pageants representing the struggle of the Spanish people against fascism. Henry Suss acted alongside MacColl in Jaroslav Hašek's *The Good Soldier Schweik*, and in Clifford Odets 1935 play *Waiting For Lefty*, a drama constructed around a group of American cab-drivers contemplating strike action. A group of American brigaders performed the play during the day of 24 July 1938, just prior to the Ebro offensive which began that night.

Henry's background was typical of the many Jewish comrades in Manchester.

> I was a machinist. I started working in clothing in 1931. I left school in 1929 when I was 14 and I worked in a merchant-shippers for about 18 months. It was the slump of 1931. I felt sorry for my boss who was paying me ten shillings for a 48-hour week. I was the youngest

of nine kids, all in the clothing industry. A learner could always get a job because they were low paid.[221]

Henry gravitated towards drama as a child because it helped him overcome a crippling stutter. He was untypical, but not exceptional, in finding his way into the Party through a left-wing theatre company. At a car showroom near Manchester Cathedral, the food-ship campaign ran an extraordinary fundraising art exhibition from 1 to 15 February 1939: Pablo Picasso's *Guernica* and 67 preparatory sketches and studies. The entrance fee was sixpence. The painting had been exhibited in London at the end of 1938 and it was a surprise that it went to Manchester at all, much less to a car showroom. The painting depicts the bombing of the Basque town on 26 April 1937 by the Luftwaffe. It was market day: farmers were there selling produce; the town was crowded. What followed was an aerial bombardment of the civilian population, among the first in modern warfare. The Nationalists had agreed to it, hopeful perhaps that the Basques would break with the Republic and make separate peace arrangements with Franco.

In this respect, the attack failed. The number of deaths is thought to have been between 200 and 300. Picasso may well have been aware of Manchester's radical traditions and confident that his work would not only be well received, but that the exhibition would be a boost to Republican sympathisers. The work was likely entrusted to a group of young artists. Many graduates of Manchester Art School during the 1930s were heavily involved in working-class politics. One of these was Harry Baines, celebrated for his public murals in the area. Shortly after the exhibition, over £3,000 was cabled from Manchester to Spain.[222]

## Wounded volunteers and dependants

A significant minority of the men who went to fight in Spain were married and some had children. Whilst they were away there was little income for the family back home. Of those that returned, many were wounded, some had lost limbs; many who were able to work were refused. As a result, in 1937 the Wounded and Dependants Aid Committee was established with Charlotte Haldane as secretary. Charlotte was a member of the CPGB and involved in the vetting and transportation of the British IB volunteers from Paris to Spain. She later wrote of the volunteers she met:

> The vast majority were men of splendid types, honest and brave, who in greater or lesser degree were conscious of being engaged in a crusade to rescue democracy from the grip of Fascism. They were not all Communists nor members of their respective parties, although the leadership was always entrusted to Party members, most of whom set a high example in discipline and devotion to the rest. To them, and to all the poorly paid workers in the organisation, the material reward was trivial.[223]

In a letter to TUC general secretary Walter Citrine requesting financial support, Charlotte outlined the Dependants Aid Committee's two main tasks: to raise money for the families of the dependants and to provide medical support for the wounded.

> There are at present five wounded members of the battalion in Middlesex Hospital and others in hospital in London and all over the country. Another 150 wounded men are expected home shortly. For all these we provide medical attention and, in many cases artificial limbs.[224]

Christmas parties were organised for children in 1937 and 1938 with co-op societies providing catering and toys at reduced prices. Children over seven years of age from London, Manchester and other large cities were given a few weeks holiday at the seaside. Welfare for veterans included clothing and food. In June 1939 the committee were able to meet medical costs for 11 men in London, including veterans from Canada, Australia, New Zealand, South Africa and Palestine. A further 47 were awaiting operations. As well as purchasing artificial limbs, crutches had to be paid for. Doctors and other specialists gave treatment free of charge; between December 1938 and February 1939, nationally 112 veterans were treated without charge. On returning from Spain, Maurice Levine was given the task of administering the Dependants Aid Fund.

> I'd have to go and tell people there wasn't much money and they'd have to take a cut. Then I was given the task when someone was killed of going to see the family. I remember going to see someone in Prestwich [in

Salford] and it was a terrible thing, you know, you go along to a mother whose son of 18 had just gone to Spain without her knowing and then you've got to come along and say he's been killed.[225]

Financial hardship was a way of life for many Party members. Despite rearmament providing security of employment for some before the Second World War, others were victimised and out of work and everyone was already paying Party dues. Absolute poverty was common in working class areas of Manchester at this time. In an area report to the Lancashire District Committee for 1938, under the section "activity with women" was recorded "work on malnutrition amongst women".[226]

After the civil war the International Brigades Association (IBA) campaigned for the release of imprisoned British and Irish IB volunteers left behind in Spain, as well as veterans who were sent to concentration camps in France. At the end of the Second World War, the IBA drew attention to the peculiar case of over 200 Spanish Republican prisoners held captive in an internment camp near Chorley, Lancashire. Many Republican prisoners held in concentration camps in France fell into Germans' hands with the occupation in May 1940. Germany used such prisoners as forced labour in their 'Todt' operations of civil and military engineering.[227] The prisoners were initially put to work on coastal defences in Bordeaux. Following France's liberation, the workers were perceived as part of the Axis forces and as such imprisoned again, falling victim to the Allies' difficulties in distinguishing between friend and foe. Consequently 226 Spanish Republicans were sent to the camp in Chorley to live in a converted mill.

Distraught at their continued imprisonment, and at the charge that they were Nazi sympathisers, in June 1945 they began a hunger strike. One internee, Agustin Soler, took his own life. Others, like Eustajio Bustos, were driven mad by their perpetual persecution. Initially the Attlee government planned to deport them back to Franco's Spain but after a broad-based campaign that included Sam Wild, leading ILP member Fenner Brockway and George Orwell, all were released. Some were sent as refugees to France, others allowed to settle in Britain. Sam was given a handcrafted wooden plaque and a Republican flag by the prisoners in recognition of his work for their cause. He later described helping to secure their release as "the greatest achievement of his adult life".[228]

## The Basque children

In the spring of 1937 a powerful lobby forced the Home Office to allow the entry of children from the Basque Country in Northern Spain into Britain. Just under 4,000 children arrived at the Southampton Docks on 23 May. Around 250 went on to be settled in Greater Manchester. The origins of the project lay in an appeal by the Basque government to foreign nations in April 1937. Spain's northern ports were blockaded, Bilbao and other Basque towns were bombarded by Nationalist forces under General Mola, and by aerial attack from German and Italian planes. Three days after the bombing of Guernica on 26 April 1937 Home Secretary Sir Samuel Hoare gave approval for 2,000 children up to the age of 15 to come to Britain.

The political drive had originated from the National Joint Committee for Spanish Relief (NJCSR), an umbrella organisation, which brought civilians out of war-affected areas and cared for refugees. Though it was a popular front initiative that the Party took part in, it by no means dominated. The Basque scheme was overseen by the Basque Children's Committee (BCC) led by the Duchess of Atholl, who had visited Spain and seen the impact of Nationalist bombing. Fundraising began in advance of the children arriving from Bilbao. Hitherto the TUC had avoided the

*Basque children arriving in Newcastle, June 1937*

issue of Spain, in keeping with General Secretary Walter Citrine's hostility to the Communist Party, but he made an exception with the Basque children, donating £5,000 to start the campaign rolling. Within a fortnight the BCC had successfully raised £2 million from the public. Finance for the care of the children throughout their stay came almost entirely from public support.

At first the children were placed in a transit camp in Hampshire built for half as many. Hoare visited the camp, which did give the initiative some official endorsement. By the end of 1937 there were Basque colonies all over the UK. Whilst some in the British press called for their immediate repatriation, public support was overwhelming. In Manchester a public meeting was held to welcome the children and their accompanying carers. A further public meeting was held at the end of May 1937 to raise money towards the children's upkeep. Labour Lord Mayor of Manchester, Joseph Toole, told his audience: "This country was famous for many things, but one great thing was the right of asylum."[229] In defending the Basque refugees against accusations that they were distracting attention from the sufferings of the native poor, the secretary of the Salford Branch of the Young Communist League argued:

> My reading of history convinces me that the British people have always welcomed refugees from political reaction, no matter the extent of poverty in our country. To do otherwise, he went on, would be foreign to the people of our great country.[230]

The refugee children were largely settled in groups: 50 in a former mansion, Watermillock, near Bolton, where 200 local people came out to welcome them; and 50 at Harold's Memorial Orphanage in Seedley, run by an independent Christian missionary group. The staff of the orphanage were overwhelmed by offers of help. A Manchester firm donated 40 high-quality dolls for the girls, sets of tools for the boys, puzzles, games, miniature pianos, saucepans and crockery. Large crowds gathered with gifts to await the children's arrival. The largest group was allocated to Holly Mount Convent at Tottington, near Bury, a school and refuge for homeless children run since the late 1880s by a Belgian Order, the Sisters of Charity of Jesus and Mary.

Manchester was understandably proud of its contribution to the Republic's cause and the enthusiasm existed well beyond the CP and its fellow travellers. An editorial in the Manchester Guardian from 1 June 1937 stated:

> In this city the cause of the Republic has been taken very much to heart; we have given our sons in surprising numbers, we have provided two ambulances and one and a half shipments of foodstuffs... money and gifts have poured into the many societies and groups organised for the purpose and Manchester people practically organised the Watermillock home for the Basque child refugees... [231]

Bella and Lily Clyne joined the YCL through the Challenge Club, though they came from a socialist family. Their father was a dissident deserter from the Russian army in the Russo-Japanese War, and their brother Joe had joined the Party in 1932.

Some refugees were also taken in by individual families. The Clyne family were a Jewish socialist family who lived on Waterloo Road in Cheetham. Their father, who was from St Petersburg, deserted from the Tsarist Army during the Russo-Japanese War. He was a supporter of the Russian Revolution and his first language was Yiddish. There were three Manchester-born daughters, Leah or Lily, Bella, and Freda and two sons, Jud and Max. The family took in two Basque refugees in 1937, a boy Angel Martinez and his sister. Lily Clyne's daughter, Hilary Jones, is to this day friends with Angel's daughter.

The episode of the Basque children sparked a national debate about how people in Britain should relate to refugees from fascist countries. In this case, the government acceded to public pressure. Children, of course, are a particular kind of refugee, but perhaps it is evidence that as the war wore on, the government's non-intervention policy on Spain had less support than they imagined. The Basque children were not the first victims of fascism to reach Britain. By 1937 there were thousands of refugees from Germany but the Basques were the first to flee modern warfare, a style of warfare which brought to mind the Japanese bombing of civilians in Shanghai, Nazi troops marching into Rhineland and Italian troops invading Abyssinia; images associated with fascist aggression. In 1937 a film was made about the plight of the Basque children entitled *Modern Orphans Of The Storm*, which was shown in Manchester in November of 1937.[232]

Andréw Thorpe's article *The Membership of the Communist Party of Great Britain, 1920-1945* concludes by asserting:

> ...the Communist Party was neither an alien organisation imported from Moscow, nor a Party totally rooted in national radical traditions but, rather, a curious hybrid of the two.[233]

The years 1936-39 was a period when, by embracing national radical traditions, and by gaining hegemony in the struggle against fascism, the Party gathered in strength and influence, its membership growing from 7,000 in February 1936 to 17,756 by July 1939. Not all the new members identified themselves as revolutionaries as they would have done in the 1920s, and so turnover in membership increased. But the Party entered the Second World War with greater buoyancy—only to be subjected to a policy imported from Moscow that would halt its march forward.

*Comrades Come Rally*

# Chapter 9

## Imperialist War in Theory

"Uncle Joe says stand on your head."
*Enemy Within*, Francis Beckett

The Second World War were the years of peak recruitment for the Party. It was transformed in size and character, moving from a party of cadre towards the basis of a mass party. However, this dramatic change applied to the period from June 1941 onwards, after the Soviet Union had entered the conflict. For the first third of the war, Party membership was static, possibly in decline because officially it refused to support the war effort. At the heart of this was the Comintern's directive of 9 September 1939 stating:

> The present war is an imperialist and unjust war for which the bourgeoisie of all the belligerent states bear equal responsibility. The communist parties, particularly in France, Britain, Belgium and the USA, which have taken up positions at variance with this standpoint, must immediately correct their political line.[234]

The above directive was initially ignored, concealed from the British Party's central committee by General Secretary Harry Pollitt. The reference to "positions at variance" refers to the initial policy of support for the war, which lasted only a matter of weeks from its outbreak on 3 September 1939. On 7 October the *Daily Worker* published a new manifesto in line with Moscow's instructions.[235]

The Party's volte-face on the orders of Moscow is one of the most, if not the most, contentious episode in the Party's history, on a par with its support for the Soviet Union's invasion of Hungary in 1956 and the suppression of the Prague Spring in 1968. It was a period of internal division and schism; an interregnum in a period when it had established unsullied credentials in the fight against fascism after combating the Blackshirts and fighting Franco. As Andrew Thorpe remarks: "The best recruiter of all, of course, was the Party's fight against fascism, both in Britain and abroad."[236] The damage to the Party's reputation was ameliorated between June 1941 and the end of the war and whilst membership may have held up or merely "frayed at the edges",[237] it was something the Party was never allowed to forget. The reversal on Comintern orders permanently cemented the fate of the organisation to the popularity or otherwise of the Soviet Union.

The imperialist war stance was a logical conclusion of the Nazi-Soviet non-aggression pact of 23 August 1939. The pact, negotiated in little over three hours, was a shock to the world and led directly to the outbreak of the war. As a document it had two sections: a public element that determined that Russia and Germany would respect each other's territories; and a private section that divided Eastern Europe into spheres of influence. Germany would have western Poland, Stalin the east as well as Latvia, Lithuania and Estonia. A week later Germany invaded Poland and Stalin telegraphed to congratulate him. The headline of the *Daily Worker* for 23 August 1939 was "Soviet's Dramatic Peace Move to Halt Aggressors". In a front-page column under the heading "What the Communist Party Says", it went on:

> 'A victory for peace and Socialism against the war plans of Fascism and the pro-Fascist policy of Chamberlain', is the description of the Soviet-German trade agreement and the negotiations for a non-aggression pact given by the Central Committee of the Communist Party of Great Britain.[238]

Like everyone else, the pact had caught the British Party off-guard, and its reaction fell back on the last resort of Soviet patriotism. Historian Kevin Morgan, who has written prodigiously on the Party's history, describes how the organisation struggled to make sense of the new situation.

> The war which ensued was inexplicable in the terms which communists had used to describe world politics.

The Peace Front was dead, though British communists were slow to realise it. Conditioned by years of its own propaganda, the CP could not but see the pact as a 'master stroke of Soviet peace policy...a genuine stand against aggression'.[239]

The Party had been campaigning for the signing of an Anglo-Soviet alliance for much of the year and continued to do so with a renewed effort, despite that in the circumstances such a call was futile. On 17 September the Soviet Union invaded eastern Poland.

When Britain declared war on Germany on 3 September the response from the Party was initially unequivocal. The editorial of the *Daily Worker* for 4 September began:

> The war is here. It is a war that CAN and MUST be won. And the people of Britain can win it. Fascism and its friends everywhere have brought this war upon us. Till now Hitler has had an easy time of it. His friends in other countries—and above all in Britain—have "opened the door " for him. Now it is our business to face him and his friends with a resistance such as he has never dreamed of. Now it is the business of the enemies of fascism to take a grip on things and fight this war to victory on every front.[240]

According to EP Thompson, the editorial was not written by General Secretary Pollitt, but by the *Daily Worker* night editor and poet, Randall Swingler.

> As the deadline for the press approached, Swingler glancing idly at the incoming ticker-tape noticed with alarm that German tanks had crossed the frontier into Poland. He tried without effect to contact [Party leaders] but each was in his separate stretch of the suburban subway. He ran down, stopped the presses and, on the stone, wrote out a defiant editorial committing the paper (and the movement) to support of the war, concluding, "This is a war which can and must be won."[241]

It might as well have been written by Pollitt. For the Party then issued a manifesto with the unanimous support of the central committee that called for a war on two fronts: a war against Nazi Germany and a war on the home front to bring down the Chamberlain government that had sought to appease Hitler. The current government, it argued, would prefer to fight the Soviet Union rather than Nazism.

> This war CANNOT be won while the "Men of Munich"— men who for years have been abandoning democracy's defences to fascism—remain in power here and in France. There is not a minute to be lost in getting for Britain at war a new Government, a GOVERNMENT THAT HAS THE UNSTINTED TRUST OF THE PEOPLE, A GOVERNMENT THAT GETS THINGS DONE.[242]

On 14 September the Party published 50,000 copies of a pamphlet written by Harry Pollitt entitled *How to Win the War*.

> The Communist Party supports the war, believing it to be a just war. To stand aside from this conflict...to contribute only revolutionary sounding phrases while the fascist beasts ride roughshod over Europe would be a betrayal of everything our forebears have fought to achieve in the course of long years of struggle against capitalism.[243]

The pamphlet declared support for Polish independence and demanded that Czech independence be restored. Pollitt's friend and comrade John Mahon was to write in his 1976 biography of Pollitt: "The line of this pamphlet and the manifesto of September 2nd were endorsed throughout the Party."[244] On the same day, a four-page press telegram arrived from Moscow exalting the Soviet system, the Soviet people, the Soviet leader and the non-aggression pact with Hitler: "Everything runs smoothly in the life of the individual and all organs of state." On page two it included the lines:

> There is no doubt whatever in the minds of the Soviet people that this war is an Imperialist and predatory war for new redivision of the world, which is waged to the tune of 'Defence of the small nations', a robber war kindled from all sides by the hands of two Imperialist groups of powers.[245]

It was at odds with the central committee's position and everything published up to then in the *Daily Worker*. Pollitt did not convey the contents of the telegram to the central committee, but it is likely that it, or a copy, was somehow seen by Party theorist and central committee member, Palme Dutt.

Dutt was a long-time close associate of Pollitt's, but someone who looked to Moscow for approval, while Pollitt looked more to the Party's standing among the British working class. As a young man Dutt was expelled from Oxford for organising a meeting in support of the Russian Revolution. Pollitt grew up in poverty in east Manchester and saw two of his siblings die. He began work at the age of 12 as a half-timer in a textile mill alongside his mother. At 13, he began an apprenticeship as a boilermaker. Harry Pollitt became a mass agitator and organiser; Dutt, editor of *Labour Monthly* and in the mid-1930s, of the *Daily Worker*. He used both publications to support Stalin's purge of Trotsky and others, praising the show trials. In light of the telegram, he argued Europe had embarked upon a second imperialist war, politically no different from the First World War and therefore, it was not in the interests of the working class to participate. When he put this position to a central committee meeting on 24 September, he received little support. However, the following day, the CPGB's representative in Moscow, Dave Springhall, returned to London with Dimitrov's 9 September directive in his briefcase. Within a week the central committee reversed their position in line with Moscow's instructions. Significantly, General Secretary Pollitt, *Daily Worker* editor JR Campbell, and the Party's only MP, Willie Gallacher, opposed the policy reversal. Pollitt was removed as general secretary, Campbell as editor of the *Daily Worker*. The responsibilities of general secretary were transferred to a secretariat headed by Dutt.

If we re-consider Andrew Thorpe's conclusion that the Party was a hybrid of an "organisation imported from Moscow", and a Party "rooted in national radical traditions", then if the latter influence was dominant from 1936 to 1939, the former took pre-eminence from 1939 to 1941. In the background was the default position that Moscow was always right. After all, the Soviet Union was supposedly immune to the economic crisis the West had just endured.

The source of the reversal was inevitably Stalin himself. Comintern Presidium Georgi Dimitrov's diaries reveal that he met with Stalin on 7 September when it was indicated to him that he should publish a thesis outlining that "the division of capitalist states into fascist and democratic states has lost its former sense".[246] On 7 October, the *Daily Worker* ran a headline and front-page article that echoed the position they had accused Chamberlain and the "Men of Munich" of holding weeks prior.

> HITLER MAKES HIS OFFER
> Conference if War Stops in West
> ...he [Hitler] therefore appealed for a peace conference of the Powers, to be held following not merely an armistice, but a demobilisation of the armies. Declaring that he had no further demands of any kind upon France, he then went on record with a flat claim for the return of former German colonies, and a denunciation of the "inequalities" between the relative extent of British colonial domination, and that of the Nazi Reich.

The tone of the article takes Hitler's words at face value. The war is described as "a war for profit" and not a war for democracy against fascism, or even a war against aggression.

> The air is thick with the speeches of the ruling class politicians. And now Hitler has spoken with his usual trust in the Almighty. From the welter of phrases there emerges the proposal for a peace conference. But Chamberlain and Daladier are demanding the continuation of the war. What are the people being called upon to fight for?[247]

The Party parroted Stalin and rationalised the Nazi-Soviet pact. The day before Stalin invaded Poland the Party produced a leaflet entitled *Britain and the Soviet Union*, in which it emphasised:

> There is not an atom of truth in the allegations about the Soviet Union getting ready to "abandon her neutrality and feed on the corpse of Poland".[248]

Roger Moorhouse in *The Devils' Alliance* maintains that the acrobatics that "loyal members" of the Party had to undergo was "humiliating".[249] Both Pollitt and Campbell wrote letters of recantation, repudiating their original position and henceforth publicly supported Dutt. The *Manchester Guardian* covered the policy reversal on 12 October.

> The British Communist Party has reversed its policy of support for the war and deposed its secretary Mr Harry Pollitt…will find it difficult to get its British sympathisers to accept this amazing right about-turn.[250]

Whilst divisions within the central committee are documented, the reaction of the membership is more difficult to assess. Soon after Britain declared war on Germany, a Manchester-wide meeting was held in Chorlton town hall. Wilf Charles and other Manchester comrades recalled a critical meeting:

> There was a big famous [meeting] just after the outbreak of war. A well-known Lancashire leader of the Party, Frank Bright, a marvellous individual, stood up and denounced the war as not in the interests of the working class—it will lead to world slaughter and called on the Party to oppose the war. I rejoiced at this. That was my natural inclination, stuff them and their war. A remarkable meeting. Frank Bright made it clear he was speaking as an individual. I don't remember a vote taken. It wasn't a decision-making meeting. It lasted most of the day with 300 members present.[251]

Wilf was a recent recruit to the Party. Born in 1916 in Moss Side, one of seven children, his father was a boot repairer. Wilf received very little formal education, joining the Party in January 1939. I interviewed him in 1992 about life in the Party during the war.

> You stumbled into it. There were so few of them then. I remember going to my first meeting, no one wanted to talk to me. They were a bit suspicious of a young fella. We were over a barber's shop on Oxford Road. They wondered how I had got there; I wondered how I had got there. They had internal fallings out, they were concerned with that. I remember coming home to me father. I says, 'They're a strange bunch,' he says, 'parties are like that, if you're any good you'll make it bloody better.'[252]

Eddie Frow had heard Bright speak on many occasions and was present at the same Manchester-wide meeting: "Frank was a tremendously powerful speaker, I was intellectually convinced, absolutely."[253] Likewise Henry Suss, even from the hindsight of 1992, believed it to have been the right decision.

> There was never heated debate like it…not in my 50 years membership. I don't recall any period where there had been intense discussions on an issue which Congress had not declared an opinion…The British Communist Party was very much divided on the question.[254]

Whilst Henry, Wilf and Eddie supported the position of Palme Dutt, Benny Rothman, at the time, a young Jewish comrade from Cheetham, supported the war effort.

> I couldn't accept the fact that the Soviet Union and the Nazis had come to this agreement. I was applying to join the Army…I joined the Home Guard round here. I think most of the people I spoke to in the factory had a somewhat similar stand, we weren't enthusiastic about the position of Palme Dutt.[255]

Mike Luft, whose father was Issy Luft, a leading Jewish Party member in Manchester, believes that the overwhelming majority of the Cheetham branch would not have supported the imperialist war stance. Frances Dean was a member of the Young Communist League at the outbreak of the war, joining the Party proper after the Soviet Union entered. Even as a "very young member" Frances was unconvinced of the Party's position.

> One of the problems then was we had the Comintern… and the Comintern had a very big influence…they designated that it was an imperialist war, and there was a certain argument for it. But when you look at what fascism meant, the destruction of democracy, the trade union movement and the labour movement in general, the subjugation of the peoples of Europe, there was another element to it and this is where the conflict came. I think Harry Pollitt was right.[256]

Hugh Scanlon was more candid: "The Party had almost

become apologists for Hitler when Hitler did the deal with the Soviet Union."[257] Hugh and Benny worked at Metro-Vicks in Trafford Park and were in reserved occupations. Consequently, Benny was turned down by the army. It is telling that he didn't tell comrades at the time he had attempted to join up, "It wouldn't have gone down too well."[258] The Manchester and district organiser for the Party at the time was Mick Jenkins. In later life Mick wrote an autobiography, *Prelude to Better Days*, in which he recalled the same Manchester meeting. He describes the row spilling out into the corridor, a comrade defending Bright and condemning Chamberlain's government.

> 'These bastards will never fight Hitler!' And no one said a word for some seconds. What answer was there to that sentiment? Inexorably we were driven to the position that the ruling class in Britain would not fight Hitler if they could help it.[259]

Except they did. They had declared war and there was already an expeditionary force in France, with another sent to Finland in November. The first year of the war included, of course, Dunkirk and the Battle of Britain, "the desperate days of the summer" as Orwell called them when Britain was perilously close to invasion. Hitler had set a date of 20 September 1940. The air battle over London and Kent on Sunday 15 September was the climax of the Battle of Britain. The Luftwaffe launched its largest raid, hoping to destroy the RAF; 1,500 aircraft took part in the fighting which lasted until dark. Cloud cover helped disperse the German aircraft which suffered heavy losses and the invasion plans were shelved. It was not Britain who sought a peace agreement with Hitler but rather the Soviet Union, which also entered into talks on joining the Axis forces. After Harry Pollitt was deposed as general secretary, he returned to his home city of Manchester and worked in the district office. Publicly he supported Dutt and the Party line, but privately he wrote of it leaving "a nasty taste in his mouth".[260] "We have not been able to treat the Warsaw resistance in the same way that we treated Madrid and Valencia and Barcelona."[261] Pollitt's fall-out with Dutt was acrimonious; according to Benny Rothman, there was also bad feeling towards Pollitt at the district level in Manchester.

In that period when he resigned, he came back to

Manchester and he was met with a frosty reception. Only a few, but some were bloody rude to him...one of the leading Party members here, Mick Jenkins, was more or less refusing to allow him into the Party offices on Rusholme Road, but he'd done more for the Party than Mick had done, up to that period or since. It was just pandering to the gallery.[262]

Most of the membership learned to live with the Party's opposition to the war, some embraced it. The Party did not shed members to the degree they did over the invasion of Hungary in 1956 or the invasion of Czechoslovakia in 1968. In all probability, membership numbers held up. Many saw a logic to it; a contorted logic confirmed by the Nazi-Soviet pact that the British government was as much a threat to peace as Hitler. During the years leading up to the war, the Party had consistently criticised the National Government as being pro-fascist. In February 1939 Pollitt wrote:

> The plain fact that Britain today is ruled by a government which prepares a way for the advance of fascism in Britain as well as supporting fascism abroad.[263]

From top to bottom the Party was convinced that the British establishment presented a threat of fascism; it did so because such a viewpoint had become embedded during Third Period Stalinism, and the turn to the politics of the popular front from the summer of 1935 had not erased previous instincts. By 1938 the Party belatedly regarded Mosley as a spent force, so anti-fascist work became directed against the government. The problem for communists at this time was not, as Orwell argued, that they failed to see the dangers of fascism, it was more that they saw the dangers everywhere; no one arguably more than Palme Dutt.

Dutt disputed that fascism was a movement from below— fascism was being put in place from above. In effect, the National Government and Mosley were two sides of the same coin. Dutt argued this at length in *Fascism and Social Revolution* (1934) shortly before Dimitrov's rendition of the Comintern's popular front strategy in August 1935. Dimitrov's new analysis contradicted Dutt's. The establishment of fascism was not the succession of one government by another but "open terrorist dictatorship".[264] Dimitrov urged communists to join others forming popular fronts against fascism, but crucially also not to...

> ...underrate the importance of the reactionary measures of the bourgeoisie at present increasingly developing in bourgeois-democratic countries.[265]

Dutt and others took this to mean fighting the National Government and it was routine to read in communist propaganda in the late 1930s that fascism was being introduced into Britain by the National Government. The writer and Labour MP John Strachey, who was a communist sympathiser throughout the period, held a particularly broad view of fascism.

> Naturally, fascism will not always be called fascism. For example, the present policy of the British ruling class appears to be leading towards an attempt to establish its unchecked autocracy.[266]

Every measure that the government took to prepare for war against fascist Germany was described by communists as encroaching fascism, including rearmament. The Party's position leading up to and during the early years of the war was always confused. A 'war on two fronts' sounded principled at face value, but what was the point of fighting a war against your own government when it alone had the means to defeat fascism? The logical conclusion of having sent soldiers to Spain was to continue the struggle by sending soldiers to France. But after Dimitrov's directive, the Party repeatedly drew parallels between the First and Second World Wars to justify their position. Labour MP Nye Bevan felt compelled to write in *Tribune* in May 1940: "They shame their own dead in Spain."[267] At the bottom of members' defence of a paradoxical policy was their unconditional loyalty to the Soviet Union. Henry Suss always remained convinced of the integrity of the Party line.

> The evidence of the first year of the war was that the British were not serious. They were stalling for any possible switch in the war away from Germany, to direct efforts against the Soviet Union. We were so concerned about the protection of the Soviet Union—for the first time in world history a revolution had taken place in

which socialists and communists led workers and peasants—that this could be endangered, had we lined up with those in support of the war.[268]

At the time Bevan was editor of *Tribune*, Orwell was literary editor. He more than anyone was to define, to portray Stalinism as not only about the ruthless imposition of the general secretary's iron will, but followers' acceptance of arbitrary decisions against their instincts and lived experience.

Every time Stalin swaps partners, 'Marxism' has to be hammered into a new shape. This entails sudden and violent changes of 'line', purges, denunciations, systematic destruction of Party literature etc. etc. Every communist is in fact liable at any moment to have to alter his most fundamental convictions, or leave the Party. The unquestionable dogma of Monday may become the damnable heresy of Tuesday, and so on.[269]

Stalinism involved stuffing reality into the suitcase of ideology no matter how difficult the fit, regardless of personal costs and sentiments. Defending the Soviet Union mattered above all else and being a communist inevitably entailed sacrifice. A classless society was not going to be won without the suffering of others or oneself, and the ruling class were not going to hand over power. One had to be tough and prepared to be unpopular.

When Harry Pollitt was in his early thirties he fell in love with Rose Cohen, repeatedly proposing. She refused him and eventually married Max Petrovsky, a Ukrainian who worked for the Comintern as a mentor for the CPGB. Rose also became a Comintern agent and travelled widely: Finland, Germany, Lithuania, Estonia, Latvia, Turkey, France, Scandinavia, conveying money and messages to communist parties. Eventually they settled in Moscow. In 1937 Petrovsky was arrested for being a supporter of Leon Trotsky then, later in the year, Rose also, for being a member of British intelligence. Pollitt had previously described the 1934 show trials of Kamenev, Zinoviev, Bukharin and others "a new triumph in the history of progress".[270] When the *Daily Herald* raised the case of Rose and the British government attempted to intervene to save the life of a subject, the *Daily Worker* criticised their efforts.

The National Government is starting up a new attack on Anglo-Soviet relations. As a pretext for this they are using the case of the arrest of a former British subject on a charge of espionage...The British Government has no right whatever to interfere in the internal affairs of another country and of its citizens.[271]

Even in a matter so personal to Pollitt, he would not break ranks. At the end of the war, Stalin declared that it had been an anti-fascist war from the start. Perhaps the reason why few members left the Party from 1939 to 1941 is that many could not envisage their lives without it. There was the Party and there was the world beyond. In *Inside the Whale*, Orwell writes about why so many intellectuals were drawn to communism in the 1930s.

It was simply something to believe in. Here was a church, an army, an orthodoxy, a discipline. Here was a Fatherland and, at any rate since 1935 or thereabouts, a Fuehrer. All the loyalties and superstitions that the intellectual has seemingly banished could come rushing back under the thinnest of disguises. Patriotism, religion, empire, military glory. All in one word: Russia. Father, king, leader, hero, saviour. All in one word: Stalin. God: Stalin. The devil: Hitler. Heaven: Moscow. Hell: Berlin. All the gaps were filled up. So, after all, the 'communism' of the English intellectual is something explicable enough. It is the patriotism of the deracinated.[272]

The Party was overwhelmingly working class in composition and the flock, if it was one, had more material reasons for joining, remaining and believing. Hugh Scanlon was 26 at the time and convenor at Metro-Vicks in Trafford Park, an engineering factory that at the height of wartime production employed around 25,000 workers. "The Party did the biggest volte-face in history. But make no mistake I swallowed the line."[273] How he and others managed to live with the line until June 1941 is another question.

*Comrades Come Rally*

# Chapter 10

## Imperialist War in Practice

> "Am just off to the Rhondda for some meetings to popularise the Party policy. I will be in a difficult position, but will manage alright." Letter from Harry Pollitt to *Daily Worker*, 18 November 1939

In Britain, the first eight months of the war were referred to as 'the phoney war' or 'the bore war'. Churchill described it as the 'Twilight War', the Germans *der Sitzkrieg* (the sitting war), a play on *blitzkrieg*; the French termed it *la Drôle de guerre*. All this ended with Germany's invasion of France and the Low Countries. The phrases had stuck, because there was no large-scale military action involving the Allies from Britain's entry into the war in September 1939 until the Battle of France began in May 1940. The feared aerial bombardment of Britain was yet to come—the gas masks were not used and children were returned from evacuation. The Communist Party interpreted the phoney war as further evidence of the National Government's reluctance to fight fascism, indeed of its sympathies with fascism. Bill Whitaker was a member of the central committee from 1938 to 1943.

> I worked for the Party in northeast Lancashire from 1938 to 1939 and was then asked to go into Manchester in early 1940... All that we were involved in was a phoney war. For a long, long period. War declared and no war, except we got chased out of Europe. And after that, there was something of a standstill.[274]

The terms, particularly from the current distance, give the impression that military action and loss of life were absent for the first eight months. There was loss and there were British casualties; there was a great deal of fear, even within the first few months. Within hours of the British declaration of war, the *SS Athenia* was torpedoed by a German submarine 250 miles northwest of Ireland on route to Montreal. One hundred and twelve passengers and crew were killed and the Battle of the Atlantic began, lasting for the duration of the war. German U-boats and pocket battleships launched attacks in the autumn and winter of 1939, sinking several British vessels, including *HMS Courageous* with the loss of 519 lives. U-boats and the Luftwaffe laid mines at the Thames estuary and attacked merchant shipping which moved in convoys of up to 40 ships with Royal Navy escorts. Elsewhere by October, Jews were being deported from Austria and Czechoslovakia into German-occupied Poland; by November 1939 every Jew in German-occupied Poland had to wear a Star of David armband. At home, the blackout had begun even before the war started, and rationing before the end of 1939.

For the Party at this time, two fronts risked their reputation. One was the ongoing economic war that Britain and France conducted against Germany, and the second was the Soviet Union's invasion of Finland on 30 November 1939. Britain and France attempted a naval blockade of Germany and also bought raw materials from neutral countries to prevent their sale to the enemy. Germany circumvented the blockade by importing what they could through Spanish ports and by being supplied with raw materials, crude oil in particular, from the Soviet Union. The Soviet Union and Germany had a growing commercial relationship right up to the invasion of the Soviet Union in June 1941. By 1939 Germany was dependent on imports for all of her raw materials and the Soviet Union was happy to oblige, particularly concerning crude oil and iron ore. In return it welcomed outside technological help that Germany could provide. In February 1940, the Soviet Union agreed to supply grain to Germany and in May 1940, Germany gifted the Soviets the battleship *Lützow*, which admittedly needed refitting, as a symbol of their expanding relationship. As far as Britain was concerned, the Soviet Union was an accomplice of Hitler and in March 1940, Britain and France began planning Operation Pike: a series of bombing raids on oil production centres in Russia. A reconnaissance mission took place and it was decided to attack the Caucasian towns of Baku and Grozny.

The plans were seized after the fall of France in May 1940, and the operation abandoned.

On 30 November 1939 the Soviet Union invaded Finland to begin what became known as the Winter War. The conflict lasted three and a half months and though they had superior military strength, Soviet losses were high. At the Moscow Treaty of March 1940, Finland ceded 11 percent of its territory and 30 percent of its economy. Though the Soviets denied it was ever their ambition to conquer all of Finland, the war exposed weaknesses in the Red Army that emboldened Hitler's invasion plans. The hand-held petrol bomb, first improvised by Nationalist forces in the Spanish Civil War against Russian T-26 tanks, owes its nickname to Finnish fighters. Foreign minister Molotov announced on state radio that Russia's aerial bombardment was not dropping explosives but rather humanitarian aid. The Finns described Russian cluster bombs 'Molotov breadbaskets' and their petrol bombs as 'Molotov cocktails'. Britain considered providing aid to Finland and scaling down trade with the Soviet Union, since exports to there were tantamount to exports to Germany, but decided that such action would only push Germany and the Soviet Union closer together. The Party felt obliged to support the invasion of Finland—here was a war it didn't want to stop. The front page of the *Daily Worker*, 1 December 1939:

> A number of buildings in Helsinki are stated to be in flames. The same sources give the text of leaflets dropped from the Soviet planes declaring that the Soviet action 'is not intended to harm Finland. It is to clear out Cajander and Mannerheim'—the Premier and Field-Marshal, both of them violently reactionary and closely linked with the Western imperialist powers, who have been mainly responsible for preventing peaceful agreement with the Soviet Union.

Roger Moorhouse maintains that the situation "tested communist credibility in Britain" and claims that people left the Party at the time.[275] There were indeed some high-profile resignations; Victor Gollancz and John Strachey left at the time of the Nazi-Soviet pact, desertions by rank-and-file members, though, are not as well recorded. Wilf Charles recalls an experience in Manchester during the Winter War.

> The attack on the Party when we opposed the war was horrendous. The event of the Finnish invasion—you had to have some bottle. I can remember a very funny incident; it didn't seem funny at the time. A lot of people disappeared. People were in vulnerable positions and didn't want to be arrested. I called a meeting on Medlock Street, centre of Hulme, with Sam Wild, there was no crowd, just 17 coppers. So, we started falling out with the coppers, Sam was laying the law down. Then a crowd came out because they saw a row with the police, and that's when we had our meeting, till the police broke it up. But we didn't get arrested or anything.[276]

Men like Wilf and Sam were not the type to keep their heads down in a hostile climate. The news editor of the *Daily Worker* at this time was Douglas Hyde. During the 1930s the paper established itself with a readership beyond the ranks of the Party. Randall Swingler's biographer Andy Croft on circulation in early 1939:

> The eight-page *Daily Worker* was enjoying a daily circulation of 50,000 (with increased sales on Saturday amounting to a weekly circulation of 377,000). Sometimes called the 'Miracle of Fleet Street', its success was due very largely to its unique relationship with its readers (the majority of whom were not members of the Communist Party).[277]

Hyde left the Party in 1948 and in 1950 published a memoir, *I Believed*, in which he described *Daily Worker* sellers at the time being "spat upon and assaulted in the streets... doors slammed in their faces, even chamber-pots emptied on their heads from upstairs windows".[278] Hyde had converted to Catholicism by this time and as Wilf Charles remarked, "memory is coloured by personal feeling". Wilf himself recalled at least a mixed reception:

> I became secretary of Moss Side branch. I used to sell the *Daily Worker* in the centre of town on Oldham Street. I can honestly say, people bought them off us. We got a few insults; you get used to that. One or two nasty

fascist types, someone like myself was pretty handy, didn't bother us. We had quite big sales.[279]

Until the Soviet Union joined the Allies, there is evidence that some Party members were reluctant to campaign for, or even defend the Party's position. They feared losing hard-earned credibility built up during the years of popular front politics, risked losing trade union positions and even their employment.

The first by-election during the war was in Stretford, Greater Manchester in December 1939. The major political parties observed an ongoing electoral truce, meaning that in the case of Stretford, Labour didn't stand against the incumbent Conservative. In light of its decision not to support the war, the Communist Party fielded a candidate, but its choice of candidate and the nature of the campaign they ran is telling. Eric Gower had previously stood as the Labour candidate for the constituency in July of the same year and, in December, described himself on his election leaflets as the "Labour Candidate for Stretford, 1938-39" rather than the Communist Party candidate. As Kevin Morgan puts it:

> Gower's aim was to gloss over political differences and thereby capitalise on the absence of a Labour candidate and popular discontent with the government. His election address contained nothing which might have alienated non-communist opponents of the war.[280]

At work, it was almost impossible to argue opposition to the war. Frances Dean who was in the YCL in 1939, began the war at Manchester's Wholesale and Co-operative Society and was then directed to work at Fairey Aviation in Levenshulme.

> There was hostility, there's no doubt at it. When you're with a crowd of people they tend to take the mickey rather than being hostile. Occasionally you got hostility. I don't think people really understood the ins and outs of Communist Party policy...People were for the war. The general public opinion was in favour of the war because of what had happened prior. The taking over of Czechoslovakia, the attack on Poland. There was no option but to respond.[281]

Benny Rothman recalled a fracas at Metro-Vicks:

> I can remember I got involved in a terrific clash with a group of workers for criticising our so-called war effort and generally being critical of the stance we had. Nearly came to blows with this chap—quite a big shot in Urmston Labour Party. It really was hot.[282]

Benny, it should be remembered, agreed with Pollitt rather than Palm Dutt and had tried to join up as soon as war was declared. Working alongside Benny, Hugh Scanlon was rapidly ascending the ranks of the AEU.

> It was almost a schizophrenic existence. Many admired the enthusiasm and conviction of Party people: what you were prepared to work for, sell the *Daily Worker* at the factory gate and have milk collections for Spain—there was more than a sneaking admiration for that. But when it came to opposition to the war, the Party was not popular.[283]

The logical conclusion of the central committee's position on the war at this time was the Bolshevik's policy towards the First World War: revolutionary defeatism. As Lenin framed it: "Transform the present imperialist war into civil war—is the only correct proletarian slogan."[284] The Bolsheviks had pulled off a revolution on the back of the premise and Party members were encouraged to read Lenin's essays on war; speakers came to branches to elucidate the theory behind an unimaginable task. Meanwhile on the shop floor at Metro-Vicks, Hugh Scanlon applied the Party line pragmatically, if not modestly.

> I can remember having air raid practices at Metro-Vicks. So, you would all go to the air-raid shelter. We would boycott that and it was a futile gesture, but that was how we would show our opposition to the war.[285]

Some comrades were reluctant to let it be known they were Party members for fear of losing their livelihood. Scanlon:

> During our opposition to the war, we were given false names—I can't remember my name—and you referred to each other as people did on the continent. I think it was a bit gimmicky. Many were convinced of the need to

oppose the war but were not prepared to be victimised for these things, and they would keep their membership if not secret, at least discreet.[286]

Richard Croucher in *Engineers at War* looks at how the authorities viewed Party activity during the first two years of the war. In July 1940 the Home Office confidently informed the cabinet:

> Although the Communist Party is opposed to the war, its members are normally careful to refrain at the present time from anti-war propaganda.

Part of the answer may be found in Croucher's comments: "...almost every shop steward who spoke about this period mentioned being watched or interviewed formally by the police."[287] The government had availed itself of emergency powers and well-known communists were prevented from joining the armed forces, directed to work elsewhere, and to a degree watched. Wilf Charles received his conscription papers in May 1940 and made his way into the recruitment hall.

> As I went in, I had a run-in with some silly sod behind the counter who told me to take my hands out of my pockets. 'Eff off' I said to him. Then they put me in this room and told me to wait. Then they came to me and said, 'You'll never be called up—you'll be directed to essential works.' This annoyed me. Then I got these letters and was sent to the Co-op with other comrades. Frances Dean, Syd Booth, Jim Cunningham. And all of us got on the [union] branch committee. MI5 came to visit the house regularly. Often, I wasn't in, so me mother made them welcome.[288]

Eric Jessop began the war in the Auxiliary Fire Service, leading an early attempt to unionise firemen in Manchester.

> I went to the fire stations I was trained at, went organising for a union. I was court-martialled along with others and dismissed. We were called in one at a time, harangued by the chief constable and told we were committing treason, 'And you know what that means.' There were around 40 of them, scared stiff. I

was followed around by Special Branch for three weeks
and then directed to Fairey's [Engineering].[289]

Margaret Gadian graduated in French and applied for
teaching jobs during the first few years of the war.

> As it was, they blacklisted me. I found out later. When
> I applied for teaching jobs and I wasn't getting any. I
> asked for a meeting with the chairman of the education
> committee, he was very embarrassed. 'You're perfectly
> competent to teach but they don't like your politics.'
> He was the leader of the Labour Education Committee.
> I worked as a clerk in the planning department. My
> immediate boss, who was very friendly with a chief
> commissioner, told me once they were watching me
> and I ought to be careful.[290]

The most important day for communist parties was 1
May, May Day. Official labour demonstrations were held on
the first Sunday in May; the Communist Party, though, held
demonstrations on 1 May regardless of the day of the week as
an indication of its influence and a demonstration of working-
class militancy. In 1940, it fell on a Wednesday and the Party
had hoped to mark it by disrupting production. In the end, most
cities' gatherings took place outside of working hours, but not
in Manchester, where some took industrial action to attend.
Here, Margaret Gadian reads from Sol Gadian's unpublished
autobiography.

> Despite no support by official labour or trade unions,
> one of the best May Day marches was held in 1940. Over
> 1,000 people marched from the centre of Manchester to
> Platt Fields. Most of the marchers had taken time off
> work.[291]

Henry Suss worked in a clothing factory in Cheetham. There
was insufficient support for strike action amongst the workforce,
yet isolated though they were, he and another comrade still left
work that day to attend the march.

> The most memorable incident was the May Day
> demonstration when we declared demonstrably our

opposition to the war. There were three comrades in our workplace, and we talked to the workers a number of times and told them we were going on this May Day demonstration. And this shop steward, who was a Labour councillor and very right-wing, went and told the boss. The boss went and put up a notice within minutes. 'Anybody who absents themselves from work will be dismissed.' We'd committed ourselves. We should have retracted. We didn't and we were sacked.[292]

The march was reported upon in Sam Wild's security file. Two arrests were made on the day and almost inevitably, one of them was Sam.

The May Day Labour demonstration held in Manchester yesterday turned out to be a communist affair. All the local well-known communists were prominent in the demonstration. One well-known demonstrator, Sam Wild, was arrested on Hyde Road by Detective Inspector Timpany, on a charge of 'Conduct likely to cause a breach of the peace' and a woman Hilda Hikin was arrested for obstructing the police during the arrest of Wild.[293]

Henry and Bill Whitaker both described a degree of hostility directed at marchers on the day. It is not surprising given the context. The spring and summer of 1940 was not a good time for anti-war propaganda. Whilst Henry and others were marching to Platt Fields, the Allies were evacuating Norwegian ports, their invasion aborted.

Though measures were taken against the Party, including in 1941 the banning of the *Daily Worker*, the British government's response was far more moderate than the response of its French counterpart to the French Communist Party (PCF) which was significantly greater in size. The Nazi-Soviet pact prompted an investigation of the PCF on the grounds that the pact had rendered the Party a passive ally of Hitler. Its newspaper *L'Humanité* was banned. Unlike the CPGB many leading members of the PCF openly condemned the pact; 21 of the Party's 73 parliamentary deputies defected and pledged to continue resistance to German aggression. The PCF's trade union, the CGT, expelled all those who refused to repudiate the Nazi-Soviet pact. Nevertheless, the French government banned the PCF when war broke out, and the dissemination of its literature was declared an offence with five years in jail. Party leader Maurice Thorez fled to Moscow and was sentenced to death in his absence; 3,000 Party members were arrested, many more sacked, and the PCF went underground.

After the fall of France, Britain was under imminent threat of invasion. In June, Germany occupied the Channel Islands; in July, the Battle of Britain began; in August, the London Blitz. Elsewhere the Soviet Union swiftly annexed Estonia, Latvia and Lithuania. Though the RAF claimed victory in the Battle of Britain in September, London was bombed throughout October. In the same month, Polish Jews were forced into the Warsaw Ghetto and Molotov began exploratory talks with Ribbentrop on the Soviet Union joining the Axis powers. Between 22 and 24 December, Manchester suffered its worst air raid of the war, killing an estimated 684 people and injuring 2,000. Thirty thousand homes were destroyed or damaged and some of the city's great buildings were hit, including the Town Hall, the Free Trade Hall, the Royal Exchange, Victoria Station, Manchester Cathedral and the Victoria Hospital. It was in this context that the Party ceased issuing demands that the war be ended and instead issued demands on how it should be won. They now demanded a 'people's war' and the establishment of a 'people's government' to secure a 'people's peace'. On the same day that the French signed an armistice, the CPGB issued a pamphlet, *The People Must Act*, which laid out nine demands including:

> Conscription of wealth and nationalisation of the principal industries without compensation; election of workers control committees in every factory to safeguard the workers' conditions and end the corruption in the production of armaments and of necessities of life.[294]

All nine demands were reprinted in the *Daily Worker* on 22 June 1940. The Party practically reverted to its initial position at the outbreak of the war: Pollitt's war on two fronts, by advocating a war against the threat of fascism from within and from without. As central committee member Bill Whitaker described it, "There was a turn when Churchill came in." Whether it was a 360-degree turn is a moot point but the following month the idea for a people's convention was born and a six-point manifesto was launched to garner much more broad-based support than previously.

1) Defence of people's living standards.
2) Defence of people's democratic and trade union rights
3) Adequate air raid precautions, deep bomb-proof shelters, rehousing and relief of victims.
4) Friendship with the Soviet Union.
5) A People's Government, truly representative of the whole people and able to inspire the confidence of the working people of the world.
6) A people's peace that gets rid of the war.[295]

The People's Convention was originally due to have taken place in Manchester at the Free Trade Hall but bomb damage determined otherwise. It took place on Saturday 11 January at the Royal Hotel, Woburn Place, London with over 2,000 delegates present. There is no doubt there was some popular support for the campaign amongst labour movement activists. On the following Monday the *Daily Mirror* went so far as to report:

They have too many grievances the government leaves unanswered. They expected Labour ministers in the government to be their champions. They are disappointed in them. Labour ministers behave like pale imitations of Tory ministers. So, the people feel themselves leaderless. They are beginning to turn to the Communist Party.[296]

The convention was very much a popular front initiative and turning up was not turning to the CPGB. Hugh Scanlon, AEU convenor from Metro-Vicks, attended as a delegate and spoke from the rostrum. The *Daily Worker* described his intervention:

Mr Scanlon of Manchester described how workers in factories had collected large sums to send delegates to the Convention. They welcomed the Convention's economic programme, realising that only the people themselves could solve their problems. The meetings at which these delegates would report back to the workers who had sent them, would be most important.[297]

In interview years later, in reply to the question, "Was there much support from your workmates for the Convention?" he replied:

> I don't think so. From the average rank and file member, Hitler had to be beaten. You could say you were an AEU member, but you couldn't speak in the name of the AEU.[298]

The convention stopped well short of revolutionary defeatism, but it was perceived by government as undermining the patriotism required to defeat Hitler. A week after the convention, Home Secretary Herbert Morrison banned the *Daily Worker* and the cabinet set up a special committee on communist activities. The committee concluded: "It is not necessary at this present time to contemplate any general action against the Communist Party."[299] The committee was concerned, however, about communist activity among merchant seamen and used Defence Regulation 18A to ban agitators from ports. The background to this was the case of George Armstrong, a 39-year-old Party member from Newcastle, arrested in Boston, USA in October 1940 after offering to supply the local German spy network with information on the Atlantic convoys. Roger Moorhouse speculates that Armstrong may have been motivated by a speech from Molotov in which he encouraged all allied merchant seamen to desert as soon as they reached a neutral port.[300] Armstrong became the first Briton to be tried for spying during the war. He was sentenced to death and executed in July 1941. Locally, in February 1941 the executive committee of Manchester and Salford Trades Council expelled nine delegates "who associated themselves with proscribed organisations".[301] The Communist Party had become the proscribed organisation. The timing might not have been related to the People's Convention but more so to the bombing of the city which had continued into January. Before the February trades council meeting, delegates had stood in respect for the dead.

Overall, there is no evidence that significant numbers of activists deserted the Party between 1939 and 1941, though in all probability there were some losses. Wilf Charles, who was secretary of Moss Side branch during the period, estimated that the branch of 40 was depleted by around 10 between 1939 and 1941. One has to factor in enlistment and other wartime disruptions. Such losses were a setback but not debilitating. Most members who disagreed with the Party's position on the war at this time were not prepared to walk away, though many that agreed were not prepared to stick their necks out and risk victimisation. Though some members were put under surveillance and the *Daily Worker* banned for a spell, the Party was not driven underground because it did not pose a threat to the war effort and neither did it attempt to. Refusing to take part in air raid practices at Metro-Vicks was a far cry from sabotage. The People's Convention and campaigns such as improved air raid shelters mitigated the damage done by its earlier, more strident opposition policy. Indeed, at times so confused was its policy that the public could be forgiven for wondering whether the Party opposed the war or not. Also shoring up membership figures in this period was the transference of the Labour League of Youth into the YCL. Ted Willis, chairman of the former, went over to the YCL taking a good proportion of the membership with him, including Frances Dean.

> I remember I was appalled at the Spanish Civil War and Munich. The first thing I did was to join the Labour League of Youth. Because the Labour Party wanted to disband it, we joined the YCL and Ted became General Secretary of the YCL. We were friendly with the YCL anyway. There's something wrong with a youngster who isn't left-wing.[302]

The Party in Manchester was made up of workplace branches as well as geographical branches. Many of the workplace branches were in engineering factories, and increased working hours and production targets, particularly from 1940 onwards, meant that workers looked to shop stewards to defend pay and conditions. They may have been less concerned about what the *Daily Worker* in the shop steward's pocket said on the war. Eddie Frow was an engineer and an AEU activist elected to the National Committee in 1941.

> Once you create an entirely new situation in industry there are all sorts of things. I once went to an engineering factory where they had ploughed along for 30 or 40 years—right in the groove. Then all at once management started making drastic changes. Well, there was all hell

let loose obviously. And that was the situation when war broke out...Whether the membership declined or it didn't, I am absolutely convinced in my mind the general situation was very good in many respects. There were some that went, but it was more in the area branches than in industry.[303]

Two months after expelling local communists, Manchester and Salford Trades Council delegates stood in silence to the memory of communist Tom Mann, who had died in 1941. Tom Mann can realistically be described as a founding organiser of the British labour movement. Born in 1856 he managed Keir Hardie's election campaign and led the 1889 dock strike along with Ben Tillett. In 1902 he migrated to Australia and became an organiser for the Australian Labor Party, returning to Britain in 1910. He was a founder member of the CPGB and his associations reached from Frederick Engels to Harry Pollitt. At the outset of the Spanish Civil War, the Tom Mann Centuria was formed, consisting of British volunteers living in Barcelona. Sam Wild spoke at Mann's funeral.

Though the Party was out of favour, it still commanded respect. However, certainly, from the fall of France onwards, the future of the nation was at risk and class differences mattered little to most people compared to the prospect of invasion and life under Nazism. Whilst the Party was not identified with the national interest, the very best it could hope to do was to tread water. All equivocation ended with the invasion of the Soviet Union on 22 June 1941, when communists threw themselves overnight into defending the realm.

# Chapter 11

## Barbarossa Begins

> "The Jew is not an organiser, but an enzyme of decomposition. The gigantic empire in the east is ripe for collapse. The end of Jewish domination in Russia will also be the end of the Russian state." Adolf Hitler, *Mein Kampf*

At 3am on Sunday 22 June, the largest invasion force in history entered the Soviet Union across an 1800-mile front with German forces attacking in three army groups toward Leningrad, Kyiv, and Moscow. As well as Germans, the 3 million Axis troops included Italian, Hungarian, Italian, Romanian, Finnish, Slovak and Croatians. It was one year to the day after the fall of France and 129 years after Napoleon's failed invasion of Russia. Russia had three times the number of tanks and aircraft Germany possessed, the Battle of Britain having depleted the Luftwaffe, but the momentum of the ground and air attack destroyed the organisation of Soviet defences. Much of their air force was destroyed on the ground, and thousands of soldiers found themselves surrounded and forced to surrender. It took several days for Stalin to come to terms with the catastrophe. He retreated to his dacha—his summer house on the Black Sea, and it was not until 1 July that he returned to the Kremlin and made his first speech. By the following day, German forces were 300 kilometres into Soviet territory and on the road to Moscow. They had cut through Lithuania and Latvia to threaten Leningrad in the north. By mid-July, German forces had advanced to within a few kilometres of Kyiv, having captured 300,000 Soviet prisoners and destroyed 2,500 tanks and 250 aircraft.

In 1940 British intelligence had picked up information that

Germany was preparing to attack Russia but Stalin ignored it. In early 1941 Stalin's intelligence and American intelligence gave repeated warnings, but when one predicted date for the invasion passed, Stalin ignored all subsequent warnings. Perhaps he refused to act for fear of provoking Hitler. Red Army generals correctly anticipated the general location of the invasion but, again, Stalin overruled them. Stalin's terror had seriously weakened the Red Army. According to Orlando Figes, over 80,000 Red Army officers were executed between 1937 and June 1941.[304] This included more than half of the regiment commanders, and it meant they were replaced by inexperienced officers who were appointed on a political basis as much as anything else.

Hitler had told the German people that he had no choice but to invade because the Soviet Union was about to invade Germany. The truth is, as far back as *Mein Kampf*, Hitler had been planning such an invasion.

> We terminate the endless German drive to the south and west of Europe, and direct our gaze towards the lands in the East. If we talk about new soil and territory in Europe today, we can think primarily only of Russia and its vassal border states.[305]

Hitler's primary focus had always been east. The invasions to the west were a result of Britain and France honouring their commitment to Poland. In the west, there were Aryans; in the east were Poles, Slavs and Jews: Untermensch. Ultimately Hitler still sought to destroy and replace the British Empire, but he believed that he had to destroy the Soviet Union first and then utilise its natural resources to return the war to Britain. The road to London ran through Moscow.

From *Mein Kampf* emerged the Generalplan Ost (GPO). Commissioned by Heinrich Himmler, it was the Nazi regime's plan for ethnic cleansing and genocide and the subsequent colonisation of central and eastern Europe by Germans. The GPO was a pre-condition of the need for Lebensraum (living space) and the necessary Drang nach Osten (drive to the east) of German expansionism for the Volk (people). Hitler impressed upon his generals that Barbarossa was not to be subject to the normal rules of war, rather it was to be a war of annihilation. The objective was to erase Slavic people through extermination, enslavement and deportation. The scale of deportation envisaged involved sending up to 31 million people to Siberia.

On 2 May 1941, seven weeks before the invasion, officials responsible for formulating Germany's economic policy met in Berlin to discuss the problems and opportunities that the Eastern Front presented. Minutes of the meeting survived in two parts. Part one begins:

> Memorandum on the result of today's discussion with the Staatssekretäre regarding Barbarossa.
> 1. The war can only be waged if the entire Wehrmacht is fed during the third year of the war.
> 2. As a result, x million people will doubtlessly starve if that which is necessary for us is extracted from the land.[306]

It was a specific hunger plan whereby food resources would be taken from Soviet territory for the German people. Millions of Russians would starve as a result. Because of military setbacks, the plan was never fully implemented; however, famine was engineered, particularly in Ukraine, and soldiers were instructed to stiffen their resolve, for food given to starving children was food denied to Germans back home.[307] Soviet prisoners of war were starved as a matter of policy.

> The most reliable figures for the death rate among Soviet prisoners of war in German captivity reveal that 3.3 million died from a total of 5.7 million captured between June 1941 and February 1945, most directly or indirectly as a result of starvation.[308]

Following in the wake of the Blitzkrieg into the east went the Einsatzgruppen (deployment groups). These were mobile killing units run by the SS responsible for the mass murder of civilians. Six months into the invasion, the Einsatzgruppen had murdered over half a million Soviet Jews, more than the number of Red Army soldiers killed in combat during that time. But it wasn't just the SS who murdered indiscriminately; many German troops viewed the war in Nazi terms and regarded Soviet people as sub-human.[309] The Generalplan Ost was designed to be...

> ...a question of existence, thus it will be a racial struggle

of pitiless severity, in the course of which 20 to 30 million Slavs and Jews will perish through military actions and crises of food supply.[310]

Its methodical slaughter led directly to the Final Solution. Seven months after Barbarossa, on 20 January 1942, 15 senior German officials met at a villa on the shores of Berlin's Lake Wannsee. The purpose of the two-hour meeting was to coordinate the genocide of Europe's Jews. The meeting was called and chaired by the Chief of the Reich Security main office, Reinhard Heydrich. In the Nazi mindset, the Wannsee meeting was a logical development of the Berlin meeting of May 1941.

Between 14 and 17 July 1943, a war crimes trial was held in the city of Krasnodar, southern Russia, in front of a Soviet military tribunal. The defendants present were 11 Soviet citizens accused of collaboration; the defendants tried in absentia were a Gestapo official and 13 SS officers. All were charged with participating in the murder of 7,000 people. The records of the trial provide a specific example of the Wehrmacht's war on the Eastern Front.[311]

Krasnodar was occupied by the 17th German army between 12 August 1942 and 12 February 1943, commanded by Colonel General Ruoff. Forces included an Einsatzgruppen (a mobile death squad) and a Sonderkommando unit of around 200 death

*Ukraine 1942. A Jewish woman and child are murdered by Einsatzgruppen while four men are ordered to dig a mass grave. The photo was mailed from the Eastern Front to Germany and intercepted at a Warsaw post office by a member of the Polish resistance collecting documentation on Nazi war crimes*

camp prisoners who were forced to dispose of victims. People, including children and hospital patients, were put to death by shooting, hanging, burning and the use of 'murder vans' that piped carbon monoxide into a zinc-lined rear storage area.

> Before being dragged from the cellar the prisoners were stripped of their clothing; then they were bundled into the murder vans 60-80 at a time. The doors of the van were then hermetically closed and the engine started... By the time the vans reached the anti-tank trench the people were asphyxiated by gas. Men, women and children were bundled into the van without discrimination.[312]

> Not only prisoners, but people indiscriminately seized in the street during wholesale raids, were put to death in the murder vans...A spectacle of particular horror was the massacre of Soviet children and adolescents. There were by no means isolated instances of Germans throwing little children into pits and burying them alive...In December 1941 the Gestapo shot 900 Soviet citizens undergoing treatment at Kharkiv hospital.[313]

The murder vans were a mobile prototype for gas chambers.

For the CPGB, the participation of the Soviet Union in the war immediately transformed it into an anti-fascist war. Pollitt returned to his former post of general secretary. After his forced resignation he had gone back to work as a boilermaker which was classed as essential war work. Leaving his job and returning to the full-time leadership of the Communist Party would have required government permission. It was swiftly granted since the government wanted the CP led by someone who wholeheartedly supported the war effort. In due course, all Party policy would be subordinated to the military context. The Party supported the Churchill government, though not uncritically, and they observed the electoral truce until the end of the war. In fact, in the Rusholme by-election of 1944, International Brigade veteran Sam Wild publicly supported the Tory candidate standing in a Tory seat. Wilf Charles recalls:

> Sam Wild, me mate, led and directed by the central

> committee, fought for "don't oppose the conservative candidate". We were playing a terrible role—nobody was for us, you see; confusion plays hell with you. Behind the scenes, there was hell to pay. They asked me to do a meeting, I refused. No way am I speaking for a bastard Tory.[314]

Sam was a district organiser for the Party at the time and for his trouble of observing the electoral truce received a letter of protest from local Common Wealth Party supporters.

> It is with dismay that we read in the *Worker* this morning that the Communist Party are to observe the political truce and support the Conservative candidate in the Rusholme election. This to us, in view of the fighting record of your Party against Tory domination is surely inconceivable, and must surely negate the efforts of your comrades who are presently engaged in the final struggle against the fascist beast.[315]

The Common Wealth Party was founded in July 1942 out of an alliance between a left-wing grouping: the 1941 Committee, the writer JB Priestley, and former International Brigade Commander Tom Wintringham. It also included a neo-Christian, Forward March Movement led by Liberal MP Richard Ackland. The Common Wealth Party opposed the electoral pact and looked to disillusioned Labour voters for an electoral base. Sam Wild would have undoubtedly been uneasy about publicly supporting a Tory candidate, but as a former soldier, he was also someone familiar with collective discipline.

For communists until the end of the war, workers' interests were subordinate to the production drive, as Hugh Scanlon put it: "We broke more strikes than we made."[316] The CPGB vied at being the party of national interest, an advocate of harnessing a total war on Germany and the most intolerant of anyone who undermined the struggle. It more than fed into the popular mood, leading in two respects: a fierce criticism of Britain's industrial inefficiency and enthusiasm for Russia's war effort. Harry Pollitt's patriotism for his own country could not be separated from his Soviet patriotism, to the point of advocating Soviet-style punishment in Britain.

The Communist Party in opening its 1942 campaign has one aim. To ensure that the people of Britain play their part in the victory over fascism, with a readiness to work, sacrifice and fight, that we will as much change the world as the epic struggle of the Soviet people has done. We are up against the most formidable and political combination of murderers and gangsters ever organised. They know no pity, love or charity, they have no territorial aim but one: world domination, and that to achieve this is to breach continents and oceans with corpses and laying the achievements of centuries to waste by fire, bomb and sword. It is an enemy with whom there can be no parley, no negotiation, no compromise; whosoever tries in any way to support this enemy, brands themselves a traitor and should be shot out of hand.[317]

Whichever way the Party turned it did so stridently, in the outside lane, and the production drive from June 1941 onwards is a case in point.

*Comrades Come Rally*

# Chapter 12

## Production Drive

> "This is an engineer's war. We are fully and personally aware of that fact. Every hour since I took office as President this has been impressed upon me." Jack Tanner, AEU president, 1940

Manchester was a key industrial centre in the war effort, a centre for aircraft manufacture, particularly the Lancaster bomber, the manufacture of which became increasingly important after the Battle of Britain. Before the war, the RAF did not have a heavy bomber at all. The Party had always had a significant presence in engineering, but during the production drive between 1941 and 1945, it became strategically the most important industry for the Party and as Richard Croucher puts it:

> The typical Party cadre during the war was an AEU member…In many respects these were the heydays of the communist engineer…Certainly in terms of numbers, positions held in workplace organisation and political influence with the rank and file, they represented the apex of Communist Party achievement…[318]

That the Party advocated reorganisation in industry during this period was of great advantage to them. Most people thought it needed it and believed that German and Russian industry was more efficiently run. The *Daily Worker* remained banned until September 1942 but the Party had an aircraft industry-based publication, *The New Propeller*, through which they attacked bureaucracy, waste and inefficiency. This was a monthly eight-page paper, expanded to 12 by the end of the war, sold at a penny a copy. Its peak circulation in 1942 was 94,000; "For 100% trade unionism" was its permanent front-page caption. Private contracts were issued by the government at a cost-plus ten percent rate. The system called into question the patriotism of employers and whether the necessary sacrifices were being made across society. It was deemed to encourage waste and highlighted a need for national planning. The government had introduced an excess profits tax but the public were sceptical of how earnestly it was applied. Each issue of *The New Propeller* had a section on "The money we earn for others". In February 1942 it began:

> Few profits of firms in our industry have been announced during the past month. The general trend revealed in those that are published shows that profits are being well maintained, despite the increased taxation.[319]

In July 1941 unemployment was at 198,000; by the end of the summer that number had been absorbed into production. Thereafter, the solution to increasing the workforce was by bringing women into the factories. In December 1941, parliament passed Bevin's National Service Act, which conscripted unmarried women between the ages of 20 and 30 years to join one of the auxiliary services: The Women's Royal Naval Service, the Women's Auxiliary Air Force, the Women's Transport Service; Women's Voluntary Service or the Women's Land Army. Alternatively, they could opt or be directed to work in munition factories. As a result, the proportion of women in engineering rose from 21.6 percent in mid-1941 to 31.9 percent in mid-1942. Thereafter further productivity increases had to be achieved by technological advance or by changing working practices. The dilution of the workforce by the introduction of women workers and unskilled men as well, meant new layers of management, new machinery, additional union members and a threat to the existing equilibrium. The Party made the case that the changes needed to maximise war production were not being made, or not being made quickly enough. What stood in the way were the priorities of profit and the status quo. Vick Eddisford was apprentice engineer and a Party member at Metro-Vicks.

The management of the factory was still the same

> people—dead legs who was appointed. Nobody to my knowledge in the factory in those days was getting up the ladder based on ability. You can have all the ability in the world, if your face didn't fit, and that was one of the worst bloody places in the world for that…the management wasn't going to change, they were only in it for the money.[320]

Frances Dean was a woman worker and Party member drafted into Fairey Aviation Company in Levenshulme, Manchester. She claims that management avoided equal pay for women even if it affected production.

> We had meetings on the fight for equal pay for women, which was a big issue at that time. I had a dispute with them. The women were doing menial work, horrible work really. Bending pipes to templates. They had a thing you had to measure up and drill various holes and the shop steward said this was semi-skilled work and we should get the semi-skilled rate for it. What they did was mark out the holes in advance so they didn't have to pay me the rate; in the end they gave the job to a man and I was on idle time. I had no work. But they still had to pay me a guaranteed amount of money—£2 10 shillings a week, which you couldn't live on. And this went on for months.[321]

Dorothy Watts worked at Metro-Vicks from the age of 18.

> It was a horrible place. There was no training given. It was a wonder we got any Lancaster bombers off the ground. I didn't know what I was supposed to be doing, sitting around hoping you were doing the right thing.[322]

The Party was determined to tackle industrial inefficiency and produced an internal document on 6 February 1942, *How to Overcome Production Obstacles*.[323] The document points to "widespread frustration among workers in industry" and "the employers who refuse to set up joint production committees in factories". These were works' councils comprising management and unions, established to improve production. In the Party document, ten proposals outline how obstacles to increasing production could be overcome. Points one to four can be summarised as seeking the support of workers and trade union officialdom in the production drive whilst avoiding "the impression that the workers are interfering with the owner's managerial rights". The remaining points deal with lobbying methods to overcome production obstacles: letters to the press, approaches to mayors, councillors, MPs and even ministers. Even some trade union leaderships were reluctant to engage in joint production committees (JPCs) but this was not the case with the AEU in which the Communist Party had considerable influence.

It is worth noting that when Bevin had suggested such a model in 1940, the *Daily Worker* had described his proposals as fascism, akin to industrial practice in Nazi Germany. After the invasion of the Soviet Union, the Party campaigned vigorously for the establishment of JPCs among the public at large and against the intransigence of the Engineering Employers Federation (EEF). Many employers saw JPCs as a threat to managerial authority in an industry with a tradition of belligerent industrial relations. The lack of enthusiasm on the part of employers was exploited in the pages of *The New Propeller* and the *Daily Worker*.

The Party's campaign for JPCs was largely run through the Engineering and Allied Trades Shop Stewards National Council and began with two regional conferences in London and Merseyside during September 1941. This was followed by a national conference at the Stoll Theatre, London on 19 October 1941 attended by 1,200 delegates from 300 factories. The opening remarks from Glaswegian Walter Swanson revealed the high hopes the Party had of JPCs' potential.

> We who meet have as heavy responsibility as the government of our country. All the delegates here have been sent by the men and women in the war factories who so desperately want to play their full part in the common struggle...can we wait until the government and employers are brought to their senses before we ourselves begin to set the example, to show what we can do on our side to turn out munitions?[324]

The conference was not countenanced by the AEU leadership, general secretary Fred Smith remarking,

> The trade union movement knows nothing of a National Shop Stewards Movement. It lends no countenance to conferences of shop stewards by any such outside body.[325]

Despite this, the size and representation of the Stoll Theatre conference is testimony to the significant credibility of the Party in engineering at the time; it had much wider influence than its number of full-time officials suggested. At the end of 1941, a Ministry of Aircraft Production memo to the cabinet's production executive remarked that some in the trade union leadership did not want JPCs because they were being sponsored by the CPGB.[326] Party pressure forced the trade union leadership to change tack—or risk letting the Party's authority grow by being at the front of a campaign that was popular beyond the factories.

As well as initial scepticism from the TUC, there was opposition from employers. In July 1941, the executive council of the AEU issued a questionnaire to shop stewards on their employer's attitudes towards collaboration. The Engineering Employers Federation reacted by sending a letter to member firms advising that no assistance be given to the stewards because the union was attempting "to obtain information which is to a large extent confidential to management".[327] Nevertheless the findings were submitted to the government and the AEU and the EEF met formally at the end of January 1942. The talks terminated without any agreement being reached, the AEU report claimed the EEF directors were adamant they were...

> ...not going to be party to handing over the production of the factory and the problems concerning production to shop stewards or anyone else...the man primarily responsible for production is the manager...there could not be divided loyalty in running the works.[328]

However, soon after, the AEU was invited to discuss the issue of JPCs in Royal Ordnance factories. It is probable that the government rapidly made it clear to the EEF that they would have to concede. Some employers' representatives were closer to governmental thinking on the subject than others. Lord McGowan, chairman of ICI, was a personal friend of Churchill, and both thought that consultation with workers would take the heat out of the debate over munitions production. In March 1942 a formal agreement was reached that excluded non-union members' right to participate in JPCs, despite the wishes of the EEF. By the end of 1943 there were nearly 4,500 JPCs in engineering and allied industries covering 3.5 million workers and the TUC were arguing for JPCs to be compulsory, though this was never to be the case.

The campaign for JPCs lifted the profile of the Party and put management on the defensive. Nina Fishman's research shows that "most, if not all... early JPCs would have been formed as a result of pressure from communist shop stewards".[329] Where there was precious little union organisation, the committees became the basis for new union recognition. Where there was already strong union representation, influence was heightened to the degree that stewards and convenors, Party members among them, were elevated towards management. Hugh Scanlon is unequivocal about the degree of incorporation of the trade union at Metro-Vicks.

> We had a committee that sat in judgement of the workers. If they were late, absent without good knowledge, we could send them to the national service officer—who in extreme cases could send them to prison. That's the extent to which the trade union movement became involved in the war effort... I'm not saying workers gained, I'm saying production increased.[330]

It was an entirely new relationship for union representatives, one which would have been unthinkable ten years before. Scanlon:

> Until rearmament, the employer was well and truly in the saddle as they are now, and I've seen the economic boot switch three times. You didn't speak to the foreman, he was God. If you wanted to approach the foreman, you did it through the chargehand and in order to curry favour with him you talked about his budgerigar or whatever. Then in 1936 you got all the developments of the rise of fascism, the threat of war and the demand of greater expenditure. Politically the left was strengthened and industrially the trade union movement was overcoming the disaster of the General Strike and the depression that followed.[331]

The situation was fraught with compromise as well as greater influence. Richard Croucher, in *Engineers at War*, identifies that a third obstacle to JPCs lay in the suspicion of average workers on the shop floor. David Whitehead, a Party member who started work in Metro-Vicks in 1942, remarked in an interview: "There was always more opposition to them than has been said."[332] Vic Eddisford, also at Metro-Vicks, believed some saw their involvement as promotion.

> The convenor almost became part of the management. Some people would do anything for a tea and a bun. They went to work in their best suits and in that factory, the class struggle was switched off. The problems were all problems of production.[333]

Eric Jessop worked at Fairey Aviation in Stockport. "There was a JPC at Fairey initiated by management and supported by the CP. Lateness created division, the Party clamped down on this, hard."[334] Benny Rothman was a JPC representative for around 1,500 workers at Metro-Vicks. Along with Vic, he observed how one or two comrades were too enthusiastic about the new management arrangements.

> One or two of our Party members became very enthusiastic and they thought they were already under socialism. They were trying to encourage people to kill them bloody selves, and that was bitterly resented by the workers.[335]

Vic Eddisford:

> I know certain CP members in certain factories who did nothing but productivity and would be termed on the shop floor as right-wing. They wouldn't support anyone farting out of tune because it might rock the boat.[336]

Both are adamant that such individuals were exceptions. Benny says that management at Metro-Vicks used the JPC and the general enthusiasm for production to try and reduce the wage bill by cutting the piece rate and increasing overtime.

> We limited overtime, controlled it very carefully. We

made sure that every encouragement was given to increase output, but that at the same time within our power that we weren't exploited, that they cut the piece rate as a result of it. The superintendent was bitter, he accused me of sabotage. We made sure they didn't ride roughshod over agreements.[337]

After the invasion of the Soviet Union the Party altered its attitude to industrial action. The directions from King Street (CPGB head office) were straightforward: involve workers in the production drive, overcome all obstacles, avoid strike action. In the summer of 1940, Order 1305 of the Emergency Powers Act had made strikes unlawful. This was supplemented by the Essential Works Order of March 1941 which restricted a worker's right to change jobs. It also strengthened an employer's capacity to take disciplinary measures. Significantly, employers were not allowed to sack workers without going to the National Service Officer. Sacking had become less of a threat in an economy that verged on full employment. With the Essential Works Order it was well known on the shop floor that the foreman couldn't sack you. Metro-Vicks' convenor Hugh Scanlon:

> The greatest challenge to management during the war was the fact that they couldn't dismiss people without the agreement of the National Service Officer.[338]

Wartime strikes occurred regardless of the legislation. In 1943, there were 1,785 stoppages and a total of 1,800,000 working days lost to industrial action; in 1944, 2,194 stoppages and 3,700,000 days lost.[339] The strikes were short and dominated by engineering and coalmining; in engineering nine out of ten lasted less than a week. There were, as a result, some prosecutions, with culprits generally fined £5. Most of the disputes were over piece rates, though there were other underlying grievances. After Dunkirk, increased overtime was worked with many workers on double shifts and inevitably the accident rate increased.

> [After the fall of France] We worked for at least a month from eight in the morning until nine at night. I was leaving at ten past seven and getting home at ten to ten.[340]

Richard Croucher maintains that the accident rate

amongst adult women and younger workers increased dramatically during 1940 and 1941. By 1941 it had almost quadrupled the 1938 figure for adult women.[341] The role of the Party was rarely to lead industrial action, but rather to attempt to dampen it. Neither did management want to have to report illegal strikes since it would be seen as a failure on their part. As a result, there were numerous, often quite small, unreported disputes. Benny Rothman credited people downing tools to poor management and incompetent union representation.

> We certainly had our work cut out to prevent disputes… The machine shop was manned almost entirely by women, completely new to industry, girls from Newcastle, from the east coast. The first time I knew there was a problem was when a little deputation of girls came to where I was working. They weren't getting any bonus. I found this clever dick of a rate fixer. I says, 'These women are going to have to get some bonus as other workers in the factory or else.' That was one occasion where we downed tools.[342]

Vic Eddisford said there were stoppages rather than strikes, on average once a month at Metro-Vicks.

> For example. His mate would clock him out, he's only trying to get his bloody dinner and that's all he's trying to do. Queue up to clock out, queue up to get your dinner, queue up to get back in. So, the foreman would decide to tighten up and catches three people and disciplines them. Knocks half an hour off their pay, you have to react to that. We'd say, we're not having that. So, we'd say, we'll stop work tomorrow at 11.30. Scanlon would say. 'Just tell me when you're doing it,' and Scanlon would disappear. I knew where he went and everyone knew where he went. Scanlon had a key to the staff [management] lavatory. Don't know how he got it. At 12 o'clock he'd go for his dinner and we'd be back at one. The management wouldn't report it. If our foreman reported it, he'd get done. So, we'd make a deal, you don't report it and we don't get docked. These struggles went on all the time.[343]

One result of full employment was that overall union membership increased by one third between 1938 to 1943, the unions involved in the war industry growing the most, none more than the AEU which had 909,000 in 1943, up from 413,000 in 1939. Hugh Scanlon:

> You have a job to find a non-unionist. You would have the odd chap who would go in arrears, but in most of the engineering shops, they were trade unionists.[344]

The situation was an opportunity for trade unions to make advances, not just in membership but in improvements in piece rates, facility time, consultation on health and safety. Vic Eddisford maintained there was no contradiction between working for full production and seeking improvements in wages and conditions.

> Because there was an enormous number of pieceworkers at Metro-Vicks, improvements in production were in workers' interests in terms of earnings as well as because it meant the defeat of fascism.[345]

The role of shop stewards in a piece work environment, he argued, was to gain increased influence over the production process, streamlining it to increase production and earnings, and consequently enhancing the negotiating strength of the union. Large sections of the working class nationwide were better off as a result of the war. There was a levelling up for many workers to the pay rates of skilled workers.

Such rapid expansion made it difficult for the bureaucracy to keep on top of local issues. The AEU had only 150 officials to handle a vast membership, which meant greater responsibility for shop stewards. Engineering shop stewards were to become key individuals, non-commissioned officers in a class war of attrition that lasted for decades after the war. They had to recruit new workers, collect subscriptions by hand, represent and resolve problems and, if it came to it, initiate and lead disputes. It was incumbent upon them, not the district or national office, to define the value of trade union membership. The Party led the unofficial Shop Stewards National Committee (SSNC) in engineering; an organisation that established itself through the campaign for JPCs and was not sanctioned by the AEU official leadership. AEU head office became increasingly wary of its power and presence, and furious when Lord Beaverbrook of the Ministry of Aircraft Production addressed the SSNC directly, acknowledging its power base. But Churchill's government was famously pragmatic when it came to waging the war. It was aware that Communist Party opposition to worker-management co-operation would have doomed JPCs, particularly in the larger munition factories. Margaret Gadian maintains the government went as far as to arrange for Party General Secretary Harry Pollitt to speak at key factories to raise workers' morale and motivation.

> When Harry Pollitt returned to his job as general secretary—he was a very powerful orator, a very charismatic sort of man—he was sent around to encourage armament workers, to put to them that we needed to produce. Pollitt would put the argument: the Russians were fighting fascism and we need to give them all the help we can and increase production. He was very effective. He was officially sent by the government, who were worried about the lack of enthusiasm for increasing production.[346]

Churchill had long been a critic of the pace of rearmament. Three days after taking office he formed the Ministry of Aircraft Production (MAP). As well as being Prime Minister, Churchill also made himself Minister for War. The MAP was led by Lord Beaverbrook who initially operated out of his own home. It took much of its staff from the Air Ministry which was moved to the Grand Hotel in Harrogate as part of a wider dispersal programme to keep defences operating in the event of invasion. Beaverbrook pushed for aircraft production to be a priority over all other forms of munitions and deliberately set out-of-reach targets for the industry, 15 percent higher than capacity, putting pressure on management and the shop floor. The widely held view that the aircraft industry was inefficient in comparison to Germany's is not supported by the facts. During the Battle of Britain, from May to August 1940, production of fighter aircraft in Britain was two and a half times greater than Germany's fighter production.[347] This was crucial because it meant the number of German fighters available for operations over England fell from 725 to 275, whilst the RAF's complement rose from 644 in July 1940 to 732 by October of the same year.[348] Aircraft production became

Churchill's pet project. At its peak, the industry employed nearly 2 million people and delivered more than 2,500 aircraft a month. In conscripting women into the factories, Britain went further than Stalin's Russia and Hitler's Germany. By 1943 it was almost impossible for a woman under 40 to avoid war work. In July 1943, Bevin announced to parliament that in order to release younger women for the aircraft factories all women up to the age of 51 would now be registered for war work. There was an outcry of opposition, but Churchill even restricted women's recruitment to the armed services to make them available for aircraft factories.

Integral to boosting wartime production was the establishment of "shadow factories". The model was to duplicate existing workplaces through public funds. The cost of land, buildings, building services and engineering was met by the state but the enterprises were privately managed. They began to be built in 1936 during rearmament and generally took two years to get into production. Between 1937 and the end of 1939, ICI had undertaken the construction of 18 shadow factories. By the end of the war there were 159 in operation, 87 of which were under the MAP. Aircraft manufacture was also dispersed, rather than concentrated in single units, so that production would be less vulnerable to being completely halted by bombing. Components for Hurricane fighter planes were made in a total of 48 different locations. Some components were made in people's homes and even in schools by children.

The period of greatest recruitment to the Party approximated with recruitment to the AEU. During the war, the largest numbers of delegates to Party congresses were from engineering. In June 1941 Party membership was somewhere between 15 and 20,000. By the end of 1942 it was 56,000. During the same period engineering grew more than any other industry in Britain. Between February and March of 1942 alone, AEU membership increased by 10,561. Significantly, the Party developed in size the most when it was not active electorally, and it was advocating a virtual industrial truce. It became identified as serving both the national interest and the interests of the working class. This was during Britain's most crucial period in modern history, when those interests were indivisible.

# Chapter 13

## Second Front Now

> "...when the folk on my native heath (Lancashire) speak of 'our great Ally' they mean Russia, but when well-to-do people use the same phrase, they mean America. The morale of our working people, he said, is very high. They will win the war for us." From *Home Front* by James Landsdale Hodson, 1944

### Military considerations

The issue of the second front, a military invasion by the Allies in Western Europe to take pressure off the Soviet Union on the Eastern Front, was the subject of cabinet meetings and international diplomacy soon after Barbarossa up until D-Day in June 1944. Churchill not only had to contend with the CP's successful broad-based second front campaign but inside his cabinet, his friend and ally, Lord Beaverbrook, was a vocal advocate for military support for the Soviet Union. Churchill's objective was always to keep Russia in the field by providing military equipment shipped via convoys to Archangel whilst continuing to erode German capability from the air. Stalking the dialogue and negotiations between himself and Stalin was the spectre of a Russian defeat, and Stalin then seeking terms with Hitler, who would then return to confront Britain with new resources at his disposal. Churchill's military strategy developed towards an allied landing in North Africa to drive the German and Italian forces east, progressing towards controlling the Mediterranean and invading Italy. Ultimately the second front in France, first raised in 1941, was delayed until June 1944 and the Soviet Union, whose Red Army, partisans and people had endured and overcome so much, arrived in Berlin ahead of the Allies.

Soviet loss of life in the Second World War is contested to this day; the post-Soviet government of Russia has put Soviet war losses at 26.6 million, around two-thirds of them civilians. There was, and continues to be, a widely held view that such losses could have been lessened if D-Day had been sooner. Whatever the veracity of this view, as AJP Taylor puts it, "What mattered was what men believed had happened, not what happened", and Churchill's reputation was made to pay, though this was the least of consequences.

Hitler's ally in Russia became Britain's ally overnight, and Churchill responded unequivocally.

> No one has been a more consistent opponent of Communism than I have for the last 25 years. I will unsay no word that I have spoken about it. But all this fades away before the spectacle which is now unfolding... Any man or state who fights on against Nazidom will have our aid. Any man or state who marches with Hitler is our foe... It follows, therefore, that we shall give whatever help we can to Russia and the Russian people. We shall appeal to all our friends and allies in every part of the world to take the same course and pursue it, as we shall, faithfully and steadfastly to the end.[349]

Anthony Eden, Foreign Secretary, told Ivan Maisky, Soviet Ambassador, that Britain would not pull out of the war as Russia feared but fight on and send whatever weapons and supplies it could to Russia. It wasn't until 18 July 1941 that Stalin recovered from the shock of the invasion to return from his dacha to reply to Churchill. Stalin was grateful for Churchill's support and immediately began his own campaign for a second front. As well as suggesting a front in France, Stalin added:

> It is easier still to establish a front in the north... We would welcome it if Great Britain could transfer to this theatre of war something like one light division or more of the Norwegian volunteers, who could be used in Northern Norway to organise a rebellion against the Germans.[350]

Then began years of demand and rebuttal, of accusation and explanation. The discourse ebbed and flowed with Russian defeats and counter-attacks as the military situation moved from desperation to perceived opportunity. On 9 August 1941, on the approach to Leningrad and Kyiv, the Germans took Smolensk with around 100,000 Russian soldiers killed or wounded and another 150,000 taken prisoner. By September, Kyiv and the armies defending it were threatened with encirclement and, in the north, Leningrad was cut off and under bombardment. In a message to Churchill via Maisky, Stalin inferred that Russia might have to seek terms with Hitler—thus freeing up the Wehrmacht to return her fire on Britain unless there was a second front soon.

> Without these two forms of help, the Soviet Union will either suffer defeat or be weakened to such an extent that it will lose for a long period any capacity to render assistance to its Allies by its actual operations ... I realise that this message will cause dismay.[351]

Ambassador Maisky read Stalin's letter to Churchill and echoed Stalin's implied threat. "This might be a turning point in history. If Soviet Russia is defeated, how can Great Britain win the war?"[352] Churchill replied angrily.

> Remember that only four months ago we in this island did not know whether you were not coming in against us on the German side. Indeed, we thought it quite likely that you would... Whatever happens, and whatever you do, you of all people have no right to make reproaches to us.[353]

Churchill's opposition to opening a second front by invading northern France was based on military impracticability. Despite fighting on an enormous front to the east, the Germans still had ample forces in France: 20 to 30 divisions and a powerful air force (a division consisting of between 10- and 20,000 soldiers). They had coastal fortifications and air support to see off an invasion before it had even made a bridgehead on land. Even after the US had come into the war in December 1941, it was viewed that a landing would be too costly. Furthermore, there wasn't yet the landing-craft for an amphibious assault, and wherever there was to be a surprise attack, the Germans could move forces much more quickly by rail and road than the Allies could at sea. They would be outmanoeuvred and there was little confidence in getting support from the French. Churchill believed that the strength of the Resistance was exaggerated and that they lacked discipline and morale. There wasn't even sufficient shipping to get enough Americans to the UK to mount such an invasion. One might also factor in that Churchill appreciated there were strategic and imperial interests to be defended in North Africa, access to the Suez Canal on route to India not the least of them. Churchill repeatedly replied to Stalin that he doubted an invasion of France could succeed, that it could be repulsed without the Germans having to move whole divisions of men away from the Eastern Front. And it would do Russia no good if the British were to lose thousands of troops for nothing. Churchill replied to Stalin via Maisky.

> Although we should shrink from no exertion, there is, in fact no possibility of any British action in the west, except air action, which would draw the German forces from the East before winter sets in. There is no chance whatever of a second front being formed in the Balkans without the help of Turkey... Action, however well-meant, leading only to costly fiascos would be no help to anyone but Hitler.[354]

For the most part, British assistance to the Soviet Union took the form of the supply of arms and equipment. By late 1941 a convoy of shipping left for Archangel every ten days. The convoy of 12 October included 140 heavy tanks, 100 Hurricane fighter aircraft, 200 Bren carriers, 200 anti-tank rifles and ammunition, 50 two-pounder guns and shells, and on 22 October, 200 fighter aircraft and 120 heavy tanks. Orwell remarked: "We are giving Russia all aid short of war."[355] But it was war that Stalin wanted, raising the prospect that Soviet Russia might make separate terms with Germany. A message sent from Churchill to Stalin on 18 July 1941 implied that a second front in Europe in 1942 was unlikely. In reply on 23 July Stalin wrote:

> In view of the situation on the Soviet-German front, I state most emphatically that the Soviet government cannot tolerate the second front in Europe being postponed till 1943.[356]

Partly to demonstrate the commitment of Britain's eventual

aim to open a second front in the west, the Allies launched operation Jubilee, a raid on the German-occupied port of Dieppe, executed on 19 August 1942. The plan was to capture the port for a short period of time to test the feasibility of a general landing. Over half of the 6,000 predominantly Canadian troops were killed, wounded or taken prisoner within hours. The infantry never got into the town, the tanks never got off the beach, the RAF lost 106 aircraft, the Royal Navy 33 landing craft and a destroyer. A German soldier observed:

> The dead on the beach, I've never seen such obscenities before. There were pieces of human beings littering the beach. There were headless bodies, there were legs, there were arms. There were even shoes, with feet in them.[357]

The casualties forced a retreat within six hours. Both Churchill and Lieutenant General Mountbatten justified the losses of almost 60 percent on the basis of what had been learned by the operation. The preferred theatre to engage Germany was fixed on North Africa. From early 1942 onwards, Britain and America began working on an invasion plan that would become known as Operation Torch. The North African goal was to clear Axis powers from the region and impose naval control of the Mediterranean to prepare for an invasion of southern Europe. The operation began on 8 November 1942 involving 850 ships, at the time the largest amphibious landing in history. The operation was commanded by US General Eisenhower.

There were American landings on Morocco's Atlantic coast and Anglo-American landings on Algeria's Mediterranean coast. The British were already battling German and Italian forces in Libya and Egypt and the landings created a second front at the rear. As the Allies invaded French colonial territory, they encountered 125,000 Vichy French troops under Marshal Pétain. In combination with Montgomery's victories at El Alamein, the operation was successful in eventually driving the Axis forces out of North Africa. Still, it failed in its hope of drawing German divisions away from the Eastern Front.

## The Party's campaign

Eddie Frow describes the second front campaign as "the single biggest political campaign we ever ran in Britain".[358] In Manchester, it involved factory gate meetings and huge rallies at

**A SECOND FRONT IN EUROPE**

TO ATTACK NOW WHILE HITLER IS BEING HAMMERED IN RUSSIA IS THE WAY TO WIN THIS YEAR

COMMUNIST PARTY POSTER

Belle Vue addressed by Harry Pollitt. The Party was successful in reaching far beyond its membership. Central committee member Bill Whitaker:

> The Party was to the fore. Packing Belle Vue with people. Moore- Brabazon was calling for Germany and Russia to wear each other out. The second front was needed from 1942, not 1944.[359]

Communists argued that Britain, Churchill in particular, was delaying an assault whilst Hitler and Stalin conducted a war of mutual exhaustion. The accusation was provided with evidence when John Moore-Brabazon, Beaverbrook's replacement at the Ministry of Air Production, expressed the hope that Germany and the Soviet Union would destroy each other. Brabazon, a Conservative MP, was forced to resign as a consequence. Though not an uncommon opinion in the Conservative Party—Churchill who himself had once said he thought the Soviet Union was best "strangled at birth", knew it was unacceptable to the war effort. As a younger man, at the time of the Russian Revolution, Churchill's hostility to the Soviet Union was deemed extreme even by those around him. He once told the Commons:

> Bolshevism is not a policy; it is a disease. It is not a creed; it is a pestilence. [Bolsheviks were]... a league of failures, the criminals, the morbid, the deranged and the distraught... a foul combination of criminality and animalism."[360]

His hostility to Nazi Germany was also obsessional. When he became prime minister on 10 May 1940, he laid down a single war aim: "The total defeat of Hitler and the undoing of all German conquests."[361] Once America had joined the war, he may have calculated that he did not need Russia to defeat Germany and, like everyone else, underestimated the pace of the Red Army's counter-attack. In the interim, Party propaganda argued that there were no plausible military objections to invading France in 1942. Trafford Park Branch issued a comprehensive eight-page leaflet in 1942: *The Campaign for the Second Front and the Arguments Against It*. It summed up the military situation: "The Second Front is practical. We have the equipment. We have the men and the fighting spirit." Those opposed to the idea were branded traitors.

> Their prejudice against Russia is so great that they try to prevent the speediest possible victory over Hitlerism in the hope that the Soviet Union will be exhausted and that Britain might be able to step in. Such a policy can only be described as treachery. Stalin would not ask for a second front and the Soviet leader considers it absolutely necessary.[362]

Whatever the veracity of the claims and counterclaims about Hitler's defences and the Allies' capability before 1944, the Party managed to help create a groundswell of opinion. During 1942 hundreds of second front rallies were organised outside workplaces and in town centres across Britain. Frances Dean:

> They certainly were interesting times. We had huge meetings in Belle Vue, Kings Hall. It held 6,000, with Harry Pollitt and Willie Gallacher, usually on a Sunday afternoon. And it was filled. And mainly from the factories. We had tremendous membership in the factories and influence. We used to have meetings outside the gate. Quite big ones calling for the second front... When the Soviet Union came into the war the

feeling was that Britain was holding back and not putting her effort into a second front which would have helped end the war quicker.[363]

The Kings Hall at Belle Vue was among the largest of venues in Manchester, and the Party repeatedly packed it. On Sunday 20 March 1942, 1,000 seats were reserved for Metro-Vicks' workers. Rothman maintained that no overtime was worked on days of big rallies. Convenor Hugh Scanlon spoke alongside Pollitt, leading the sale of tickets and putting pressure on shop stewards to sell them.

> At that Belle Vue rally, with the possible exception of Pollitt in Trafalgar Square, I think his speech was the best political speech I've ever listened to. The gist was, 'I was wrong, I've learned my lesson, I'm now back and we've all got a job to do.' The appeal to work and get busy was truly inspiring. We all had to be Caesar's wife—above suspicion and really work.[364]

In May 1942, 50,000 attended a second front demonstration in Trafalgar Square. On May Day there was a factory gate meeting outside Metro-Vicks and on 21 May an open-air meeting in Piccadilly Gardens, Manchester, chaired by Fairey's convenor Ernie Hope. As Metro-Vicks made equipment for the northern convoys to Archangel, they received a visit from a Russian trade union leader. Benny Rothman:

> When a Russian trade union leader visited Metro-Vicks the support he got was enthusiastic beyond imagination. He was invited to come down to the directors' dining room but he wanted to go to the workers' canteen instead, and he was very warmly and genuinely cheered. No question about that.[365]

In a Party-led 'production week' in November 1942, a delegation from 17 factories lobbied the Stretford mayor to call for a second front. At the Fords plant in Trafford Park during 1942, there was an Aid for Russia week, a joint effort by management and shop stewards. Hugh Scanlon summed up the prevailing climate in the factories:

> Not so much 'we support the Red Army'—although

there were slogans like 'Joe for King', but it manifested itself by two things: a demand for the second front and working to ensure maximum war effort. The flow of arms was always a substitute.[366]

As part of the Soviet's campaign for a second front, they sent Ludmilla Pavlichenko to the US, Britain and Canada. Twenty-six-year-old Pavlichenko was credited with 309 kills and was nicknamed 'Lady Death'. She had fought at the Siege of Odesa and the Siege of Sevastopol in the early stages of the war. In America, she met Roosevelt and his wife, in England she went to factories in the Midlands where £4,516 was raised for three X-Ray units for the Red Army.

Although armament factories were materially linked to the question of a second front, there was gathering political support beyond the shop floor. Margaret Gadian:

> They were under pressure. Willie Gallacher was constantly raising it, and other left MPs. There was quite a broad campaign. They held off as long as they could. There was an enormous feeling. Harry Pollitt was sent officially to tour the factories in order to increase the enthusiasm for 'tanks for Joe'.[367]

*Pathe News* covered Pollitt speaking at a second front rally but what the film didn't show was Pollitt arguing that Soviet society was better equipped to deal with war. Britain, he argued, was a class-divided society and sectional interest was hampering the war effort.

> Inheriting all the obstacles of a society based on the division of classes and of the anarchy and monopoly interest of privately owned industry, we have to find the way to organise the united endeavour of the nation and all sections of the nation in the war effort, and the most efficient organisation of the war effort, in such a way as to overcome and break down the crippling influence of sectional interest.[368]

In Hugh Scanlon's view, though, Barbarossa exposed Russia's unpreparedness for war; Britain had defeated the Luftwaffe with the aid of radar technology.

Just as the Party had brought International Brigade volunteers back from Spain to address meetings on Aid for Spain, members of the French Communist Party and the Resistance were smuggled in and out of Britain to meet British Intelligence Services and speak at Party meetings. Bill Whitaker recalls it was a much more perilous undertaking. "We had the French Resistance in meetings in Manchester. One of the two men were killed; they didn't get through."[369] Margaret Gadian, who had read French at university, acted as interpreter.

> Some of the communist deputies who were in the Resistance... at intervals they came over. They were flown over from France to be given a rest, because in the Resistance they were never in more than one place for one night at a time. On one occasion a group of them including Marcel Cachin came over to Manchester and was looked after, and I acted as an interpreter, which was fascinating.[370]

An unlikely and unexpected ally in the second front movement was the owner of the *Express* group of newspapers and cabinet minister, Lord Beaverbrook. He was a personal friend of Churchill, and his unexpected and very forthright interventions criticising Churchill's stance were an embarrassment to the government and Churchill personally. In September 1941, Beaverbrook sailed from Scapa Flow around the north cape to Archangel and then undertook the 600-mile overland journey to Moscow to discuss military aid to Russia. The meeting influenced Beaverbrook to be in favour of opening a second front. Churchill had forewarned his friend:

> All ideas of 20 or 30 divisions being launched by Great Britain against the western shores of the continent or sent round the sea for service in Russia have no foundation of reality on which to rest. This should be made clear. We have every intention of intervening on land next spring if it can be done.[371]

On his return from Russia, Beaverbrook attacked the government position through his newspapers, the *Daily Express*, the *Sunday Express* and *Evening Standard*, all three papers campaigning for a 'Second Front Now'. There were several *Daily Express* mass meetings at which he spoke alongside figures of the Left like Manny Shinwell. In April 1942 Beaverbrook made what was, for him, an extraordinary speech in New York.

> The war can be settled in 1942. Communism under Stalin has produced the most valiant fighting army in Europe. Communism under Stalin has produced the best generals in the war.[372]

In spring 1942, Churchill went to Washington to impress on the Americans that North Africa, not France, should be the way to engage Hitler's army. Just as he returned, news came through of the fall of Tobruk. Tobruk, a Libyan port, was taken by the British from Italian forces in January 1941. From April 1941, German forces under Field Marshal Rommel laid siege to Tobruk until it was finally overrun in June 1942 with 30,00 Allied prisoners taken. It was an embarrassing defeat and Beaverbrook thought that Churchill might have to be replaced as prime minister. He orchestrated a motion of censure in the commons, Aneurin Bevan arguing that the prime minister was deceiving the Russians over a second front. The motion was heavily defeated; there simply was no alternative to Churchill. Fortunately for Churchill, defeat at Tobruk was followed by victory at El Alamein under the leadership of General Montgomery. Montgomery put the Germans in full retreat in Egypt and on 15 November 1942, church bells rang out across the country to mark Monty's victory. Churchill famously said: "Now this is not the end. Not even the beginning of the end. But it is perhaps, the end of the beginning."[373] He was proved correct and later said: "Before Alamein, we never had a victory. After Alamein, we never had a defeat."[374]

## Red wave

The intervention of William Maxwell Aitken, 1st Baron Beaverbrook, was an expression of what historian Angus Calder describes as the "move away from the Party" during the war. A major cause of this was a widespread sympathy for the Soviet Union; a political enemy yet a military ally. As Calder remarks: "The enthusiasm for Russia swept over and past the Communist Party."[375] Churchill had set the tone with an emotional broadcast at the outset of Barbarossa: "The cause of any Russian fighting for his hearth and home is the cause of free men and free peoples in every quarter of the globe."[376] Lady Churchill headed an Aid for Russia campaign from October 1941 onwards. The public intellectuals Sidney and Beatrice Webb were advocates for the Soviet Union, but it was not their message that resonated with the wider populace. What people knew was that the Russian leader, Uncle Joe, wore a taxi driver's cap and his country was devoid of upper-class blimps.

The unexpected resistance of the Red Army and the leviathan efforts of the Russian people strengthened the Party's arguments daily. More than any other medium in the war, newsreels contributed to the development of this powerful tide of pro-Russian feeling and were effectively part of the second front campaign. Russia issued a total of 450 newsreels between June 1941 and September 1945; 40 Soviet cameramen were killed in the process. British cinema audiences were exposed to a constant supply of films of the fierce fighting on the Eastern Front. The BBC audience research department, mass observation, Gallup, and the Home Intelligence Service all assessed wartime opinion and found sympathy for Russia on the second front question.

The high point of pro-Russian feeling in Britain and internationally was the Red Army's victory at the Battle of Stalingrad in February 1943; it amazed the German army and the world. Militarily it turned the tide of the war in Europe. Thereafter the Wehrmacht was driven back at an increasing rate. The victory was celebrated in Britain on Red Army Day 23 February 1943, a huge expression of Anglo-Soviet friendship. The Royal Albert Hall hosted a pageant on 21 February to commemorate the 25th anniversary of the establishment of the Red Army, including a fanfare written by William Walton and a poem by Louis MacNeice, *Salute to the Red Army*, the piece conducted by Sir Malcolm Sargent. A commemorative bejewelled Sword of Stalingrad was forged and inscribed by command of the king as a token of homage from the British people to the Soviet defenders of the city. On 29 November 1943 it was presented to Stalin by Churchill at the Tehran Conference. In the autumn of 1943, the Sword of Stalingrad did a triumphal tour of Britain, and at Westminster Abbey people queued for hours to see it. The Party took a leading role in all this because it possessed supplies of films and photos of the Soviet Union, but even Tory MPs praised Stalin. For example, the National Government's Board of Education issued a memorandum encouraging teachers to teach Russian affairs. The education minister at the time was RA Butler, a high-ranking Tory.

Regardless of the veracity of the assertion that a second front would have been viable from 1942 onwards and that Churchill delayed matters for eventual geopolitical advantage, the longer the delay, the more the Party benefited. Emotion, it seems, was ever-present in the debate, from cabinet level to the factory gate. Contemporaries repeatedly refer to a 'feeling' abroad. It was sympathy for the suffering of the Russian people, admiration for the onslaught they eventually overcame.

> Everywhere—in the armed forces, factories, offices, the streets—it was seen in a visible relaxation of tension, a renewal of hope. A bond of sympathy grew for the unfortunate Russian people.[377]

After Hitler moved east, Britain could have bowed out of the war, sought terms with Germany but it didn't; it didn't want to.

The ban on the *Daily Worker* was lifted in September 1942 and the paper re-emerged with a print run of 120,000, which meant that up to half a million people a day would have had access to the paper. In May 1943 Stalin dissolved the Comintern to reassure his allies. The Communist Party of Great Britain became simply the Communist Party and anglicised its structure: the central committee became the executive committee, and the members' names were made public. The politburo became the political committee; factory cells became groups or branches. In December 1943, the Party recorded its highest ever membership figures at 55,138. By 1945 it had dropped nearly 10,000 as it struggled to absorb and manage such numbers, such growth also creating tensions within the organisation. The members who had joined between 1941 and 1943 did not do so to become seasoned Bolsheviks. Often the only contact newer members had with the Party was through the factory group. They might not want it known at home or in the local they were Party members. Eddie Frow, a member of the Party since the 1920s, remarked on how much autonomy the factory branches had, and Hugh Scanlon, who worked at Metro-Vicks, had little or nothing to do with the local geographical branch.

> I worked within a factory branch and I did not know what the activities of a pure branch was like. You met

as trade unionists and as members of the Party. I never held a position in a [geographical] branch.[378]

To be a member of the Party meant something different, arguably something less than it had ten years prior and Vic Eddisford describes the discontent held by some.

> I was never for this elitist concept. I didn't join the CP because of this tendency of elitism. It was the undoing of the CP. They had this influx of members that they were proud of. We'd get a factory branch of 250 and then they'd have the nerve, some of them, who had been in since before the war, scathingly to refer to them as 'Red Army volunteers'. 'They won't be here after the war.' That included me.[379]

It was the case that the activism expected of a comrade may not have been welcome for some recruits and they never committed themselves to the Party. The failure to retain new members was sufficiently concerning for the central committee to write an open letter to all Party members in August 1942. This was followed up by a leaflet critical of existing comrades' inability to welcome new members, and a call to change the tone and step of the organisation.

> There has undoubtedly been a serious lack of that solicitous attitude to comrades joining the Party which comrade Stalin declared must be a characteristic feature of Party work. This has led to a situation where:
> • no more than 70 percent of the membership has fully paid-up dues;
> • a large number of new Party members have been left for a long period of weeks before being given membership cards;
> • There has been a serious lack of comradely personal contact with new members and assistance in drawing them into the first forms of political activity;
> • A tendency has been shown to judge new members by their readiness or otherwise to attend internal Party meetings... [380]

A major part of the problem was, like the AEU, the Party just did not possess the required number of officials to cope with the influx.

At this time, the Party was associated with the Soviet Union more than any other period in its history. The leaflet above tells members it is comrade Stalin himself who they are letting down. Eric Jessop was the secretary of Fairey Aviation factory branch in Stockport.

> We got a degree of acceptance. Particularly those of us who had been in the Party since before the war. We'd been struggling against hostile elements. To find ourselves in a position where, the mere fact that we were accepted, the leadership of the Party accepted, I think that's how support for Russia expressed itself.[381]

The personification of that victory, of Russian heroism, was Stalin: seemingly resolute, humble in attire, fearless and proletarian. It was an image that was to become contaminated inside a decade, but one that members remained loyal to, for it was a feature inside the communist family. Sam Wild's son Mike was born in Manchester in 1940 and when Stalin died in 1953, the Party celebrated the Soviet leader's achievements in the Free Trade Hall, Manchester. Mike recalls that there was a photograph of Stalin in the front room "looking down on them" at home, and he asked his father if he could speak at the event.

> Stalin died; the papers were full of it. And at that time Stalin was still in good odour and the Left wanted to honour his life and acknowledge it... As a young kid I was at Manchester Grammar school. Me dad put me forward, I was asked to say a few words, I was 13 in short trousers. I was in my Manchester Grammar school uniform but I didn't want other kids to know, didn't want teachers to know. I didn't want to be bullied, be in the Evening News. I wrote a speech; my general theme was the role of the Russian people in the war. I got up and said, without Stalin, we wouldn't have won the war.[382]

Between 1941 and 1945, in Manchester and elsewhere, small communist factory groups that had withstood the ban on the *Daily Worker* were rapidly transformed into substantial factory branches that sustained themselves without much or any contact with geographical branches. In Greater Manchester and elsewhere, this changed the character of the Party. The next chapter provides a case study of a factory branch regarded by King Street as exemplary.

# Chapter 14

## Factory Fortresses

"We were in such a strong position. I've never been in quite that position even though I've been in charge of a factory." Party member Eric Jessop, shop steward at Fairey Engineering

### Fairey Aviation, Stockport

The Fairey Aviation Company was established in the Heaton Chapel area of Stockport in 1934, on a site previously owned by Crossley Brothers Ltd, a motor manufacturing company. Aircraft had been built on the site during the First World War, but it had returned to vehicle production after. The director in charge of the new aviation project was Major Thomas Barlow, who had served in the Royal Naval Air Service before becoming chief technical officer at an RAF experimental centre. The company began by building 14 Hendon bombers and then moved on to the more successful Fairey Battle, a light bomber with a single Merlin engine. During the Second World War, Fairey Aviation, 'Faireys', became an important manufacturer of military aircraft across five sites: Reddish, Manchester Ringway, Hayes near London, Heaton Chapel and Erwood Park near Stockport. A Battle Bomber built at Heaton Chapel chalked up the first downing of a Luftwaffe aircraft during the war: a Messerschmitt 109 over northern France. Production of the Battle ceased in 1942, and the factory moved on to the Fleet Fulmer.

Soon after the outbreak of war, the government completed the construction of the Erwood Park works, a shadow factory opposite the Heaton Park site. Erwood Park made Bristol Beaufighter night fighters. The first Beaufighter left the lines in January 1941, and 500 were built before the site moved on to building Handley Page Halifax heavy bombers. In all, 660 Halifax bombers were delivered to the Royal Air Force. Heaton Chapel provided Fleet Air Arm with over 1,000 Barracuda torpedo dive bombers towards the end of the war. They were employed for wide-ranging, anti-shipping attacks, the most spectacular being a successful raid on the German battleship *Tirpitz* on 3 April 1944. The original Heaton Chapel works employed between 1,000 and 1,500 workers; the Erwood Park works, eventually over 2,000. The shadow factory buildings around the country were standard 2,000-feet long redbrick built sheds, with a central aisle and jagged roofs glazed on the north-facing side. Built quickly and primarily to increase aircraft production during World War Two, they became a feature of Britain's industrial suburban landscape for the next 50 years.

Engineering was a hierarchical industry with skilled workers doggedly defending their craft status and position. Trade union membership itself was demarcated. The time-served skilled workers who held the appropriate AEU green membership cards were concentrated at Heaton Chapel, whilst the Erwood Park shadow factory had a preponderance of semi-skilled men and women workers. Women workers were prevented from joining the male-only AEU until 1943 and joined other unions, mainly the Transport and General Workers Union (TGWU) and the Electrical Trade Union. Semi-skilled men at Erwood Park held red AEU membership cards. Management refused to negotiate with a works committee that represented both sites throughout the war. There were, therefore, two joint shop stewards' committees, which provided the Communist Party with two arenas to intervene in from one factory Party branch, with Erwood Park being by far the more militant of the two sites. It was an environment that provided an opportunity for women shop stewards to cut their teeth as trade union activists in industry.

On some issues, the Party sought conflict; on others, it sought to extinguish disputes, for it held common ground with the employer in desiring to increase production. Communists would have reprimanded their workmates for tardiness and pushed them harder than management. But if this engendered hostility, it did not override the respect and popularity the Party won during this period at Faireys. At the beginning of the war, there were a handful of members at Heaton Chapel; by October 1942, the factory branch had 140 members and 280 by 1944.

*Aircraft factory in west London*

Mick Jenkins was born in Cheetham, Manchester, in 1904. He joined the Young Communist League in 1924 and by 1939 was the Manchester district organiser of the Party and working at Faireys.

> The Erwood Park works was a huge, newly built shed with a concrete floor, divided into shops, with some large doors for wheeling big aircraft out. Scores of workers were entering the factory every week. Alongside the Erwood Park works was the old Fairey factory still producing Fairey National Aircraft and expansion was taking place there.[383]

Mick worked in the aircraft erection department along with around 800 other workers. Eric Jessop had volunteered for a government-run basic engineering course and was transferred to Erwood Park on completion. He had joined the Cheetham Hill branch of the Party in 1932. Before the war, he was a Young Communist League representative on the Party's district committee and a member of the YCL's national committee. By the time Eric arrived at Faireys, he had served an apprenticeship in the Communist Party rather than the AEU.

> Fred Flood, an old Party member and I, we started organising things. It went well... so much so each

> department had its own collector of Party subs. The first meeting we had of the factory branch was in Levenshulme Town Hall and we got 300 people. It was a remarkable experience. Fantastic. I was Party branch secretary. I became shop steward in the jig assembly section.[384]

The jig assembly section at Erwood Park employed skilled AEU workers. For Eric to become shop steward, he would need a green AEU membership card, even though he had never served an apprenticeship.

> I had a green card as opposed to a red card. It was a bit of a fraud. The Party said look, 'we want us as shop stewards.' I got myself a green card by attending a [AEU] branch meeting and someone said they knew or swore that they knew I'd worked in a certain factory and served an apprenticeship. It was very much a closed thing in those days.[385]

In engineering nationwide, shadow factories tended to be more militant and better recruiting grounds for the Party than the original workplaces. Workers were drafted in not only from the locality but also from outlying areas. Those new to factory life did not possess the sectionalism, and neither could they subscribe to the craft elitism, of time-served AEU members. Eric Jessop summarised it as: "Heaton Chapel was the great divide."[386] Brought into new workplaces in large numbers, where wages were probably an improvement for most, and where the foreman couldn't sack them, dislocation created conditions for trade unionism to flourish. For many of these workers, particularly young women workers, this was an introduction to working life. They had not been moulded by the workshop regime of the 1930s when the employer had the whip hand. Foremen had to police long hours of routine labour by workers who were not necessarily frightened of them. In general, around the country, where the dislocation of workers was greatest, Party membership grew the most. Frances Dean became a shop steward at the Erwood Park site for the TGWU.

> Most of the women were in the T and G, but it was a joint shop stewards committee. We had a more or less full-time convenor and a chair of the shop stewards committee.

> First of all, you had the responsibility of collecting the cash. And then you took up grievances they had with the convenor or directly with the foreman, and you represented people on the shop stewards committee. In that department, I was collecting from around 50. We used to have meetings at the factory gate calling for the second front. We had meetings on the issue of equal pay for women which was a big issue at that time.[387]

The Second World War brought women into industry in a similar way to the previous war. Women workers' contribution became important in securing suffrage at the end of the First World War. Though equal pay in law would take a generation to arrive after 1945, its case had begun to be taken up by socialists and trade unionists during the 1940s production drive. At Faireys, it was won before the end of the war with one woman worker being awarded retrospective pay of £200. This was a considerable achievement considering how male-dominated engineering was at the end of the 1930s.

The wives of skilled engineers may not have worked at all; their factories would have been entirely male environments with a given language and behaviour to suit. In working-class culture, a woman working was evidence that her husband was poorly paid; it was a mark of shame. Women in the workplace were considered a distraction and a temptation, an opportunity for the employer to reduce the wage bill, for a woman's wage was in all probability a second income. Allowing women to join the AEU in 1943 was as much about protecting male engineers' pay and conditions from the dilution of the workforce by unskilled women workers as giving women's grievances representation. Frances Dean:

> I got the pay of an unskilled worker even though I was doing semi-skilled work. I was ignorant about engineering…We had some women from the Channel Islands, who were really refugees in Manchester. There were a lot of dilutees in the factory, men who had never been in engineering; they had to accept it in the more craft conscious sections. My father was a boilermaker and the boilermakers union was very craft conscious. Women were allowed to join the union but they had no rights whatsoever. They couldn't go to a meeting or

anything, they were just tolerated.[388]

The Party dominated the shop stewards committee of around 20 men and women at Erwood Park. The convenor, David Ainley, and the chair both had full-time union positions which were paid the shop average. The committee met monthly. At Heaton Chapel, though the Party was less influential, the convenor there, Jack Wilding, was also a Party member for some time. Eric Jessop:

> The workers knew me. One occasion typified the situation. I was told to go to somebody's office and they said: 'Jessop, we've called you in because we understand you're carrying out subversive activities.' I said: 'Who said so and what activities?' 'We've got information.' 'What information and where did you get it from? .... You're talking bloody nonsense and I don't want to listen to any more of it.' I turned on my heels and walked out. Before I got very far down the shop, 'What did they want you for Eric?'[389]

On the first Wednesday of the month, directly after work at 6.30 pm, the Party branch ran evening classes on Marxism above a tea shop around the corner from the factory. As Frances Dean admits, this did rule out attendance from some women members who had childcare responsibilities. Mick Jenkins led many of the classes:

> Attendance varied, but there was nearly always a room full of 30 or 40, and at times more than 100 members would crowd the stairways as well as the café.[390]

The factory branch committee met each week, composed of shop stewards and departmental contacts who collected Party dues. The branch as a whole, because of its size, would meet at Levenshulme Town Hall. It had five departmental literature secretaries who covered the two factories between them.: "250 copies of a popular pamphlet was considered a poor sale."[391] The branch also ran a book club with members paying a weekly shilling. Departments with large enough membership ran their own book clubs. The Party's engineering paper, *The New Propeller*, was not popular at Erwood Park because most of the workforce didn't identify as engineers. They knew they would be leaving the factory once the war was over. The branch got around the *Daily Worker* ban by printing leaflets. Eric Jessop's previous employer had been the printer manufacturer, Gestetner, and he managed to acquire some equipment. Because he'd been under surveillance by Special Branch in the past, he used different addresses to which printers could be delivered. When the ban was lifted in September 1942:

> Hundreds of copies went into the factory daily. It was a common sight to see 20 to 30 copies of the *Daily Worker* sticking up in the vices in some departments.[392]

With around 10 percent membership at the Erwood Park site, the Party calling a meeting was almost as effective as the convenor calling a trade union meeting. If the Party called a meeting on the second front in works time in the canteen and management forbade it, they were strong enough to walk much of the workforce outside without any fear of disciplinary repercussions.

> There was a personal feeling you had. In many respects, the Party owned the factory. They [management] were only too keen to come to some arrangement with us. For example, the Red Army Choir should come into the factory and give a concert in the canteen. The Red Army Choir. And they did. It was almost unheard of.[393]

At the beginning of July 1942, the joint union and management works committee sent a letter to the Russian government congratulating Russian workers in their struggle against Nazi aggression. In November 1942, a further letter was mailed to sniper Ludmilla Pavlichenko, informing her that Faireys' workers had raised £1,200 for a mobile X-Ray unit for "your gallant Red Army".

Non-union labour was turfed out of the factory. In one case, a fitter who refused to join was about to cause a stoppage before management intervened and presented the alternative of conscription to the army. After three months, the individual was removed from the factory, and the works committee wrote to the AEU district office to make sure he was not allowed to work in any other engineering factory. The Party's position on production meant in practice at Faireys, and elsewhere, confronting both shop floor and management norms. King Street's advice, as outlined in *How to Overcome Production Obstacles*, warned against treading on management's toes. At various times during the production drive at Faireys, the Party both supported management and undermined it as well. Erwood Park convenor David Ainley was an influential individual, a charismatic trade unionist and communist who could extinguish disputes through negotiation or lead them when required. Eric Jessop:

> David Ainley solved a lot of problems before they got to a dispute. Failing that, arbitration. Disputes were never allowed to get out of hand. There was a willingness to sort matters out… David had an amazing hold; he was deeply respected on both sides. By the management—respect for the power that he held and particularly amongst the workers. He had an ability to motivate that was quite remarkable.[394]

In July 1941 the works committee at Heaton Chapel noted, "that if it were not for the shop stewards and trade unionism, production in this factory would be increased by 20 percent".[395] The same day a mass meeting at the site called by convenor Jack Wilding, also a Party member, passed a vote of no confidence in the management of the factory. By the beginning of 1942, the shop stewards committee requested officials from the Ministry of Aircraft Production (MAP) to meet them to discuss improving production.

> Failing this being done by Friday morning, the stewards will lead all the idle time men and women down to the Labour Exchange on Friday afternoon to protest against lack of work, when the country is in dire need of planes and 100 percent production being called.[396]

Eventually, a deputation of eight workers lobbied parliament, visited the Ministry of Aircraft Production offices and then held a press conference arranged by the Shop Stewards National Council, attended by the industrial correspondents of all the leading national newspapers. Within a fortnight Colonel Llewellyn from the MAP visited Faireys, and consequently Mick

Jenkins remarks that the "time estimated of the changeover from the Beaufighter to the Halifax bomber was cut by a third".[397] The production campaign by stewards was the subject of debate in the House of Lords. Jenkins believes it was the primary cause of the sacking of top management across the five Fairey sites in England. The company director's concerns may not just have been about a degree of disorganisation, but the political capital that communists were able to make from so many workers placed on idle time. One of the fruits of the campaign was that the trade unions established a combine committee to coordinate efforts nationally across the five Fairey Aviation sites. At the beginning of the war, management had maintained a division between Heaton Chapel and Erwood Park, which were separated by more than railings.

Nationally the CPGB attempted to develop a Stakhanovite culture after June 1941, but it wasn't something that resonated much on the shop floor in Britain. Aleksey Stakhanov gave the Stakhanovite movement in the Soviet Union its name. He was a Russian Soviet miner who apparently, on 31 August 1935, exceeded his quota 14 times over by mining 227 tons of coal in a single shift. He was heralded as a model for other workers to follow, and a national Stakhanovite movement dedicated to exceeding production targets was born. During the war, the Party called for 'shock brigades' to work double and treble shifts, 36 hours in total, to overcome bottlenecks in production. Such efforts were undertaken at Faireys. In Eric Jessop's view, they were "more of a political demonstration rather than an effective productive effort. That was the impression I had". In 1988 the Soviet newspaper *Komsomolskaya Pravda* ran an article claiming that other workers had assisted Stakhanov, and that his record was staged to boost morale and production. At Faireys, absentee committees were established across the two sites with Party involvement. Eric described comrades as being "in hock with the management". It was a situation that was not popular, even with the Party's factory branch, and the committee at Heaton Chapel resigned their positions in October 1942 "tired of the bad feelings towards them".[398]

Communists saw industrial relations in the context of a war against Nazism, as a weapon in the struggle for the second front in Europe, which would lessen the slaughter. Maximising production would enable a second front. Stoppages just helped Hitler; unenthusiastic workers were little better. Mick Jenkins contrasts the veteran skilled craftsman who "spent most of the day evading the foreman and not doing a stroke of work"[399] with the semi-skilled new entrants that made up the shock brigades. As ironic as it seems, communists became shop stewards to prevent industrial action at this time. But the implementation of 100 percent trade union membership and effective representation over piece rates and other bread and butter issues would make it easier, so the theory went, to convince the audience of its historic task. Underpinning this was the belief that the working class could prove it was the superior force in society, better able to defeat fascism than the capitalist class.

The Erwood Park works were closed at the end of the war, and the factory branch dissipated. Mick Jenkins was appointed election agent to Pat Devine in the constituency of Preston for the 1945 election. In 1947 he was appointed East Midlands District Secretary for the Party and moved to Nottingham. Eric Jessop went back to Gestetner but not before leading a works 'swords into ploughshares' demonstration in London.

> We had a demonstration in London to find alternative work at the end of the war—to the Air Ministry. We got great support within the factory, we always did—but not a lot outside it. A great march but not successful. It was indicative of the spirit that existed. So sad to see it disintegrate. Largely because we didn't make things a political issue enough, more a practical issue.[400]

Factory branches were integral to the success the Communist Party experienced during the war and the unfulfilled expectations at the end. The factory branches benefited the most from the Party's growth between 1941 and 1943. Early in the war, they were described as factory groups, sub-groups of the nearest geographical branches, but after the Soviet Union entered the war, they evolved into branches with their own officers. The Lancashire district report for 1942 shows that by the end of the year, 60 percent of the district's membership were in factory branches. A result of this was that men outnumbered women by a ratio of more than four to one. Though Party members who were shop stewards may have been chiefly concerned with trade union issues, political education was well organised in larger factory branches like Faireys. After Faireys, the second biggest factory branch in the

Manchester area was Metro-Vicks, where Vic Eddisford was an apprentice.

> We had capable people who looked after sales of literature, looked after sales of the *Daily Worker*, one looked after recruitment of members, one looked after sales of *Soviet Weekly*, another looked after education of members and we ran a library. I ran a library in my department for people who have so much a week and bought a book a week. Then we had meetings where we discussed these books.[401]

Metro-Vicks was in Trafford Park industrial estate, one of several factories where branches totalled over 500 members. There was also a nearby Stretford geographical branch, "and our wives were members of that". The Party had offices on the edge of Trafford Park at Trafford Bar.

> The bottom part was a bookshop, premises for meeting above it, and a family lived in it; at one stage, I lived in it. Various people lived in it and looked after it. We had meetings in there in the evenings. We also had an association with the Stretford branch. They helped us. If we needed the factory leafleting, they did it. We worked closely.[402]

## Industrial retreat

By the end of the war, the CPGB was approaching considerable influence, if not control, over large parts of the trade union movement in Britain. It had muscle at official and shop floor level, and factory branches played a crucial role in this balance. There was, then, some surprise and no doubt objections when, in March 1943, King Street proposed draft rules for members to belong to the Party branch where they lived rather than where they worked. The policy was implemented in 1945 when all factory branches were dissolved. Harry Pollitt later referred to this as a serious mistake. Richard Croucher comments: "The results were disastrous...this move led to the dissolution of possibly the CP's greatest asset."[403] Some members didn't make the transition. Viv Eddisford recalls the toll it took on the Metro-Vicks group.

> The members of our factory branch who lived in

Stretford went back to the Stretford branch; if you lived in Salford, they went to the Salford branch. This was the problem. We'd made 250 members at that factory who were members of the CP at work but weren't members at home. The families didn't have to know they were members. So suddenly they get transferred from an environment they'd developed in, into a Salford branch. These local branches were mainly run by the old pre-war elitist comrades. Comrades who had gone through it since before the war. It was suddenly a different world for them. We lost them all, nearly all.[404]

In some cases, where factories had closed after the war and workers were redeployed elsewhere, the transition to geographical branches was not possible. But there were political objectives at play as well. The factory branches built during the war were desired in the 1920s and 1930s. By the time they arrived, the Party had begun to change direction. During the 1920s and early 1930s, the Party made much of rank-and-file organisation, forming the National Minority Movement in August 1924 to overcome the small number of communists within industry. It was an attempt to emulate the shop stewards' movement of the First World War, to represent workers across industry and develop a bargaining base. However, during the 1930s, the role of full-time union officials became more decisive, and power shifted away from the shop floor. Union officials were under pressure to deliver a more disciplined, ordered and dispute-free workplace.

It was a process that accelerated during the war years as the Party swelled the growing ranks of union officials attempting to catch up with the influx of members. Furthermore, the popular front strategy adopted from 1936 onwards forced questions about the self-activity of a rank and file risking alienating influential allies. By the end of the war, the Party also had electoral aspirations that proved unrealistic and vain hopes of Labour Party affiliation. In that sense, factory branches were not particularly valued. King Street chose to reorganise the Party on a constituency basis.

Significantly, the years of most significant recruitment for the CPGB occurred when there was little class conflict when it had to balance allegiance between class and country. Eric Jessop

### FACTORY GROUPS. Lancs District. April 1st 1942.

| BRANCH | FACTORY | MEMBERS | No. of workers. |
|---|---|---|---|
| Blackley | A.V.Roes, Chadderton | 55 | 16000 |
| | I.C.I. | 32 | 5000 |
| | Crumpsall Hospital | 8 | 1200 |
| | Connolleys | 3 | 1000 |
| Trafford Prk. | Metro Vickers | 96 | 25000 |
| | M.V.A's | 18 | 2000 |
| | Fords | 62 | 12500 |
| | Hills Aircraft | 6 | 1000 |
| | Taylors Bros. | 13 | 1500 |
| | Clovers Cables | 4 | 2500 |
| S.Manchester. | Faireys | 138(19) | 7,000 |
| | Hans Reynolds | 19(3) | 3,500 |
| | Trams | 19(6) | 800 |
| Moss Side | Dunlops | 6 | 2,000 |
| | Rails | 1 | 1,000 |
| | Tyrams | 5 | 400 |
| Cheetham | Rosenfields Aircraft | 17(3) | 500 |
| | Transport (Queens Rd.Depot) | 31(14) | 500 |
| | Wallworks, Toolmakers | 5 | 200 |
| | C.W.S. Optical | 5 | |
| Platting | West Gas | 7 | 500 |
| | Mather & Platts | 4 | 2,000 |
| | Trams, Rochdale Rd.Depot. | 6 | 800 |
| | Ferrantis, Moston | 20 | 3,000 |
| E.Manchester. | Vickers Armstrong | 140 | 4,700 |
| | Crossley Motors | 56 | 1,600 |
| | Ferguson Pailin | 20 | 1,000 |
| | English Steel | 35 | 1,500 |
| | Electric Motors | 8 | 700 |
| | Gorton Tank | 6 | 3,000 |
| | Rails Group | 7 | 500 |
| | Trams | 7 | 800 |
| | Crossley Gas | 4 | 2,500 |
| Swinton | Magnesium Electron | 45 (7) | 1,600 |
| | Burtons | 12 (4) | 1,200 |
| | Chloride | 45(6) | 2,000 |

*courtesy WCML*

believes this affected the degree of political consciousness amongst new members.

> The drive for production meant there were no strikes. No class conflict, no change in consciousness... Workers were allied to production, their wages allied to production. They saw production as a means of improving earnings. The first characteristic was that people were getting more money.[405]

There had been no such fight during the war; as Hugh Scanlon put it: "The class struggle was switched off." Growth in the number of engineering workers, the AEU and consequently the Party came on the back of government contracts and a labour shortage.

But none of that should detract from the Party's achievements after 1941. Without their instincts and leadership, the gains in wages and working conditions, in trade union organisation, would not have been made. They were tangible gains made after the hungry 1930s, gains that benefited workers decades later. Communists were at the forefront of establishing a determination among working people in 1945 that there would be no going back to pre-war society.

The Party paid significant attention to record keeping. The above is from a Lancashire District Report to Centre of 9 November 1942. It concerns the factory branches in the Manchester area as of April 1942. In April, across the Lancashire district, there were 109 factory branches with 1,925 members. By November, the numbers had swelled to 126 factory branches with 3,486 members. At the same time, the document identifies 13 geographical branches in the city, with the largest branch being East Manchester, which is recorded as having 706 members. Lancashire District-wide membership is reported as increasing from 4,776 in April of 1942 to 6,244 by October of the same year.

## Apprentices' strike of March 1941

In the spring of 1941, when industrial action was unlawful, apprentices between the ages of 14 and 20 from 16 factories across Greater Manchester took strike action over pay. It was part of a national dispute which involved more than 25,000 apprentices. At the centre of the dispute in Manchester was Metro-Vicks Trafford Park, and the leadership of the apprentices there were members of the YCL. The strikers had little support from their trade unions or adult workers and formed their own independent negotiating committees. The Manchester leaders were threatened with prosecution and conscription but refused to back down. Ultimately the action was successful, and the strikers' demands were met nationwide.

Metropolitan-Vickers Electrical Company was established in 1919, the Trafford Park site initially employing 20,000 workers. The work was mainly but not exclusively the manufacture of electrical turbines and generators for electrical power; and transformers and switchgear for industrial and public services. Most of the company's work was classed as heavy engineering, such as hydro-electrical generators weighing over 200 tonnes. There was also highly delicate mechanism work, electrical instruments and relays and scientific equipment such as X-ray apparatus, microscopes and radar. During the war, an extension of the factory built over 1,000 Lancaster bomber aircraft. At its peak, this shadow factory employed 8,411 people, of whom 3,250 were women. The company's workforce as a whole expanded to 30,000 workers in 1943-1944. Metro-Vicks was contracted to manufacture a power plant worth millions for the Soviet Union. In 1937 there were 11 Party members working at Metro-Vicks; by the end of the war, there was a factory branch of around 250.

In the first year of the war, the inflation rate meant that engineering workers put a lot of hope on the national pay award. This was particularly true of apprentices since they only received a proportion of the settlement. The grievances felt in workshops were aggravated during the war by dilution in the engineering trade. In practical terms, this meant they had to work alongside co-opted trainees, older than themselves, and women workers new to industry, all of whom needed help from apprentices but were paid more. As Richard Croucher explains in *Engineers At War*:

> It was stretching their patience too far to expect them, as skilled men in the making, to continue to do this while receiving lower wages. Their pay did not reflect their status in the shops, they felt, and soon after they learned of the increases due to them under the national award they took action as a previous generation of apprentices had done in 1937.[406]

The dispute that engulfed apprentices in Manchester was one in a series of strikes across industrial Britain. The vanguard of the action was on the Clyde. At the beginning of February 1941, apprentices elected their own representatives to present a list of demands to their employers, refusing to allow union officials to negotiate on their behalf. Eight of the nine representatives on the Clyde Apprentices Committee were members of the YCL, and the apprentices' autonomy in Scotland was characteristic of all the strikes. As the Clyde apprentices settled, the strike spread to England and Northern Ireland. But the lessons learned from Scotland were not about to be wasted as Clyde lads spoke to apprentice meetings elsewhere. When Lancashire apprentices struck, they had the precedent that national negotiations had already taken place over disputes elsewhere. Metro-Vicks convenor Hugh Scanlon describes the AEU's attitude to the dispute:

> The attitude towards strikes before Russia came in was that, they were supported by the left and there was neutrality by the right. Perhaps more than anything there was a need for apprentices to organise because the employers had always argued they were bound by their indentures and that they couldn't be represented by a trade union. In general terms, the employers' attitude to apprentices was: "You're a serf bound by the articles of your indenture." The apprentices' strike? The district committee [AEU] supported it unanimously. The question of official recognition by the national executive was another matter.[407]

On Friday 14 March 1941, strikers from Scotland addressed a Metro-Vicks factory gate meeting of around 300 apprentices. The same evening 40 apprentices elected a negotiating committee with YCL member Dick Nettleton as chair.[408] The apprentices' claim consisted of a threepence per hour increase for all ages up to 20 and two and five shillings per week for the first six months of the final year of the indenture. The claim was put to management on the following Monday and promptly rejected. On Wednesday 19 March, 600- 800 Metro-Vicks apprentices walked out on strike joining apprentices from, amongst others, AV Roe in Newton Heath, Ferranti, Mather and Platt, and the textile machinery trade in Rochdale. A mass meeting of around 3,000 was addressed by the secretary of the strike committee, Ken Warburton. By the evening, there were 9,000 apprentices on strike in Manchester, by the end of the week, 1,000 of them from Metro-Vicks, including Vic Eddisford:

> There was a branch of the YCL. Dick Nettleton, Warburton and Bob Watts were all leaders of the strike and they were all young communists. I'd just started getting involved in the apprentice movement, I was 16 then. Do you want to hear a funny story? I was on the apprentice committee for my section. I eventually became chair and a strike was bubbling... we had a meeting at the local co-op hall. It was the night I went

dancing and I really resented it, but the lads said, 'You're our representative, you must go and tell us what goes on.' There wasn't a lot there, but the leadership were there, Nettleton, Bob Watts and Warburton who was American, don't know how he even got there, ended up in the American Forces I think. And the lads from Scotland were there. We decided we were going to have the factory out the next day and tactically how we were going to do it. There was a common way that everyone had learnt to get factory apprentices out. It had been done since 1937. You just marched round shouting 'Out, out, out!' Pull them out. All you need is one department to go and you walk through like a snake, just like the pied piper and they all come. If you can't do that, you're not going to get a strike. You didn't react like men, go out to a meeting, discuss it and vote, you go out then vote when you're out. The tactic was to work in this way. I went off to my dance.

The apprentices' method of taking strike action is testimony to their independence. It was an autonomy partly born of necessity, for they were not permitted to hold their meetings in the factory and union officials were not about to organise one. Somehow Metro-Vicks management had got word that a walk-out was anticipated.

In the factory the next morning the management got all the representatives of the Apprentice Committee together. Had us together for two hours trying to explain why this strike was wrong and what could happen and so on and so forth, and they held on until dinner time, 12 noon. And I noticed Nettleton wasn't there, Watts and Warburton wasn't there, and quite a few others weren't there—so I knew what they were doing, they were carrying out the decision. The management thought they were keeping the apprentices in by keeping the Apprentice Committee in, the leadership, so they couldn't do anything. The other lads had walked round and had the other lads out. I got back to my department at ten past twelve. The journeymen just got hold of my bag with the sandwiches in, threw it at me, whistled and said 'Out!' Those that weren't out were kicked out by the men.

The initial walk-out did lever some response from the employers. The Apprentices Committee, with whom management initially refused to negotiate, were told that further discussions on the claim were to be held at the Employers Federation on Friday 21 March. A return to work was agreed, pending the result of those negotiations. The result was that the employers offered one shilling per week increase for 17-year-olds and between four and eight shillings for 18 to 20-year-olds. However, there was nothing for 14 to 16-year-olds and the unequal wage increases were seen as an attempt to split the lads. The strike at Metro-Vicks resumed with increased support; 2,000 Metro-Vicks apprentices stopped work on 27 March. Duncan Hallas started work at Metro-Vicks in January 1940, aged 14.

> I started working in January 1940. Almost everyone could get a job (they had introduced conscription for men, and then for women with some qualifications). At the shop I worked in—the turbine machine shop of Metro-Vicks—all the electrical work was done by women, whereas all the machine work was done by men. Lots of them were new or had not worked for a long time. At its peak it had 30,000 workers... I started at 14 shillings and sixpence a week. By the age of 16 I had reached the grand total of 20 shillings a week. There were a series of grievances about relative privileges. What precipitated the dispute in Manchester was the fact that the employers decided to abolish the Shrove Tuesday half-day holiday, which had existed since before the industrial revolution. That was the last straw.

Hallas believes that the employers were keen to settle because they feared the action might spread to adult workers, officially or unofficially driven. Perhaps they understood that action breeds militancy and radicalisation, as was the case with Hallas himself.

> So we raw youth were instructed in the art of picketing and had the first scab bicycled into a ditch. Of course, we loved it. The dispute lasted about a week. The management caved in, not because we could beat them—our parents would have forced us back—but because of the owners'

general assessment of the situation in the factories. They didn't want the dispute to spread, because a lot of disputes were simmering. My radicalisation came after the 1941 dispute. I joined the Young Communist League. I was never in the CP, but I stayed in the YCL until 1942.[409]

The spread of the dispute in Manchester is described in a Manchester area Party information sheet that lists the number of apprentices "on holiday" between 27 and 29 March.

Thursday 27th March
An apprentices meeting on Donkey Common, Manchester was attended by 4,000 apprentices from the following factories: M.Vs; Ferguson, Pallin's, Mather and Platt, Cravons (2 factories); English steel; AV Roe's; Crossley Gas. Ferranti's, West's Gas; Beyer Peacocks; and four big Rochdale factories and one factory in Birch.

Friday 28th March
Special meeting of apprentices called for Donkey Common for 2pm. 5,000 present.[410]

Another 740 apprentices from seven factories are reported joining the dispute on Saturday 29 March. At the meeting on the common on 27 March, AEU divisional organiser Fred Siddall advocated a return to work. Vic Eddisford: "He got booed down. He was the guy Scanlon stood up against in the election in later years and beat him out of office." Siddall was eventually censured by the AEU district committee (DC) since it had already pledged support at a previous meeting. Dick Nettleton addressed a DC meeting who then pressed the union's national executive committee to approach the employers to re-open negotiations. Adult support for the apprentices was patchy and limited to a levy. Vic Eddisford:

In 1941, they were booted out of the factory. The adult movement booted them out.

*They wouldn't strike in support?*
Well, they weren't expected to. They weren't asked to; there was no suggestion they would.

Hugh Scanlon's meter department in Metro-Vicks held a

meeting on 2 April in Stretford Trades and Labour Club after working hours. Roughly 120 attended and agreed to support the striking apprentices by a levy. A Party document from 29 March provides some evidence of how adult union activists and comrades perceived the dispute.

> A feature of the first action in Manchester was the lack of any real support to the lads from the adults in the form of guidance or financial aid. When the award ultimatum became known, it was extremely difficult to hold the lads, who were indignant at the terms of the boys of 14, 15, 16, and 17, and practically unanimously took the decision to resume their holiday on March 27th. There is now in existence a widely representative Apprentice Committee, which appears to have the whole thing in hand. As yet however, the AEU District Committee and the adult organisations are not pulling their full weight.[411]

The distance between the Apprentices Committee and the AEU officials was never really breached. The apprentices were contravening the law, and paid officials would not sanction their actions. The local AEU believed the lads should have confined their action to a one-day demonstration and not gone on to strike. They were undoubtedly concerned by the lads' autonomy; they produced their own strike bulletin, which they sold for a penny and their own press statement. The bulletin was headlined:

> 10,000 APPRENTICES OUT ON STRIKE
> On Thursday March 27th, 5,000 lads stopped work in Manchester, over 1,000 in Rochdale. They have since been joined by several thousands more.[412]

It went on to request financial support from "trade union branches, Co-op Guilds and other organisations", appealing over the head of the AEU. In the statement to the press, the Apprentices Committee point out that they have the support of AEU shop stewards from their quarterly meeting. On 3 April the Apprentices Committee went to London to see Minister for Labour Ernest Bevin. They were introduced to top civil servant Sir Frederick Leggett instead, who told them to negotiate through their union.

The apprentices returned to work on 7 April. At the mass meeting that voted to return, a letter was read out from the AEU, which promised to pursue outstanding grievances regarding younger lads with the employers. Pressure was applied to the leadership when five members of the committee, some of them Metro-Vicks' lads, were summoned to appear in court on 4 April. They were charged with unlawfully taking part...

...in a strike in connection with a trade dispute not reported at the Ministry of Labour and National Service in accordance with the provisions of Article 2 of the Conditions of Employment and Arbitration Order 1940 contrary to Article 12 of the Order made under Regulation 58AA of the Defence Regulation (General) 1939.

In addition, call-up notices were issued for some older apprentices. The five committee members were bound over on 4 April and negotiations on apprentices' pay was resumed in September. The 1941 agreement did eventually establish a national rate of pay for apprentices, a victory for unofficial and spontaneous action. The apprentices' action across workplaces and regions was spurred by legitimate grievance, youthful energy, cohesion and disregard for officialdom, whether the AEU or the Ministry of Labour. In the case of Metro-Vicks, the role of the YCL in initiating action was pivotal. YCL members would have demanded that Nettleton and his comrades lead the strike. The Party provided contact with older time-served engineers, who would have given advice. Nettleton and others would have doubtless spoken to comrade Hugh Scanlon who organised a levy in support from his department. Their leadership and the strike's success would have improved the profile and membership of the YCL in the factory and beyond. On return to work, the Party's district committee produced a document on the significance of the dispute.

The action of the lads has had a tremendous effect upon the entire working class movement in Lancashire and the country and is clear evidence of the fact that there is great dissatisfaction among young people at the miserable wages and conditions. The action of the lads is the strongest possible reply to those who feel today that there is little or no dissatisfaction in the country or chance of mass movement.[413]

The issue the document highlights the most is the attack on the right to strike by the prosecution of the strike leaders and the "call-up papers to a large number (unspecified) of the boys". It goes on to outline a series of proposals including: shop meetings "aimed at everyone" to defend the right to strike; Manchester and Salford Trades Council to call a conference on the question; the Manchester and area Apprentices' Committee to be made a permanent organisation "with careful attention to building apprentice committees in all factories".

The Party saw a political potential in the apprentices' movement that it wanted to tap into. Still, there is no evidence that it agitated for strike action by adults when the dispute was underway. As Vic Eddisford remarks: "It wasn't expected." The AEU would have tried to prevent it, and there might well have been consequences, including imprisonment, for those proposing industrial action. A strike by adult engineers would have disrupted war production, in the case of Metro-Vicks, the manufacture of Lancaster bombers. Few workers would have countenanced that on behalf of apprentices. The Party would have made organisational gains in the factories as a result of the dispute, but it also sought to make political capital regarding civil liberties and the right to strike, and campaigning for the forthcoming People's Convention.

# Chapter 15

## Labour landslide

"The fear of death was departing; the fear of life was returning." Angus Calder, *The People's War*

Victory in Europe was declared on Tuesday 8 May 1945. Victory in Japan was yet to arrive. British and American paratroopers had dropped into France in the small hours of 6 June the previous year. At 6.30am the same morning, allied seaborne troops went ashore in Normandy. The second front had finally arrived. Soviet soldiers raised their flag over the ruins of the Reichstag, Berlin, on 2 May 1945. The race to Berlin was only between Soviet marshals. The capture of the German capital by the Red Army was not contested by the Allies. The USA concentrated its forces to the south of Germany to fight what was left of the Wehrmacht and make sure a Nazi government didn't decamp to the Alps. Around 200,000 combatants died in the two-week Battle of Berlin, as well as 22,000 civilians. As it had elsewhere on German territory, Soviet soldiers committed mass rape of German women and children and female Soviet forced labour. The most often quoted figures are 100,000 for Berlin and 2 million women and children on German territory as a whole. Such was the extent of the atrocities that Article 218 of Germany's penal code that forbade abortion was ignored for the victims. Historian Anthony Beevor, whose books have been banned in Russian schools and universities since 2015, describes it as the "greatest phenomenon of mass rape in history".[414] The atrocities provoked a wave of suicides and, in the case of the town of Demmin, a mass suicide.

In Britain, 9 May was declared a public holiday and people danced in the streets. Eric Jessop: "People were so glad the war was over, there was a sense of elation." In London, crowds massed in Trafalgar Square and outside Buckingham Palace. Churchill took his place on the balcony alongside the King and Queen. Princess Elizabeth and Princess Margaret wandered incognito among the crowds. Regardless of their politics, many assumed that a general election sooner rather than later would return Churchill as prime minister. There hadn't been an election since 1935, and Conservative MPs pressed Churchill to call off the coalition as soon as was practicably possible. Initially, Attlee suggested the coalition should continue until Japan was defeated. But Churchill's response was that it could take another 18 months and offered a July 1945 election. Labour's national executive committee was keen to go to the polls, and Churchill tended his resignation on 23 May. The demobilisation of service personnel, 'demob', began on 18 June. There were 5 million men and women to return home and the process was undertaken in stages. Those in the Far East and India had to wait longer and this provoked strike action by RAF personnel in South East Asia. There was a world shortage of food, hunger across Europe and famine in India. In Britain there was less meat on sale at the end of the war than in 1944. The bacon ration was reduced from four ounces to three, clothing coupons were reduced because of the shortage of textile workers. There was, however, more fish available as trawler men were released from the navy.

## Turning the town upside down

Churchill's approval rating with the public was high, and the Tories election campaign rested heavily on his wartime record. They were confident of victory and were genuinely shocked when the result came. The Tories hadn't proposed anything new when there had never been such a desire for change, and the electorate was able to distinguish between Churchill's record and that of his party. Significant voting swings and big majorities are often the result of larger parties underestimating their electorate, particularly their memory. The Tories had been in power for 24 of the previous 27 years since the First World War. They governed during years blighted by mass unemployment and the Means Test, of inadequate housing and health care. They were also tainted by appeasement; some considered there might not have been a world war if Hitler had been stopped earlier. There was a widespread conviction in 1945 there should be no going back to days when life and livelihood were at the mercy of market forces, the whim of the landlord and the foreman. The state had managed almost every aspect of public life during the war; people believed it should play a more significant role in the peace that had been won. Homes had not been fit for heroes after the First World War, but this time it was going to be different.

Much of the difference desired was contained in a report, *Social Insurance and Allied Services*, written by the social economist William Beveridge, published in November 1942. The report went beyond the brief the author had been given. Beveridge had worked at the charitable organisation Toynbee Hall in the East End, and seen social inequality first-hand. He'd concluded that philanthropy was an inadequate response to the scale of the problem and began writing widely on unemployment and social security. In 1933 he was appointed Master of University College, Oxford; in 1936 he was appointed as senior civil servant for the National Government by Minister of Labour Ernest Bevin. The essence of what became known as the Beveridge Report was establishing a minimum standard of living "below which no one should be allowed to fall". Bold in ambition and grandiose in style, it identified five giants to be slain along the road to reconstruction: want, disease, ignorance, squalor and idleness. He proposed that all people of a working age should pay a weekly national insurance contribution; in return, benefits would be paid to people who were sick, unemployed, retired or widowed.

One of Beveridge's assumptions would be that there would be a health service for all citizens, regardless of income. The Ministry of Health was already working on this. The war had necessitated a centralised state-run Emergency Hospital Service established in 1939 so, by 1945, the idea that the state should run health services was familiar. On 21 March 1943, Churchill broadcast his plan for post-war Britain, *from the cradle to the grave*, speaking of the need to establish a national health service. The National Government set to work on the legislation in March 1944, publishing a white paper, *A National Health Service*, on which the National Health Service Act of 1946 was closely based. Opposition to public health care was to come, not from within parliament but from the medical profession in the shape of the British Medical Association. Before the war, healthcare was a mixture of private, municipal and charity schemes; it depended on one's ability to pay. Henceforth, it would be 100 percent funded by taxation.

William Beveridge became a Liberal MP, but his ideas appealed across the political spectrum. Employers were reassured that the scheme would make for a healthier and more productive workforce. Another underlying premise of Beveridge's scheme was that there should be full employment, defined as not more than 3 percent unemployment. Implicit in this was the need for state intervention to protect jobs; private employers alone could not be expected to secure full employment. This was the heyday of Keynesian economics when it was accepted that governments should regulate the business cycle through a fiscal policy.

Churchill was sceptical of Beveridge's proposals from the outset. He disliked the universal nature of the scheme—the millionaire and his state pension. The Tories thought it was economically irresponsible and were concerned that its advocates were encouraging the public to expect a post-war golden age when, in fact, austerity and rationing were set to continue for the foreseeable future. The Beveridge report was released to the public in January 1943; Ministry of Information intelligence revealed that there was widespread approval and support for the plan, though a proportion of the public were sceptical it would ever be implemented. Factory gate and union meetings demanded its implementation. It is significant that the plan was published shortly after victory at the Battle of El Alamein in November 1942, which had followed a series of defeats. The victory was a turning point in the war in North Africa, as Beveridge's report was a turning point on the home front. Combined, they were viewed as lifting morale and resolve. *Picture Post* went as far as to comment: "The report, designed to cast out fear from the people of Britain, brought terror to the rulers of Germany, Italy, Japan."[415] Labour adopted Beveridge's plans for the 1945 election and promised widespread nationalisation, more for efficiency than class warfare, for some in Labour had cold feet about such wholesale economic change. Churchill described the plans as "borrowed from foreign lands and alien minds" and believed the proposals to be out of step from public opinion.

The Communist Party responded to the publication of the report in December 1942 with its programme: *Guidelines on Post War Construction*. Henceforth the Party was increasingly drafting policies on post-war planning. In May 1944 it published *Britain for the People*, which included a call for proportional representation. At the end of the war, its overenthusiastic support for peaceful co-existence led it to call for the temporary continuation of the National Government. Eden and Churchill were thought of as progressive Tories; a position borne of international communist thinking, the continuation of popular front politics as coalitions took power across the continent after German occupation. The Communist Party also still had an ambition to affiliate to the Labour Party, which was technically possible at the time. They applied on three occasions: 1935, 1943, and 1946. At the 1945 election they approached Labour to propose there be only "one working-class candidate" in each constituency. Not surprisingly, Labour declined the invitation yet the Communist Party entered the general election trying to strengthen political unity, reducing its number of parliamentary candidates from 52 to 21 and actually had little to say that was different to Labour. Perhaps more than the Labour Party, the CP leadership believed and desired that the national unity of the war could be continued. Hugh Scanlon for Stretford was one of the candidates who had to withdraw.

> Party candidates were dropped. I hadn't a chance of being elected. I was told to stand down. The Labour candidate was a naval commander. He was very left-wing in his views.[416]

Vic Eddisford believes that in the case of Stretford, it was the right decision:

> There was a certain correctness in pulling Scanlon out. In the sense that we wanted a Labour government, we'd been involved in selecting the candidate and we were in a constituency that had never been won for Labour but we thought we could. The national leadership was correct in our case.[417]

As in many other areas of the country, it meant large Communist Party branches campaigning for Labour. The Party shied away from establishing themselves as a separate electoral force nationally, in a head-on collision with Labour, yet had recently closed down factory branches for electoral reasons. Vic explains how the Party's initial call for continuation of the coalition government was a mistake "that life proved ridiculously wrong", and one that wasn't made by the Stretford comrades. The experience on the ground, on the shop floor, had made them realise:

> ...we could win it for Labour. We'd been involved with the Labour Party in choosing a candidate we thought worth fighting for...He was a supporter of Shinwell and Aneurin Bevan which made it as far as we were concerned, the right kind of candidate. We'd done so much work for Scanlon, we could swing it behind Labour...I knew Stretford like the back of my hand...We were a young, active, virile force in that town and we could turn that town upside bloody down. And we did do.[418]

Voting took place on 5 July 1945, though because of the overseas vote, including troops in Burma, counting was delayed until 26 July. It was the first election in ten years and the outcome wasn't decided during the campaign, it was decided during the war, probably by 1943. By February 1945 Labour had an 18 percent poll lead over the Tories. Both Churchill and Attlee attended the Potsdam conference in 1945 which ran from 17 July to 2 August, convened amidst the ruins of Berlin. Stalin expected Churchill to win and said of Attlee: "I do not think he looks forward avidly to taking over your authority." But when the two leaders inspected British soldiers, it was the Labour leader that was greeted with the loudest cheers. In the coming days Attlee won a remarkable landslide with one of the biggest swings in British electoral history; a net gain of 239 seats and 47.7 percent of the popular vote. The Tory working-class vote shrank, leaving them with 213 seats to Labour's 393. Churchill was the people's leader for the war but not for peace and reconstruction. Stretford was taken from the Tories by Labour. Hugh Scanlon and his comrades from Metro-Vicks no doubt made a significant contribution towards the election of Lewis Austin, not only at the time of the campaign, but throughout the war as they pushed the centre of gravity to left, day after day, week after week. The Party was the industrial base of Labour's 1945 campaign.

Standing for Labour in Manchester's Hulme constituency was Fred Lee, chair of the Metro-Vicks works committee and a member of the AEU national executive. Benny Rothman and his comrades in the factory branch campaigned vigorously for Lee.

> People had had a bellyful of the other class. They wanted them out. We certainly put Fred Lee into the House of

Commons. We were responsible for getting a whole load of Labour candidates elected from the factories. We had a high degree of organisation. We had a meeting every Friday dinner time, about 100 stewards, men and women. We'd discuss problems inside and outside the factory. Fred Lee as chairman of the works committee would come down and nod sagely. And the Friday after he was elected, he came down and said, 'Now comrades, I'm leaving this committee, and I'm going to another in Westminster, but I can assure you you'll see me here on every occasion on a Friday to discuss national issues.' We never saw the bugger once. Instead, he went to see the directors. If ever there was a man who did a somersault. It was sad to see.[419]

The move away from the party was well and truly over. It was the first time the Labour Party had won an outright majority, "the crowning achievement of two generations of political activity",[420] and it had won it on a manifesto entitled *Let Us Face the Future*, of nationalisation, economic planning, full employment, a welfare state and the establishment of the NHS. Ironically, the man that helped to win the election for Labour, William Beveridge, lost his seat. The *Daily Express* had promised a "Gestapo in Britain if socialists win". This echoed something that Churchill had said in the campaign that had backfired badly. In general terms, Labour benefited from being identified with care for ordinary people in a way the Tories were not.

Maurice Levine was serving in Belgium at the time of the election, and his politics were well known to other soldiers.

When the result of the 1945 general election was announced the colonel sent for me. He said, 'Levine, you are coming out with me for a drink tonight. I think you know something about what is taking place in England.' The colonel couldn't understand why they had thrown Churchill out. He was very interested, a very intelligent man.[421]

The Communist Party won 100,000 votes, averaging 11 percent in the seats in which it stood, winning in two: Phil Piratin joined Willie Gallacher in parliament after winning Stepney. Two-thirds of the Labour MPs were new MPs, and about a dozen of those were thought to be secret members of the CP. On the first day of the new government, Gallacher and Piratin and the crypto communists inside the Labour Party stood up and sang *The Red Flag* in the Commons.[422] The Party had helped Labour to victory in two ways. They campaigned on the ground for Labour candidates. The *Daily Worker* slogan for the election was Harry Pollitt's instruction to "Vote as red as you can". And though the CP was numerically far smaller than the Labour Party, most of its members were activists who would have been on the knocker and soapboxes for Labour. They also contributed to the landslide in a more generalised way. From the Spanish Civil War onwards, they earnestly put the case for socialism and against fascism; for state control of welfare, health, and industry. They railed against those who had sought to appease Hitler and Franco, and as the horror of the Holocaust came to light, the dichotomy they claimed the world faced, of socialism versus barbarism, was seen by many to be correct.

## Labour in power

The Party's initial attitude to the Attlee government could be described as unconditional support. It continued its policy of a moratorium on strikes for the first few years after the election, something not welcomed by Metro-Vicks' convenor Hugh Scanlon.

> There were times when I could have cheerfully hung Attlee and Bevin from the nearest lamppost. I thought they were betraying all we'd fought for in the war. We wanted the new Jerusalem now. The real crux of workers' power was still evading us. That's how left you were in those days. All the things we'd talked about in the war...we wanted them in the life of the new Labour Government.[423]

Britain in 1945 was bankrupt. During the war, there had been a Lend-Lease scheme in operation whereby the US government provided Britain with food, oil and weaponry in return for leases on army and naval bases in Allied territory. Attlee hoped this would continue, but it ended soon after the surrender of Japan. The cushion of a £4 billion loan was spent within two years. During the war, the country had lost two-thirds of its export trade; now that there was peace, exports needed to rise. So, when there was a series of disputes on the docks across the country, mostly unofficial, the government came down firmly on the side of the employer and used troops to break the strikes. Wilf Charles recalls Party district secretary for Lancashire and Cheshire and the Communist candidate for Preston in 1945, Pat Devine, urging dockers and others back to work.

> I worked in an industry that was so strike prone, steel erecting—building bridges; six got killed at Barton Bridge. You got paid what you could get. We used to have a saying in those days, the three Fs. Fogged off, frosted off and fucked off. Then a big upheaval came and the dockers were very well led. The Party was quite strong in the docks. Now to get on a platform like Pat Devine did, on the top of an air-raid shelter, and say 'No more strikes!'[424]

Senior Party members like Pat Devine were not merely officials in a hierarchy, they were comrades of considerable experience, held in high esteem, imbued with authority over other activists. Pat was born in Motherwell and left school at 13 to go down the pit. He served in the Royal Flying Corps and was a founder member of the CPGB. He was active in the 1926 General Strike in Scotland and went back and forth to the United States to help the fledgling communist party there. He became general secretary of the National Textile Workers Union, leading a strike at the Lawrence Textile Mills in Massachusetts. He was arrested and sentenced to 15 years in prison, but after a year was deported back to Scotland. Within months, he was again imprisoned for his involvement in the National Unemployed Workers Movement. Back in England, he worked with Isobel Brown in the Aid for Spain Movement, and then became an east London organiser against fascism and was in the leadership of the battle of Cable Street in October 1936. Pat Devine had the kind of clout in the CP that was required to tell striking workers what they didn't want to hear. During the same period, there was a dispute at Metro-Vicks where the Party officials responded in the same way. Vic Eddisford recalls:

> I think it was a very bad period the CP went through. It was swinging from extreme to extreme, from not thinking a Labour government would be elected, to not having any struggles while a Labour government was

in. That was the worst period. Much worse than your Joint Production Committees and the war. The biggest thing that split the CP in that factory was a big dispute; it was 1946 or 1947. There was a six-week day-work strike there, part of the struggle led by Scanlon, a communist, the convenor, the factory comrades behind it and then the CP pulled us into line and said, 'It's a Labour government don't rock the boat.' The CP official came down and told us to get back to work, 'You're gonna ruin the Labour government.'

The dousing of disputes was in part an attempt to improve the Party's chances of Labour Party affiliation, but was destined to make no difference. Attlee desperately needed to increase productivity and exports, and though he would have welcomed the Party imploring dockers to load ships in London and Merseyside, he and his government shared a long-held hatred of the CP and its fellow travellers. Labour was more interested in security intelligence on them than the Tories because they feared their infiltration. When the CP applied for affiliation in December 1942, Labour's national executive committee refused to accept the proposal, or even discuss the matter. Then following the dissolution of the Communist International in May 1943, the NEC urged the CP to:

> Follow the example of the Comintern and dissolve itself, thereby contributing to the further development of a great consolidated party of the left: the Labour Party. [425]

Despite such a stark rebuttal, the request for affiliation made its way on to the Labour Party conference agenda in June of the same year. An anti-affiliation campaign was launched that didn't pull its punches, publishing a pamphlet, *The Communist Party and the War: A Record of Hypocrisy and Treachery to the Workers of Europe*, which was sold in bulk to local parties. Herbert Morrison asked the conference to distinguish between Stalin, "one of the world's greatest men", and the leaders of the British Communist Party, who he described as "unclean".[426] The Communist Party had the support of the Miners Federation of Great Britain but lost the conference vote convincingly.

The 1945 landslide had given the Labour leadership the impetus to try to put an end to the splintering of the Left, leaving them as its sole representative. In the 1945 election, the Common Wealth Party had stood 23 candidates with one elected where there had been no Labour opposition. The Independent Labour Party (ILP) managed to get three of its five candidates elected but of these, one died in 1946 and the other two joined the Labour Party in 1947; thereafter the ILP ended its electoral ambitions. It is worth adding that 12 of the 21 CP candidates lost their deposits. D N Pritt, the left-wing lawyer, summed it up by saying of Labour, "We're the only cock on the dunghill."[427] At the end of 1945, the CP applied for affiliation for the last time. Labour Party General Secretary Morgan Philips wrote to Harry Pollitt on 23 January 1946:

> The gulf between us has not been narrowed to any degree since the general election of last year which amply demonstrated the ineffectiveness and political incapacity of the Communist Party. That election also showed that a united labour movement behind the Labour Party has been achieved in Britain.[428]

Labour believed that any collaboration with the CP would permit communists to cause disruption within its ranks, which was broadly correct. Individual membership of the Labour Party rose from 265,763 in 1944 to 487,047 in 1945 and 908,161 by the end of the decade, more than tripling in size. In 1946 the NEC passed a resolution that prevented other political groups from affiliating to the Labour Party. In the local elections of autumn 1945, the CP increased its number of councillors to 206, doing better in Scotland and Wales. But it didn't, and would never, control a single council in Britain.

Elsewhere in Europe after the war, communist parties were represented in government, and party membership numbers were much higher than in Britain. A major reason for this was that communists had been at the forefront of resistance and liberation movements against the Nazis. In France it was the PCF that made up the cadre in the military resistance to German occupation. The Allied landings in Normandy in 1944 were accompanied by a national uprising that saw communist-led resistance forces liberate large parts of the country, including Paris. An interesting footnote is that among the first Allied troops to march through Paris in August 1944 were Spanish Republicans. They were the soldiers of 'La Nueve". The 9th

Company consisted of the 160 men under French command, 146 of whom were Spanish refugees from Francoist Spain and enlisted in the French army based in North Africa. The majority of the company were socialists, communists or anarchists and were permitted to wear the tricolour of the Second Spanish Republic on their uniforms. Daubed on their vehicles when they paraded down the Champs Elysees were the names of civil war battles: Guadalajara, Brunete, Teruel, and Guernica. As a significant force, the PCF was among the leading parties in the elections of 1945 and 1946, entering into a coalition government. Its membership grew from 292,701 in 1937 to 616,348 in 1945.

In Italy, after the fall of the Mussolini regime in July 1943, the Italian Communist Party (PCI) was legal once more and took on a major role in the national liberation movement Resistenza Italiana, dominating most of the partisan groups. PCI members of parliament were involved in the post-war government in 1944-47, with PCI secretary Palmiro Togliatti serving as deputy Prime Minister from 1945 to 1946. Party membership grew from 402,000 in 1944 to over 2 million in 1946. In Greece the National Liberation Front (EAM) was led by the Greek Communist Party (KKE). Their military wing, the Greek People's Liberation Army (ELAS) fought nationwide. From 1943 onwards, the liberation movement was beset by conflict between different factions with communists achieving the upper hand and controlling much of the country until, in late 1944, British forces arrived to suppress the communists and install an anti-communist government which ultimately resulted in the Greek Civil War of 1946 to 1949. Communist parties grew in Austria, Finland, and Japan and the US. The Soviet Union had gained prestige across the globe for its endurance and victories on the Eastern Front, and though it had abolished the Comintern in 1943, communist parties around the world continued to look to Moscow for direction.

When Stalin dissolved the Comintern, he instructed communist parties to support the wartime alliance to defeat the Axis. Post-war, Stalin desired a continuation of the alliance based on spheres of influence agreed between Britain, the US and the Soviet Union at Yalta in February 1945. Britain and the US were assured that Stalin would not be attempting to ferment international revolution, but rather wanted to secure the Soviet Union through a buffer zone of Eastern European states. Chris Bambery argues that such a policy acted as a restraint on domestic communist parties at a time when there were possibilities for radical political change.

> In brutal terms, Stalin was willing to restrain the hands of the Communist Parties to get Eastern Europe. This can be traced in the histories of the French, Italian and Greek Communist Parties.[429]

In France, General De Gaulle granted a pardon for the leader of the PCF, Maurice Thorez, who had been in exile in Moscow, on the understanding he would not pose a threat to national stability. Thorez committed the PCF to 'la France éternelle' through a battle for increased production. Like Pat Devine at the London docks, Thorez told striking French car workers to get back to work.[430] In 1944, the Italian Communist Party agreed to set up a government of national unity and abandon the socialist armed struggle that had helped defeat the Axis powers. What became known as the Salerno Turn was a compromise between the PCI, the monarchy and Prime Minister Pietro Badoglio, who had been head of the Italian armed forces under Mussolini. In the January 1946 elections, the Christian Democrats became the major party in Italy, and the PCI agreed to the recognition of Catholicism as the state religion, a ban on divorce and recognition of the privileged position of the Vatican.

By the spring of 1947, the post-war agreements of Yalta and the governments of national unity began to unravel. On 12 March President Truman announced to the US Congress his pledge to contain communist expansion. The 'Truman doctrine' became the foundation of US foreign policy and led to the forming of NATO and the Cold War. In May of that year, in a widely repeated move, both the PCF and PCI ministers were dismissed from government. In October 1947 the Communist Parties of the Soviet Union, Poland, Czechoslovakia, Hungary, Yugoslavia, Bulgaria, Romania, France and Italy met in Poland to found the Cominform, the Communist Information Bureau. This was not a reincarnation of the Comintern. Its principal activities were to encourage co-operation and mutual support for communist organisations but also to frustrate the objectives of the Truman doctrine and the Marshall Plan—a US initiative to restore European economies lest they succumb to revolution and communist control. Several states in the Soviet Union's 'buffer zone' were attracted to US economic aid and influence, and Stalin perceived a threat.

Seven weeks after the Axis powers abandoned Greece in October 1944, Britain had helped drive out the communist-run resistance forces from Athens, providing support for the Greek government's Hellenic army. A civil war followed from 1946 to 1949 in which the much larger government-run army was victorious. Though Churchill and Eden had begun the intervention, it continued under Attlee. Stalin had agreed not to support communist forces in Greece, but the insurgents did receive supplies of weapons from Tito's Yugoslavia. Britain formally withdrew from Greece in 1947. Many of the defeated Greek communists fled over the border into Albania, which was under communist rule. In 1949 Attlee sent agents into Albania to initiate a coup, but the mission failed and resulted in the death of the agents and their supporters. The civil war in Greece marked the first post-war involvement on the part of the Allies in a Cold War arena and by this point the CPGB's truce with the Attlee government was over. Vic Eddisford:

> In one minute in 1945, they don't think a Labour government can get elected, so we were with a coalition. Then in 1947, 'Get your gloves off, you can have a go.' The Cold War had really started then. Once the Cold War started, you can have a good working-class struggle.[431]

Coinciding with the advent of the Cold War, Britain's underlying economic problems came to the surface and hamstrung the Attlee Government. Post-war Britain hung on to the appearance of one of the three great world powers alongside Russia and the US, but economically it had the resources of a defeated nation. It had around 2 million men worldwide in fleets, garrisons and air squadrons that it couldn't afford to pay for. The Marshall Aid that Britain received after the US loan was used to fund this strategic role instead of modernising infrastructure and industry. Labour began to cut social services and capital investment. As it began to embrace the Cold War, helping to crush risings in Vietnam, Malaya and in particular, Greece, proved expensive. By June of 1947, Party membership had declined to 38,579 and Young Communist League membership was a third of its pre-war size. Vic Eddisford feels the Party retreated at the end of the war.

> My experiences were about working for a mass party in that period. A lot of people had their head in the

clouds. They didn't know what was happening. The elitists didn't really want a mass party. I think if the CP had not gone back into its shell at the end of the war and built on some of those experiences, if it had more confidence in some of the newer younger forces that weren't embracing Leninism and idolising Stalin.[432]

Had they stood more candidates in 1945, it is doubtful they would have won more seats. But it remains an open question what might have been sustained and built on had the Party, instead of unsuccessfully seeking to merge with Labour and therefore soft-pedalling on its criticisms, prepared its members to resist the austerity that was reimposed by the late 1940s. If they had not closed down factory branches and called a moratorium on strikes under Attlee, it is probable they would have further strengthened their position with the trade unions. At the end of the war, communist Arthur Horner became general secretary of the miners' union, the first to lead a major trade union. The TUC general council had its first-ever communist member in Bert Papworth of the TGWU, and the Party had pretty much full control of the Fire Brigades Union, the AEU, and the Electrical Trades Union. But whilst it captured positions in the trade union bureaucracy, it lost members on the shop floor.

At the end of the war, Maurice Levine returned to the work he had left when he went to Spain in 1936.

> I began work again at a small clothing factory in Cheetham Hill Road in January 1947. Everywhere looked drab and shortages were apparent. In that bitter winter, the country was short of coal; electricity was restricted, millions were temporarily laid off work. Rationing was to continue for a further five years. The slow and difficult return to normality was beginning.[433]

*Comrades Come Rally*

# Chapter 16

## Jewish Comrades

> "To be a Jew means always being with the oppressed and never the oppressors." Marek Edelman, one of the leaders of the Warsaw Ghetto Uprising

Jews were over-represented in radical politics during this period and before, and they were particularly over-represented in the leadership of communist parties across Europe. In Poland, Jews were just under 10 percent of the population in the 1930s but constituted 25 percent of the Polish Communist Party; by 1935 most of the central committee were Jewish. In Russia, even in the wake of Stalin's purges, Jews still formed 10 percent of the central committee despite being less than 2 percent of the general population. Jews were also prominent in communist parties in Hungary, Ukraine, Belarus, Romania and Lithuania.[434] The Communist Party in Britain and its branches in the Manchester area were no different. In the heyday of the CPGB, Jews constituted as much as 10 percent of the membership—ten times the population as a whole; in the 1940s, nearly a third of all district secretaries were Jewish. Communist MP Phil Piratin's Mile End constituency in Stepney, east London, was a Jewish enclave.

### Forefathers from the Pale

Before the Russian Revolution and the creation of European communist parties, there was the Jewish Labour Bund. Bund was an abbreviation for the 'General Jewish Workers Union in Lithuania, Poland and Russia'. Formed in 1897, it was a secular Jewish socialist party seeking to unite all Jewish workers in the Russian Empire. In make-up, it was a working-class party; in outlook, it rejected the assimilation of Jews into Russian society and any alliance with other Jewish political groups with religious objectives. It rejected the sacred language of Hebrew and chose to speak Yiddish, the language of Eastern European Jews. The Bund renounced the notion of Jews returning to a Holy Land, believing that Jewish life had to be lived out where they were.

As such, it opposed Zionism whilst campaigning against antisemitism and defending Jewish cultural and civil rights. At its height in 1917, the Bund had 40,000 members, mainly within the area formerly known as the Pale of Settlement. The Pale was a broad stretch of land reaching from the Black Sea to the Baltic where, under Tsarist rule, Jewish people were legally entitled to reside. At the time it was home to 40 percent of the world's Jews. Any Jew in the Empire that didn't live in the Pale was forced to convert to Russian orthodoxy.

Even before the years of the Bund, Jewish workers in the Russian Empire tended to be more radical and militant than non-Jews. Tony Cliff from his biography of Lenin:

> In the regions of heavy Jewish population, strikes became very frequent, reaching a high point in 1895, in a textile industry strike in Bialystok, which involved as many as 15,000 workers. In fact, Jewish workers were far ahead of Russian workers in terms of trade union organisation. While as late as 1907, only 7 percent of the St. Petersburg workers were organised in trade unions, in 1900 20 percent of Jewish workers in Bialystok were organised in trade unions, 24 percent in Vilna, 40 percent in Gomel, and 25-40 percent in Minsk.[435]

Such was their reputation; employers became reluctant to hire them.

> Jewish workers were often hired last because they were considered to be too quick to organise, strike or revolt. A Jewish factory owner in Vilnius explained: "I prefer to hire Christians. The Jews are good workers, but they are capable of organising revolts against the boss, the regime and the Tsar himself."[436]

It was from this context that the political organisation of the Bund emerged, a context of rapid industrialisation and antisemitic oppression that included not just the confinement of the Pale. From the 1880s onwards, there was a succession of pogroms against Russian Jews. In 1902, in Vilnius, Lithuania, Jews who attended a May Day demonstration were flogged on the orders of the city's governor. A Bundist youth subsequently shot the governor. During the Russian pogroms of the early 20th century, the Bund became the principal organiser of Jewish self-defence. Between 1903 and 1904, Tsarist police arrested and jailed 4,500 of its members. However, it recovered during the revolution of 1905, becoming the largest socialist group in the Russian Empire to publish a daily newspaper, *Undzer Tsayt* (*Our Time*). The Bund implicitly saw Jews of the Russian Empire as a nationality defined by the Yiddish language and culture.[437] It was hoped that the eventual socialist revolution would deliver national autonomy for all oppressed nationalities in a Russian federation. With the split between the Mensheviks and Bolsheviks in 1912, the Bund initially remained with the former. The Bolsheviks proposed that Jewish workers should be integrated into the wider workers' movement; that all workers, not just Jews, should take up the fight against antisemitism.

With the revolution of 1917, the relationship between the Bund and the Bolsheviks changed. The revolutionary government decreed the abolition of national discrimination and withdrew all antisemitic legislation. The Pale was abolished, and Jews were permitted to live across the country. During the civil war, White Armies orchestrated pogroms across the country.

> In regions such as Ukraine, Byelorussia, Crimea and the Caucasus, the very fabric of the economic and social existence of Jewish communities was torn to shreds in the course of a merciless confrontation between Reds and Whites—the latter mobilised under the banner 'For Holy Russia, against the Jews!'[438]

The Bolsheviks treated antisemitic pogroms as counter-revolutionary violence and imposed martial law on the perpetrators. Many Jewish workers began to join the Bolsheviks, encouraged to take up positions in the structures of the Party and government. Esther Rosenthal-Schneidermann, a young communist of Polish origin, arrived in Moscow in 1926 to take part in the first congress of Jewish activists specialising in education. It was a liberating step for Esther:

> Up till then, I had never seen a Jew in the role of high official, not to say an official speaking our everyday mamelosh, Yiddish. And here on the podium in the congress hall of the People's Commissariat for Education, there were top officials speaking Yiddish, in the name of the colossal Soviet power, of Jewish education that the party placed on a footing of equality with the cultural assets of other peoples.[439]

Some became key figures. Five out of 15 members of the central committee of the Bolshevik Party were Jewish in 1918; at the Party's tenth congress in March 1921, out of 694 delegates, 94 were Jewish. In 1921, after heated debates both with the Bolsheviks and inside the organisation, the Russian Bund dissolved itself completely.

Much has been written about the relationship between Jews and socialism, both from an abstract perspective, alleging similarities between Judaism and Marxism, and a more evidential approach, that looks at the experience and testaments of individuals who moved between Jewish communities to the community of communism. The English historian Barnet Litvinoff writes of a 'Jewish infatuation' with communism.[440] Others have argued that communism was a means of casting off an identity that imposed traditions upon its subjects. Marxist historian Isaac Deutscher described communism as a place of denial and himself as a "non-Jewish Jew".

> Religion? I am an atheist. Jewish nationalist? I am an internationalist. In neither sense am I, therefore a Jew. I am, however, a Jew by force of my unconditional solidarity with the persecuted and exterminated. I am a Jew because I feel the pulse of Jewish history; I should like to do all I can to assure the real, not spurious, security and self-respect of the Jews.[441]

Whilst the relationship is confirmed, it should not be overstated. Ros Livshin remarks in the obverse: "Although there have been few radicals among Jews, there have been many Jews among radicals."[442] Conversely, whilst the Manchester Party had a disproportionate number of Jewish activists, there were also many in the Jewish community in the city who were hostile to socialism.

## Cheetham

By 1933 the number of self-identifying Jews in Manchester had stabilised to around 35,000. Most were second- or third-generation descendants of Eastern Europe migrants.[443] A mile from the city centre, the area of Cheetham had undergone a wave of Irish immigration during the famine (1845 to 1852). In the late 19th and early 20th centuries, Jews came to the area, fleeing persecution in Eastern Europe. The area hosted the first-ever Marks and Spencer store in 1893, and nine synagogues in the early 20th century. The Methodist chapels of the previous century became furniture and tailoring workshops. Maurice Levine was born in Cheetham in 1907, in a block of tenements known locally as 'the dwellings', occupied by immigrant families from Poland, Russia and Lithuania.

> My parents came to England from Lithuania with my two elder sisters and brother about 1895… On the day they arrived, my brother, who was about five years old, ran into the street to see something of this strange new neighbourhood. He saw a skinned rabbit hanging in a greengrocer's shop and ran home to tell his mother that people here ate cats.[444]

In Lithuania, Maurice's parents lived in a shtetl, in a wooden hut with an earthen floor, sleeping on benches near the stove, in a country where Jews were forbidden to own land. The family lived in the area for generations and handed down history.

> My father told me that his grandmother was born towards the end of the 18th century and when Napoleon's army was retreating from Moscow in 1812, French soldiers passed through her village. The troops were starving and some French officers knocked at the door offering a gold watch for some potatoes.
>
> It was a history where they were always second-class citizens.
>
> My father told me of attacks on Jews in his shtetl, which was in Kovno, now Kaunas, and I remember washing his back when I was a child and seeing a mark on his skull, from where a gang of youths had set upon him.[445]

Growing up in Cheetham, Maurice encountered fights between Jewish youth and non-Jewish gangs that came into the area to attack and intimidate residents.

> I remember the fights between Gentile and Jewish youth during the First World War. The Battle of the Somme in 1916, with its tremendous number of English casualties, sparked off a certain amount of antisemitic feeling in the area, probably because some of the people had German-sounding names…Gangs of youths came from the other side of Hightown to attack the Jews. They were known as 'scuttlers'…Later on, the 'nappo' gangs came…But the firstborn of the Jewish immigrants, the down-to-earth working-class people could also fight.[446]

Maurice left school at 14 to make caps in an attic, read Joseph Conrad, Rider Haggard and the American writer Theodore Dreiser. As a teenager, he attended YCL meetings but didn't join the Party until 1931. He was one of a generation of Manchester's leading Jewish communists, most of them from the Cheetham area, including Jud Colman, Mick Jenkins, Sol Gadian, Gabriel Cohen, Hymie Lee, Vic Shammah, Benny Rothman, Bert Masky, Frank Allaun, the three Ainley brothers and the Clyne sisters. Some would hold senior positions in the Party and trade unions, one became a Labour MP for almost 30 years, and some would fight in Spain, never to return. Most of the above were members of the YCL before the Blackshirts' arrival and the rise of antisemitic fascism on the continent. They were drawn to communism through reading, attending meetings and social events, and they would have recruited one another.

A vibrant reading culture amongst young comrades in Cheetham created intellectual bonds and equipped some for leadership. Manchester Central Reference Library was a 20-minute walk away; slightly closer was The Bomb Shop, a left-leaning bookshop on Market Street selling classic Marxist texts and a predecessor of Collets. Ben Ainley formed a reading group called 'The Pioneers', which met on a Sunday afternoon. They read Marxist literature, Tom Paine, political fiction by Jack London and Upton Sinclair, and classical literature including Tolstoy and Dostoevsky. Jack Cohen bought the first issue of *Young Communist*, the YCL's monthly periodical, at The Bomb Shop, and decided to set up a local branch in 1921. The *Workers*

*Weekly*, which was the paper of the Party from 1923 to 1927, was initially sold from the house of Gabriel Cohen on Carnarvon Street, but then as the YCL and the Party branch proper began to prosper, they sold the *Daily Worker* on street corners, outside factories and even from door to door. From 1935 a branch of Collets bookshop opened on Hanging Ditch near Manchester Cathedral. Collets was owned by left-wing publisher Victor Gollancz, and the shop became a focal point and a meeting place for activists in the city.

Collets also sold *Russia Today* for the Friends of the Soviet Union (FSU), a monthly illustrated magazine promoting Soviet life. On the tenth anniversary of the Bolshevik Revolution, the FSU was formed as a vehicle for Soviet propaganda. Communists established FSU groups across Manchester, including Cheetham, holding meetings in the local town hall and showing films in supporters' houses. During the Moscow show trials between 1936 and 1938, Pat Sloan, author of *Soviet Democracy* (1937), came to speak in support of Stalin. Frank Allaun was inspired by what he read in *Russia Today* and made several visits to the Soviet Union but began to pull away from the Party due to the show trials and the Nazi-Soviet pact. Jud Colman was 20 years old in 1936 when he went to fight in Spain: "We used to get these beautiful old magazines about Russia ... wonderful pictures ... this is what we wanted."[447] Jack Ribbon, a Jewish communist, became the Lancashire organiser of FSU, followed in the mid-1930s by H Shrager of Cheetham. Maurice Levine was a member of the group:

> For many young people in the late 1920s and 1930s, the Communist Party was the political party to join. At the beginning of 1930 it was only very tiny, with around 3,000 members, but suddenly started to grow very rapidly in Manchester and elsewhere. It had a great deal of attraction for Jewish youth in the Cheetham area; they set up their own premises in Hightown and in other parts of Cheetham later on... For a lot of young people, the Communist Party was a university. There were discussion groups and we were meeting older people who were familiar with books and contemporary writers.[448]

Cheetham YCL opened up the Challenge Club on the upper floor of an old workshop on Herbert Street, the Hightown area of Cheetham, in 1935. The club hosted dances, cultural events, political meetings and classes. Ben Ainley was the club's main tutor and, amongst others, he ran a course on public speaking that included street meetings. Before radio and television, street meetings were part of popular culture. They were a platform for radicals but not exclusively. Frances Dean recalls the regular meeting spots in Manchester in the late 1930s.

> There were open-air meetings in Platt Fields at the outbreak of the war. There was a tradition of regular pitches in Platt Fields and at Alexandra Park gates in Moss Side and Stevenson Square. It used to be a regular meeting place, like Hyde Park. All kinds of people spoke. Religious people as well.[449]

YCL members from Cheetham would attend Stevenson Square meetings on Sundays to listen to speakers and sell communist pamphlets and papers, and for Mick Jenkins, they were formative events.

> I know that they implanted in the hearts and minds of thousands a hatred of capitalism that was real, that lived, that grew, and eventually that wanted to overthrow capitalism.[450]

Mick and others began organising their own street meetings in Cheetham, standing on a chair or a box putting the case for anti-fascism, for peace and communism whilst others gave out leaflets and sold literature. The regular spot was a waste ground known as Marshall Croft in the Hightown area of Cheetham, used by various groups including the socialist Zionist group Hashomer Hatzair. It was where Maurice Levine was first attracted to communist ideas. The YCL branch in Cheetham initially operated out of the Jenkins home. Mick was born in 1904, joining the YCL in 1924. He became the Party's district organiser in Manchester, playing a major part in organising support for the International Brigade's volunteers and their families and the Aid for Spain campaign. During the Second World War, he worked with David Ainley, Eric Jessop and others at the Fairy Aviation factory in Stockport.

Probably more than most branches, Cheetham YCL had an active social side, organising rambles and camping trips into the countryside, often led by Benny Rothman who became secretary of the Manchester British Workers Sports Federation in 1930. Benny was born in 1911, the middle son of five children of Romanian Jewish parents. His father died when he was 12, and Benny left school before he could matriculate to help support the family. Growing up, he read the novels of Upton Sinclair and *The Ragged Trousered Philanthropist*. In the summer of 1925, aged 14, he cycled to North Wales to see Mount Snowdon. It was the beginning of a lifetime love affair with the British countryside alongside campaigns to improve access rights. Benny joined the YCL in 1929 and was a leading anti-fascist in the early 1930s, fighting Blackshirts on Manchester's streets. He was a shop steward and leading comrade in Metro-Vicks throughout the war.

During one camp near Glossop in 1932, Benny and his rambling group were stopped in their tracks by gamekeepers. In response, they organised a mass trespass on 24 April, which attracted hundreds of walkers. Confronted by gamekeepers in the approach to the Kinder plateau, this time Benny and others pushed their way past, onwards to their objective where a second group of trespassers from Sheffield met them. Later, in the village of Hayfield, six of the group were arrested and taken to a local lock-up, charged with breach of the peace and unlawful assembly. Four of the six were Jewish, the judge sentencing Benny and four others to between two and six-months imprisonment. Alongside Benny at the forefront of the campaign were Cheetham comrades Maurice Levine and Sol Gadian.

The severity of the sentences drew public attention and public sympathy. The campaign for access continued, Maurice's memoir recalls, "the Ramblers Association got more militant", and in 1949 the Attlee government legislated for the creation of national parks and access agreements to open country. The first national park was the Peak District, and the first access agreement negotiated was for Kinder Scout. One-time Labour home secretary Roy Hattersley described the 1932 Kinder Scout trespass as "the most successful direct action in British history".

The Party kept no records on the number of Jewish comrades in Manchester, but most Cheetham and Salford members would have been Jewish, and the report to the district committee in 1938 recorded 68 Party members for Cheetham and 44 for Salford. YCL membership would have been roughly the same, if not larger in both areas. What sustained that membership in Cheetham and elsewhere in the 1930s was the fight against antisemitic fascism and the growing periphery that the Party and the YCL drew around it. The establishment of the Challenge Club may have been a direct response to the Comintern's popular front initiative of 1935 since it opened in the same year; more likely, it was a function of the evolution of radical politics in the community. Either way, the club was also frequented by non-communists. Issy's son, Mike Luft:

> They had a club in Hightown, a gathering point of people on the Left, all of them friendly to the CP and the YCL, but not necessarily members. The YCL created an enormous periphery. It was popular front politics. Because they had joined the Party early on, they didn't have the excesses of class against class, but they had the positive things, the combativity and militancy.[451]

The YCL's well-earned reputation for driving the BUF off the streets of Cheetham earned it respect and support, particularly amongst younger, more secular Jews. But within the broader Jewish community, there was some disapproval of confrontations with Blackshirts. Nathan Laski, president of the Council of Manchester and Salford Jews, advised locals, "not to be alarmed by the activities of fascists...we must always be on the watch that the Jewish name should be safeguarded".[452] There was concern that Benny and his comrades were giving Jews a bad reputation. Indeed, Benny faced hostility from his own family because of his actions and had to leave home to live with his newly acquired in-laws. Though it is the case that many in the immigrant community in Cheetham and elsewhere in Manchester initially opposed street fighting, sentiments may have changed later in the decade.

## German refugees

In the late 1930s, a new influx of Jews into Britain began: those fleeing Nazi Germany. The rise of Nazism in Germany took the best part of a decade, but German Jews did not leave in large numbers until close to the war's outbreak. Many thought that the regime would not last; many had nowhere else to go. Two events precipitated an exodus in 1938: the Anschluss—the reunification of Austria and Germany in March and, during the first week in November, Kristallnacht. Kristallnacht, 'Crystal Night', was so-called because of the shards of broken glass on the street after Jewish homes and businesses were destroyed throughout Germany, Austria and Sudetenland. The scale of the Holocaust, film footage and its epithet has relegated the event to a night of vandalism, but it was the inception of organised mass murder. The death toll is uncertain and depends upon whether one counts just the murders or the suicides as well, but it was in the mid-hundreds. 30,000 Jewish men were also arrested and taken to concentration camps, most to be murdered. The attacks were triggered by a German diplomat's assassination by a 17-year-old German-born Polish Jew living in Paris. Kristallnacht was a culmination and a turning point in the oppression of Jews. Before this, discrimination had been primarily political, religious and social; with Kristallnacht, it became physical and murderous.

Attacks on the rights of Jews in Germany began soon after Hitler became Chancellor in January 1933. Discriminatory legislation was implemented against all those judged to be Jewish, including those with at least one Jewish grandparent. It included those that had long abandoned any links to Judaism. People were assaulted in the street; property was seized. The Nazis demanded expulsion.

The problem then for German Jews was finding a country that would take them. No individual government launched a rescue plan, and high unemployment was a deterrent to taking an unknown number of migrants. In Britain, the right of entry was limited to those who could prove they had work to go to or would have someone's financial support, so they would not depend on the state. One possible destination outside Europe was Palestine. During the First World War, Britain had encouraged and supported an Arab revolt against the Ottoman Empire that controlled the region. With the armistice, Britain and France divided the Middle East into spheres of influence, and in 1920 Britain was granted a mandate for Palestine approved by the League of Nations. Three years before, the government's Balfour declaration had committed Britain to acknowledge a 'natural home' for Jewish people in Palestine. This principle became incorporated into the preamble of the 1920 mandate, and thus Britain had a dual obligation towards Jews and Arabs. As more Jews moved to Palestine during the mandate years, two social systems, a Jewish one and a Palestinian one, developed under the same political authority. Each society had its welfare, educational and cultural institutions, becoming two societies independent of one another. Throughout the 1920s and 1930s, violent confrontation between Jews and Arabs occurred, and Britain began to review Jewish immigration into Palestine.

In Britain's case, perhaps 10,000 German Jewish refugees entered the country before 1938, another 60,000 arriving from Germany, Austria, Czechoslovakia and Poland between 1938 and 1939. For Manchester, this meant 500 before 1938 and 6-7,000 after Anschluss. The Manchester numbers included 1,000 of the 10,000 children allowed into Britain on the Kindertransport from Berlin, Vienna, Prague and Warsaw.[453] Alongside Jews fleeing the Nazis were political refugees: socialists and communists, even liberals, any opponent of the regime. Amongst the Czech refugees were experienced members of the German Communist Party (KPD) who had initially fled to Prague, then onto Britain. They regrouped in Manchester, and eight comrades formally constituted themselves as the German Communist Party's Manchester branch.[454] In *Jews and Other Foreigners*, Bill Williams compares the Party's response to Jewish refugees to the Basque children that arrived in 1937 (see Chapter 8, Aid for Spain). The Basque children drew more attention than German Jewish refugees, and Williams suggests the Basques' plight suited Party propaganda better than German Jews, who had the means to escape and who were not part of the resistance to fascism.

> Unlike Hitler's German-Jewish victims, who might be seen as accepting their fate or, at any rate, as not challenging a fascist regime, some of the fathers and elder brothers of the Basque children, it was often pointed out, were fighting and dying for democracy. It was perhaps because they could not be portrayed, in contrast to the Basques, as politically motivated class warriors against fascism that Hitler's Jewish victims appeared so rarely in the anti-fascist propaganda of the CPGB.[455]

Was it possible that there was another factor at play? When Jews were leaving Germany, Stalin exploited antisemitism in his campaign against the Left Opposition in the Soviet Union. During the purges, Jews had been removed from official positions, and limits were placed on the numbers of Jews admitted to educational institutions. Trotsky's essay, *Thermidor and Anti-Semitism* (published February 1937), describes how Stalin enlisted a prejudice deep-rooted in Russian society.

> In the months of preparations for the expulsions of the Opposition from the party, the arrests, the exiles (in the second half of 1927), the anti-Semitic agitation assumed a thoroughly unbridled character. The slogan, "Beat the Opposition" often took on the complexion of the old slogan "Beat the Jews and save Russia". The matter went so far that Stalin was constrained to come out with a printed statement which declared: "We fight against Trotsky, Zinoviev and Kamenev not because they are Jews but because they are Oppositionists," etc. To every politically thinking person it was completely clear that this consciously equivocal declaration, directed against "excesses" of anti-Semitism, did at the same time with complete premeditation nourish it. "Do not forget that the leaders of the Opposition are—Jews." That was the *meaning* of the statement of Stalin, published in all Soviet journals.[456]

It is impossible to ascertain whether such attitudes in Moscow filtered down to King Street.

## Spain

It is estimated that up to 25 percent of all the International Brigade (IB) fighters were Jewish. It is difficult to be sure of the numbers, for they weren't recorded as such, and some Jewish volunteers changed their names. Jews were less than 1 percent of the British population at the time, but at approximately 350 out of the 2,550, they made up 14 percent of the British Battalion. The proportion from Greater Manchester was at least 20 out of a total of 130, or 26 percent.[457] Cheetham Communist Party branch and YCL sent at least 15 volunteers of whom seven were killed.

The reason why Jews are so over-represented amongst IB volunteers, as with their over-representation in radical politics, is the source of much discussion and conjecture. They would have volunteered as communists, as anti-fascists and indeed as Zionists. Giles Tremlett identifies an underlying historical experience that led them to the battlefield.

Their experience of historical bigotry and forthright anti-Semitism of fascism meant that the knowledge of oppression was greater than that of other working-class people who travelled with them, and with deeper roots.[458]

That knowledge of oppression manifested itself at different times in the 20th century in support of communism and Zionism.

Benny Rothman volunteered to be an ambulance driver after attending a talk one evening by the works doctor at Metro-Vicks, a supporter of the Republican cause. He was, however, turned down because despite working at a garage, he couldn't drive. He was then also turned down by district organiser Mick Jenkins to be a volunteer combatant. When the Second World War came, Benny was in a reserved occupation but joined the Home Guard.

> I was still smarting that I wasn't in the IB. I didn't get to Spain. There was a little bit of that washing off on me. A big number of the lads where I lived volunteered for Spain—and quite a number were killed. They hadn't a cat in hell's chance. So many from Cheetham where I lived. It was very sad.[459]

Most of the Manchester volunteers who were children of immigrant Jews were in an age range between Maurice Levine, born in 1907, and Vic Shammah, born in 1914. One exception to this is Bert Masky, born in 1893 and whose life reads like a character from Victor Serge's *Memoirs of a Revolutionary*. Bert's grandson, David Mason:

> The collective comments of family members who knew him, describe him as five foot seven tall and powerfully built, not easily roused but with a violent temper. He was a competent boxer with a powerful punch and always carried a Danish flick knife. In complete contrast to all of this, he was very charming and kind, always neatly dressed with a clean collar every day.[460]

Born Barnett Maransky in Vilnius, Lithuania, he came from a family of Jewish silk merchants, receiving a relatively good

## Jewish Comrades

| | |
|---|---|
| **Arrived Dec 1936** | |
| Bill Benson | *Killed in action Jun 1938* |
| Jud Colman | |
| Ralph Cantor | *Killed in action Jun 1937* |
| Maurice Levine | |
| Edward Swindells | *Killed in action Feb 1937* |
| George Westfield | *Killed in action Oct 1937* |
| **Arrived Jan 1937** | |
| Bert Masky | *Killed in action Feb 1937* |
| George Brown | *Killed in action Jun 1937* |
| **Arrived Feb 1937** | |
| Benny Goldman | |
| Cyril Bowman | *Killed in action Jun 1937* |
| Bernard McKenna | |
| **Arrived May 1937** | |
| Wilfred Winnick | |
| **Arrived Feb 1938** | |
| Benny Goodman | |
| Sol Simon | |
| Monty Rosenfield | |

education and speaking Russian, German, French and English. One of his brothers was involved in the socialist movement and may have been a Bolshevik Party member. Bert was politically active as a teenager and was imprisoned by the Tsarist regime for distributing radical pamphlets in 1907, aged just 14. On release, he went into exile, first in Germany and then to London, arriving in 1912. Conscripted into the British Army, he spent most of the war in Charlton Park, London, as the battalion barber. As a German speaker, he was employed in questioning German prisoners. However, his attendance at the prisoners' socialist meetings and his urging of others to attend them led to his premature demobilisation.

In 1918, the then Bert Masky married miner's daughter Sarah Boon. They moved to Cheetham in Manchester, opened a barbershop and had two children together. At that time, women who married 'aliens' had to relinquish their citizenship and carry a registration booklet, so Sarah Masky from Staffordshire became a Russian citizen. After some six years, Bert began a relationship with Hilda Wild, sister of Sam Wild, and they had a son together. He lived between two houses for the next decade and eventually settled with Hilda. After Bert's decision, Sarah spent considerable time trying to regain British nationality, which she did on 3 February 1933.

Meanwhile, the barber's shop became the unofficial headquarters of Cheetham CP and YCL, and a library and bookshop specialising in left-leaning European literature. From the shop, Bert collected money for the Workers Loan to Soviet Russia, a scheme established in 1921 to raise funds for famine relief in Russia. Bert joined the Party in 1922 and would invite Russian sailors he met at Salford docks to speak to audiences at the Free Trade Hall, acting as a translator. Not surprisingly, he came under Special Branch's watch and was arrested and imprisoned in Brixton prison, awaiting deportation as an undesirable alien. The problem for Special Branch was that the Soviet Union labelled him a Trotskyite because of the activities of his elder brother and wouldn't accept his repatriation. Bert was released from prison and put under surveillance. Manchester's detective chief inspector King made a habit of having his hair cut at Bert's barbershop until Bert lost the shop in a game of cards.

Like Maurice Levine and others, Bert learned to box through the Jewish Lads' club and fought the Blackshirts on the streets

*Sarah Maransky's passport (courtesy David Mason)*

of Cheetham until in 1936, he went to fight in Spain, convincing Hilda's brother Sam Wild to go with him. The circumstances of his death are unknown, but it is thought that because he was a Yiddish speaker, he may well have been employed as an interpreter and killed when headquarters came under artillery fire. Regardless, his body was never recovered, and his grandson David Mason has speculated he might have even fled to the US to join his elder brother in Baltimore. Sarah's next battle, after Bert's death, was supporting their two sons. The state would have demanded a death certificate for Bert before giving her any support, and it is doubtful if a letter from Harry Pollitt would have been acceptable. The 1938 minutes of the Women's Section of Blackley Labour Party include a report of an IB widow with two children who had been begging for money. And in 1944, Sarah became secretary of that Women's Section. In 1980 Sam Wild replied to a letter from Bert's grandson about Bert's short time in Spain.

> We were in the same group until we arrived at the IB training base in Spain. We separated when Bert was transferred to headquarters as an interpreter with his knowledge of Russian, French and German. Bert was killed on 12 February, on the first day of the Battle of Jarama. I was wounded on the same day. I had a great liking for Bert and nobody knew him better than me.[462]

When Maurice Levine returned from Spain, they wouldn't give him his old job because he had left without permission. He managed to get some paid work from the Dependants Aid Fund, which meant breaking the news to mothers that their sons had been killed in Spain. Many of the fallen he had known personally: Ralph Cantor from Cheetham, Alec Armstrong from Hulme, Fred Killick, Bert Maskey and, in particular, Victor Shammah. Born in South Manchester, Victor came from a Syrian Sephardi family who were cotton merchants. He went to Clifton College, a public school with a Jewish house but had to return home due to the family's financial difficulties following his father's death in 1932. Victor Shammah became the secretary of the Didsbury YCL and the first Manchester Challenge Club organiser. He was a clerk when he volunteered to fight in Spain in January 1937 and was killed on the Aragon front in March 1938, aged 24. Maurice wrote: "His death was a great blow to his sisters and family; he was only a young man, quite an intelligent young fellow."[463]

Frank Allaun had been Shammah's best friend and said that his death changed him forever. To raise funds for the Dependants Aid Committee, Maurice arranged for Paul Robeson, who was touring the UK at the time, to sing at the Free Trade Hall. He also managed to find work at the co-operative society but left to go back to garment making.

> I left the Co-op after a certain amount of hostility. I was one of only two left-wingers and I was the only Jew working there. The fact that I had been in the Spanish Civil War didn't go down well with some of the employees.[464]

When Maurice was called up for the Second World War, he requested to join the navy but was refused entry because his parents were not naturalised. He joined the army instead and asked to be admitted to the parachute regiment. At interview, he spoke about his combat experience in Spain, yet despite passing as A1, was given a menial job as a billet orderly. After complaining to MP Willie Gallacher, Maurice was transferred to a Royal Army Service Corps involved in the Normandy landings and became a regimental policeman.

Towards the end of the war, he was part of a committee that attempted to set up a forces parliament in Germany based on the one in Cairo. In Egypt, British officers had encouraged discussion groups among the men. By February 1944, the groups had developed into a more formal debating society based on the structure of the Westminster Parliament, with hundreds of troops attending the debates and a speaker appointed. A mock general election was held that produced a large majority for a Commonwealth and Labour Party coalition, which then proposed policies for the nationalisation of banks, land, mines, and transport.

The Labour 'Prime Minister' of the Forces Parliament was Henry Solomons, a Jew from Stepney, east London. Solomons was eventually to become a Labour MP in the House of Commons. The two other individuals most referred to as drivers of the Parliament were Leo Abse, a Jewish Welshman descended from Polish émigrés, and communist Sam Bardell, secretary to the Parliament. At a meeting of some 600 troops, senior officers arrived with military police to shut down the Parliament. The ringleaders were detained and posted elsewhere. Two other smaller parliaments emerged at Mhow and Deolali in India, and the movement has echoes of the Putney debates of 1649. Maurice's attempts to set up a forces parliament in Germany were never allowed to get off the ground.

It is worth noting that it was significantly more difficult for Jewish women to get involved in politics than Jewish men. In the Party, Jewish women were a minority within a minority. There was pressure upon Jewish women from parents and religious authority to stay at home and within the bounds of their community. Most families in Cheetham were orthodox or moderately observant. Significantly, many Jewish men who became communists married outside their community. Communism was a means of rebellion and a passage into broader society. One way that young Jewish women could meet with communists and other radicals was through social events organised by the Challenge Club. As well as hosting meetings and reading groups, it had a vibrant social life with 200-300 young people attending Sunday night dances. There were *Daily Worker* bazaars and days out rambling led by Benny. One suspects young Jewish women were there with or without their parents' knowledge.[465]

The Clyne sisters remembered unemployed men hanging around Cheetham looking for trouble and how Jewish youth were driven out of a local ice rink by Blackshirts. Jewish girls did not generally get involved in physical confrontation with fascists, though at aged 17 Lily Clyne was arrested for obstructing the police when they tried to arrest her father for hitting a fascist.

Lily was fined five shillings, her father 20 shillings. Often the girls would provide first aid to injured male comrades.

Rather than being drawn to communism by a sense of Jewish consciousness, it seems more likely that Jewish comrades made their way there because of the same historical circumstances as non-Jews. They were no doubt subject to a higher sensitivity because of the growing threat of antisemitic fascism, the experience of their parents and their own everyday experience of prejudice. Whilst the official arbiters of Jewish consciousness, the Board of Deputies and the *Jewish Chronicle*, were stridently opposed to communism, even anti-fascist activity, their authority was opposed by the sons and daughters of émigrés driven out of Eastern Europe. They were Jews for whom Judaism or Zionism did not provide salvation.

# Chapter 17

## Culture Front

> "'We must take the theatre onto the streets,' we said, 'we must take theatre to the masses.' So how should we go about the task of forging ourselves into a weapon for the class struggle?" Ewan MacColl, *Journeyman*

The logic of the popular front demanded communists intervene in their national culture. Culture was an arena in which fascism could be opposed and socialism built, not just through cultural production, but by creating alliances with intellectuals and artists, thereby enlisting their reputations and influencing their work. The Party in the 1930s and 1940s was overwhelmingly a workers' organisation; middle-class individuals and intellectuals were aware of their minority status. However, from the mid-1930s, academics, actors, writers and musicians were recruited to the Party and terms such as 'Bloomsbury Bolshies' and the 'Mayfair Marxists' came with them. Their involvement extended the reach of communist ideas and provided a new audience for the artists. For some, it proved a good career move; for others, the association was damaging.

Communists believed in the 'democratisation of the arts', making high-culture available for working people. They were also pro-Soviet and wanted others to make that point. The world was understood as increasingly dividing into two camps: fascist and communist, and it was time for people of conscience to act. Many, if not most, bohemians were left-leaning, some seeing communism as an exotic ideology; both emerging and well-established artists gave their support, though some fleetingly. There was also the context that capitalism was perceived as failing economically and socially. The Party's cultural activities appealed to an anti-American and anti-commercial ethic that existed in such circles at the time. During the two decades, the Party exercised an influence well beyond its size in political and industrial spheres. This was achieved through hard work by members and the alliances made in broad-based campaigns; the same was true of the cultural sphere.

## Left Book Club

The Left Book Club (LBC) was not strictly a Party initiative. The majority of its members and activists were probably not Party members, who were busy building CPGB branches. However, it was closely aligned in most people's minds if not indistinguishable from the CPGB, and the Party significantly contributed to the success of the enterprise.

Its creator was London publisher Victor Gollancz who was closely aligned to the Party but never joined. He worked alongside Labour Party member Harold Laski and another communist sympathiser, the journalist John Strachey, to create Britain's first national book club in May 1936. Members paid two shillings and sixpence for a 'left book of the month', chosen by Gollancz and his two colleagues. The orange, cloth-covered editions were inexpensive for the time, previously unpublished and frequently explicitly written for the club. In its lifetime, it published 257 new books; titles included *The Struggle for Peace* by Stafford Cripps, *Days of Contempt* by André Malraux, *The Labour Party in Perspective* by Clement Attlee, *Spanish Testament* by Arthur Koestler, and *The Road to Wigan Pier* by George Orwell. Subscribers, who had to accept the monthly choice of the selection committee, also received a copy of a monthly magazine, *Left Book News*. Each edition contained a lengthy review of left literature by either Strachey or Laski and an editorial by Gollancz, a summary of club activities and a monthly survey of the Soviet Union. The LBC's published aims were:

> To help the struggle for world peace and a better social and economic order and against fascism... by increasing the knowledge of those who already see the importance of the struggle, and... adding to their number the very many who hold aloof from the fight by reason of ignorance or apathy.[466]

The club had three main areas of coverage: the threat of

war, the danger of fascism, the blight of unemployment. To save on postage the books were distributed to members through bookshops and the participation of LBC activists was necessary for the project to succeed. A previously untapped audience drawn to affordable left-leaning texts was also sought, and quickly found. Gollancz's target club membership was 5,000—after one month they had achieved 6,000 members, and at the end of the first year there were 40,000 members. In broader publishing, few books at the time sold 50,000 a year. LBC was producing 40,000 copies of 12 titles a year—nothing short of a revolution in publishing.

Frank Allaun, who had joined the Party in 1935 and worked at Collets bookshop on the edge of Manchester city centre, placed an advertisement in Left Book News in July 1936, announcing the launch of a Manchester group. By the end of the year there were almost 1,000 members. Such large attendance at central Manchester meetings made discussion of texts impractical, so as an alternative, national speakers were invited. The first speaker in November 1937 was Sylvia Pankhurst. Frank Allaun:

> Manchester LBC… held meetings attended by up to 200 at the Burlington café opposite the university. AJP Taylor, Professor Laski, Willie Paul, introduced the discussions.[467]

Other speakers included Ellen Wilkinson, Aneurin Bevan, Gollancz, Strachey and the scientist JBS Haldane. Whilst the central Manchester LBC was effectively running monthly political rallies, other smaller groups across the city were able to have discussion groups. Soon these were organised by Frank Allaun in advance, and the backroom of Collets had gone from a place to distribute books to an administrative centre for the LBC. Comrade and secondary school teacher Ted Ainley, who had run classes on Marxism at Cheetham Challenge Club, led training sessions for discussion leaders in Manchester and day schools for those further afield. Ainley provided a critical appraisal of each monthly book, suggesting questions to be considered. These were circulated to discussion leaders across the city. As well as being extremely active as a discussion leader himself, he consequently became influential at meetings at which he was not present.

Before long people from the same occupations organised themselves into discrete groups. There were LBC groups for teachers, rail workers, taxi drivers, poets, engineers and others. The national poetry group launched a magazine, *Poetry and the People*, "20 badly duplicated pages inside a hand-drawn cover".[468] A Manchester LBC poetry group was formed in July 1939 by engineer Ray Watkinson. Watkinson was born in Flixton and studied at the Manchester Regional School of Art. During the war he was a technical illustrator at Manchester's Avro aircraft factory. He became an art historian, an expert on William Morris and the Pre-Raphaelites.

The poetry group organised readings, and published one issue of a magazine, *The Plough*. Eddie Frow set up an engineers' group in Salford. A host of supplementary activities were generated by the LBC: social events, Russian language classes, theatre trips, education classes. Pre-existing societies, such as local photography and chess clubs, affiliated to the LBC. By 1938 there were over 4,000 booksellers nationwide involved in distributing books; *Left Book News* became *Left News* and issues were running up to 48 pages in length. One of the most successful outcomes of the LBC was establishing the LBC Theatre Guild, a network of amateur theatre companies committed to producing political theatre. By September 1939, there were some 300 theatre groups established across Britain. Manchester LBC Theatre Guild's first recorded performance was *On Guard for Spain*, a massed chant by Jack Lindsay, performed after a meeting on 20 September 1937.

The movement came at an auspicious time. A Popular Front Government which included communists was elected in France in May 1936, and British interest in the Spanish Civil War began. Whilst there was little opposition to the National Government, the LBC offered people a sense of hope and direction, and it invited and supported self-organisation. What started as a national book club became a political movement and a system of education. At the Ashton Under Lyne LBC, east of Manchester, money was collected for Aid for Spain and a member of the International Brigade addressed members. Along with the AEU, the CPGB and the Women's Co-operative Guild, the Ashton group set up a conference on 'Spain and the European Situation'.[469] The central Manchester group set up the Manchester China Protest Committee in response to Japan's invasion in 1937. In west Manchester, Urmston and Flixton LBC organised a China relief campaign. A national LBC rally in London in 1937 filled the Albert Hall with several thousand left outside. The Manchester contingent organised a train for the event, and a local rally was held in the city in March of the same year. From the back of Collets bookshop, Frank Allaun even organised LBC trips to the Soviet Union.

> I organised three boat visits to Leningrad and Moscow. Whole ships were filled in this way. They were so successful and remunerative to Collets that it was decided to set up a separate travel agency in London.[470]

Working alongside Frank at Collets was Bessie Wild (née Berry). Bessie joined the Party in the mid-1930s after a visit to the Soviet Union, possibly organised through the LBC. "I was so very impressed with what I'd seen in the Soviet Union. I had no background in the Labour Movement."[471] Bessie's son, Mike Wild, who was born in 1939, remembers LBC titles in the home decades later. "Our walls were covered in orange books. I read some as a kid, *The Distressed Areas* by Wal Hannington and *The Road to Wigan Pier*."[472]

The Nazi-Soviet pact of August 1939 destroyed the unity of the movement, and it destroyed its credibility. The LBC had argued, like the Party, that there was an irreconcilable conflict between fascism and communism, yet here was a compromise. For three years, it had fed members that a pro-Soviet alliance against fascism was the solution for peace in Europe. The leadership of the LBC split. Gollancz and Laski supported Britain's war effort; John Strachey supported the Party line that it was an imperialist war. Pro- and anti-Soviet groups developed in the Club, and when it began publishing anti-Soviet literature, communists began to leave. By 1940 membership had dropped from 57,000 to 36,000. In 1936, Ben Ainley had believed the popular front was the "paramount issue of the day" and he had sat as the CPGB representative on the local branch of the National Council for Civil Liberties, campaigned for CPGB affiliation to the Labour Party and above all else, had been active in the LBC. In 1939 his activity in the club ended. Frank Allaun, who had moved to London to work for the recently launched Collets tour operator, returned to Manchester and found himself out of work.

The LBC was on the front line of a cultural conflict. It created an influential movement that contributed to the election of the 1945 Labour government: there were 11 LBC authors in Attlee's cabinet, including the prime minister himself. Some of the books published, such as Morton's *A People's History of England*

and Orwell's *The Road to Wigan Pier*, became established titles. Engineer Eddie Frow had six LBC members in his toolroom, and he would cycle down from Salford to pick up books for them from Frank Allaun. Ruth Frow:

> Many years later, when as Manchester district secretary of the union, he visited a factory and walked through the toolroom, a man he recognised opened his cupboard to show the volumes which were still being read 30 years later.[473]

Eddie himself, like many of his comrades, became a bookworm, an autodidact. The Party appealed to self-educating working men and women, operating as an Open University of its time. Culturally, the most important popular front initiative the Party was involved in was the LBC. In Frow's case, it proved to be a seed that gave birth to a precious archive.

## Pageants and Patriotism

People rarely make pageants these days. We are too fractured, and our history too contested to accommodate them. They were a pursuit born of Edwardian England, the Sherborne pageant of 1905 being one of the earliest events which would become a staple of public cultural life until the 1950s. A pageant was commonly understood as a mass spectacle event where participants performed, in costume, scenes from history. There was usually a musical accompaniment as well as scripted dialogue, narration and verse. The historical scenes were expected to be germane to a locality, an anniversary or a theme. At Sherborne in Dorset, there were 11 episodes, the first dramatising "The Coming of Ealdhelm" in AD705, the last the arrival of Sir Walter Raleigh in 1593. There were 90 speaking parts and five performances in the ruins of Sherborne Castle.

Some outdoor pageants were preceded by processions, but processions alone were not considered pageants, despite what the poster might have said. Choirs often sang hymns and many pageants included church representation or dramatised episodes from religious history. The hymn *Jerusalem* was popularised by being sung at pageants, as was *Land of Hope and Glory*. Pageants were mass affirmations of historical tradition.

By the 1930s, pageant making was commonplace across classes and rural and urban settings. Reviewers wrote in terms

*Culture Front*

*courtesy WCML*

*CPGB pageant Manchester, 18 June 1938 (courtesy WCML)*

of a pageant season. The centenary of the Liverpool Manchester Railway was celebrated by a mass *Pageant of Transport* in Liverpool in 1930. The pageant master was Edward Genn, his director Matthew Anderson, and together they worked on large-scale pageants across the north between 1926 and 1934. The Party saw an opportunity for a more radical interpretation of history, and the norm of turning audiences into actors appealed. In September 1936, the London District Communist Party organised a processional pageant involving up to 20,000 people marching from Embankment via Hyde Park to Shoreditch. Banners were carried depicting the Peasants' Revolt, Thomas More, Cromwell's New Model Army, Peterloo, and the Chartists. There was a portrait banner of Felicia Browne, comrade and artist who was the first British casualty of the Spanish Civil War.[474] The *Daily Worker*'s perspective was that communist involvement in pageant making provided the working classes with their rightful place in English history. As the paper put it:

Historical elbow room, gained for the English proletariat in its historic mission, was one dearly bought by struggle on England's very own soil.[475]

Banners on the march declared: "The Communist Party fights for democracy and progress" and, "The Communist Party fights for peace and freedom and a merry England."[476] It is unclear, arguably doubtful, that there were any dramatised scenes at Hyde Park or elsewhere.

In July 1937, the Lancashire District of the Party held a *Pageant of English History* in Manchester. Between 1,500 and 3,000 people marched to Debdale Park, Gorton, carrying banners portraying the struggle of Lancashire people: images of Peterloo, of crippled children in mills and the Rochdale pioneers. The banners of 18 Party branches formed a semi-circle around a platform from which Harry Pollitt spoke, standing in for an ensemble cast. The following year Manchester City Council held a *Manchester History Pageant* to mark its centenary. There were 70 actors, a chorus of 27, an extensive musical accompaniment and ten performances. The event did not include a commemoration of Peterloo. A week before, the Party had held its pageant on Fallowfield sports fields with a banner dedicated to the massacre of 1819. On this occasion participants were in costume and there was community singing but, once again, it seems the only drama were the speeches by Harry Pollitt and Tom Mann.

In the spring of 1938, to no avail, the local Party proposed that the official May Day demonstration should involve a political pageant. It was a rebuttal that has to be seen in the context of a TUC circular of January 1934 barring communists from admission to trades councils. The Party termed this the "Black Circular" and, in Manchester, it resulted in expulsions of Eddie Frow, Ben Ainley and Syd Jenkins from Manchester and Salford Trades Council.

Whilst in Manchester the Party was flirting with the form, in London the composer Alan Bush and the poet Randall Swingler, both comrades, were pageant makers for the Royal Albert Hall, working alongside national and international talent including WH Auden and Paul Robeson. In 1939 they collaborated to produce a large-scale *Festival of Music and the People*. It was ambitious in scale, seeking to be both popular and politically committed. The programme consisted of three concerts, Swingler writing the historical pageant, Paul Robeson and

Parry Jones the principal singers, with 500 other voices from 23 London Co-operative choirs. There were also 100 dancers. Swingler's text was set to music by 12 composers including Vaughan Williams, and scenes were dramatised in tableaux. Party historian Andy Croft:

> It was part theatre, part recruitment meeting, educational, propagandist and enjoyable. Amateurs worked with professionals and the audience was itself part of the spectacle, their history the subject of the performance as real historical figures 'played' themselves on stage.[477]

Involvement in pageants did help to push the parameters of ideas inside and outside the organisation. Communism claimed a place in English history, by suggesting a communist element was present, hidden from us by the establishment. And likewise, it permitted comrades to embrace their nation's past. People sought authenticity through pageants, folk music and pastimes such as Morris dancing, but it was always a manufactured authenticity, and sometimes they tried too hard. During the *Music and the People* pageant, for the French Revolution scene, Woodcraft Folk children danced around a guillotine. In 1948 Alan Bush and Montagu Slater produced a *Communist Manifesto Centenary Pageant* at the Royal Albert Hall. It was described as "a largely inward-looking affair".[478] Another planned for the following year on the English Civil War was cancelled. The Cold War put an end to communist pageants as film and television would bring the curtain down on pageants themselves.

## Ewan MacColl

Jimmie Miller was born in Salford in 1915, changing his name to Ewan MacColl in 1945. He left school in 1930 during the Depression and found it almost impossible to get work. His parents were Scots, his mother possessing a repertoire of traditional folk songs, and his father was a trade unionist who had been blacklisted in Scotland. MacColl became best known as a singer and writer of folk songs, a key figure in the British folk revival in the 1950s and 1960s. He is the author of numerous plays and songs, including the very popular *The First Time Ever I Saw Your Face* and *Dirty Old Town*. The *Manchester Rambler* was inspired by the Kinder trespass of 1932.

At 14, MacColl joined the Clarion Players, an amateur

socialist theatre group in Salford. They took their name from the Clarion cycling clubs of the late 19th and early 20th century, part of a socialist cultural movement born of Robert Blatchford's 1890s newspaper *The Clarion*. The group met and rehearsed at the house of Lance Helman. Lance's father, Morris Helman, a ladies' tailor, was born in Kovno, Russia in 1879. He had been a Bundist in Russia and brought his radical political ideas to Manchester. The Helmans were part of a cultural movement centred around the playwright Henrik Ibsen, naming all their children after characters in Ibsen's plays.

In his mid-teens MacColl was more interested in politics than in Ibsen and soon split from the group. He had recently joined the YCL and wanted to get involved in the Workers Theatre Movement, a national network of radical theatre groups aligned to the Party. Actors performed sketches in non-theatre spaces, even from the back of a coal lorry to picket lines and demonstrations. A group of seven, including MacColl, all unemployed, formed an agitprop company calling themselves the Red Megaphones. The name was taken directly from Das Rote Sprachrohr, a Berlin company that collaborated directly with the propaganda department of the German Communist Party. It was the first of four companies in five years that MacColl would be involved in.

Agitprop developed in Russia and Germany, the word a compound of propaganda and agitation and its practice was to evoke an emotional response in the audience over a political issue. It was mobile revolutionary art, theatre taken to audiences distant from playhouses. It went back to where theatre began—on the back of a cart rolling into a village—back to the avant-garde. It relied on repetition, short phrases and stark imagery, possibly because the performers were in front of inattentive audiences. The Red Megaphones rehearsed in a disused cellar beneath Salford Workers' Arts Club. "It was cold, dark, dirty and it smelled bad. We rehearsed by candlelight."[479] Eddie Frow describes their performance style.

> ... it was really a method of putting over a message to a crowd of people outside that was different than just one person speaking. Four would get up on the platform and the first one would shout out a slogan, the second one would pick it up, the third one would carry it on then they would all do it in unison. Something that was

like a drill, it had a tremendous dramatic effect because you must remember that there was a tremendous tradition of open-air meetings. There were many, many places like Stevenson Square and innumerable places in Salford. There were traditional meeting places from the time of the Socialist Movement and earlier than that. Another big meeting place was outside Labour Exchanges where you had to go and sign on twice a week, you'd nothing to do with your time.[480]

In 1933 the Red Megaphones transformed themselves into Theatre of Action. They wanted to move beyond agitprop sketches to produce plays, and they wanted to move from the back of the cart onto a stage and develop as actors, writers and producers. They spent a great deal of time in Salford Arts Club cellar, and MacColl spent a great deal of time in Manchester's central reference library reading drama. He was also preoccupied with RADA trained Londoner, Joan Littlewood, who joined the group as a co-producer from Rusholme Repertory Theatre. A week after she walked out of repertory, they were married. Together they embarked on a quest for theatrical forms that would suit their purpose of engaging working-class audiences in political theatre. They looked back, even as far as the Greeks, but also to "the country rituals, the mumming plays, mysteries and moralities from which our classical theatre had evolved".[481] They also read how the Russian Revolution had transformed theatre in the Soviet Union.

Vsevolod Meyerhold was a leading theatre director in Tsarist Russia. The opening night of his production of the Russian classic, *Masquerade*, at the Alexandrinsky Imperial Theatre in Petrograd coincided with the first night of the February Revolution, gunfire audible to the audience. The Bolsheviks appreciated theatre's importance to the struggle for communism, and soon after the October Revolution, theatres were nationalised. Over 100 artists were invited to a meeting in Petrograd to discuss the relationship between art and communism, but only a few attended, including Meyerhold, who was awarded a senior position in Petrograd theatre. The revolution had precipitated a groundswell of new theatre-making and in audiences, a "craze for theatricalisation...there are reports of villages with as many as five theatres".[482] New audiences create new possibilities for dramatists. Peasants and workers who had never been to the theatre had fewer pre-conceptions on what to expect. The new theatre saw its function as informing people about the new political situation, thus the "living newspaper" emerged, with actors dramatising events and proposing social action.

The Bolsheviks had a civil war to win and had little time to oversee the arts, leaving the dramatists free to experiment. Meyerhold began to develop physical theatre practice, employing what he called *biomechanics*, stylised movement based on ballet. Another method that emerged at this time was the breaking down of the division between actor and audience. Mass spectacle events were produced, for example, Nikolai Evreinov's *Storming of the Winter Palace* (1921), which involved 10,000 performers and an audience of 100,000. In a more traditional context, actors would walk out of character to introduce the play and then return; performers would be planted in the audience to bring them into the narrative. Turning spectators into actors was central to the new practice.

In Manchester, Ewan MacColl and Joan Littlewood researched and absorbed these ideas and applied them to their work. MacColl explains in his autobiography *Journeyman*:

> Meyerhold and Vakhtangov had explored uncharted areas of stage and audience relationships. Stanislavsky had found psychological solutions for the actors' problems, while Meyerhold had attempted to solve them in another way—via the circus and the commedia dell'arte. Biomechanics was an attempt to escape from naturalistic acting.[483]

The company recruited a dance teacher, and in the confines of the Salford cellar, actor and roof slater Alec Armstrong from Hulme tried so hard to escape from a naturalistic setting his head hit the ceiling. Eighteen-year-old Henry Suss from Cheetham joined the company in 1933. At the time he was not a member of the Party or the YCL and his interest in theatre was partly drawn from necessity.

> I became interested in the theatre because when I was a lad, I had a terrible stammer. I could not complete a sentence within a minute or two. These alternative medical people said "Speak, speak, speak and keep

speaking. That will restore confidence". There was a school play, it was called *Fresh Fields* by Ivor Novella. I only spoke about two lines but I had this stutter and coped with it.[484]

He first saw Theatre of Action at a Harry Pollitt meeting in Manchester performing a mass declamation.

Mass Declamation is poetry with a militant message. I was intrigued by that. I thought this is my cup of tea. I was young and so I joined them. We used to go to all sorts; co-operative societies. There was a Communist Party member, the Rev. Étienne Watts of All Saints, Manchester, and he would invite us to his church hall.

Henry was among the youngest members of the ten-strong company. "Only two were communists", including IB volunteer Victor Shammah's sister, Esther. Henry performed in "Blackburn, Warrington, Bolton, Preston. Audience size: between 30 and 80 people", until he got married aged 23, by which time he had joined the Party. In 1935 they produced the British premiere of Clifford Odets' *Waiting for Lefty*, which attracted new talent to the company. MacColl and Littlewood then went to London to teach their methods with hopes of travelling to Moscow to learn more. They were unsuccessful in both regards.

In 1936 they returned to Manchester and formed Theatre Union. Their first production was *Miracle at Verdun* by Hans Schlumberg, staged at the Friends Meeting House for Manchester Peace Week. Austrian playwright Schlumberg had served in the First World War as a young lieutenant. He survived to write a series of anti-war plays. In *Miracle at Verdun*, the French and German dead rise from their graves and walk home carrying their crosses to a world that doesn't want them. In a dreadful irony, during a rehearsal of the play in Leipzig, Schlumberg fell into the orchestra pit from the stage, dying of his injuries. Aid for Spain events provided a subject and a platform at venues like the Free Trade Hall. MacColl:

As the Spanish Civil War dragged on, we found ourselves becoming more and more involved with it and soon we were staging pageants and specially written dramatic episodes for public meetings and demonstrations.

> Indeed, some of the dramatic interludes staged at Medical Aid for Spain rallies rank among our most successful experiments. In them we carried the agitprop form to new heights.[485]

Vsevolod Meyerhold was arrested in June 1939 for accusing the Soviet authorities of eliminating art. Whilst in prison, his wife was murdered by agents from the NKVD (People's Commissariat for Internal Affairs). Sixty-five-year-old Meyerhold was tortured until he confessed to spying and then shot. In the same year, Alec Armstrong was arrested for taking part in a banned demonstration that attempted to lay an anti-war wreath at the Manchester cenotaph. In February 1937, he was killed in Spain at the Battle of Jarama. In 1932 the security services opened a file on MacColl and MI5 informed the BBC, preventing both him and Littlewood from working there for a spell. In 1940, MacColl and Littlewood were arrested when police stopped a performance of a living newspaper piece called *The Last Edition*.

The war years are omitted from MacColl's autobiography; they are a contentious episode. His security file, now in the public domain, provides the Army's side of the story. MacColl, or Private Miller, enlisted in July 1940 and deserted on 18 December 1940. Upon enquiry, the Lieutenant Colonel of the King's Regiment reported to his Major that Miller was:

> Well educated but boastful of his knowledge regarding military matters... Has made no great effort to influence fellow soldiers but appears to have interested them by his wide knowledge of Soviet Russia... Regularly receives copies of the *Daily Worker*... His talks on Soviet Russia to his fellow soldiers could reasonably be considered under this heading... He was employed as a clerk but was returned to his duties for lack of interest in his work... He served in the International Brigade in the recent war in Spain.[486]

He hadn't fought in Spain, but he may have received letters from Alec Armstrong during the few months before Armstrong was killed, and he would also have picked up plenty of details about the fighting from the *Daily Worker* or rallies that Sam Wild and others addressed. The police made several attempts to arrest Miller by calling at his family home and believed him to be inside but didn't force entry. The army wasn't desperate to have him back. At the end of the war, when he and Littlewood launched the company, Theatre Workshop, Miller renamed himself MacColl, which he may have seen as a necessity to avoid attention and a prison sentence. MacColl and Littlewood divorced in 1953, with MacColl devoting himself to creating a vibrant folk music revival and Littlewood establishing a home for Theatre Workshop in east London. Whilst working there she wrote *Oh, What a Lovely War* (1963), a musical, experimental in form, utilising an electronic newspaper behind actors, who invited the audience to join them in singing music hall songs.

## Arms and the poet

Of all art forms, poetry is best known for taking a political stand in the 1930s. Comrades turned to it to express their deeply held convictions and career poets rallied to the cause of anti-fascism, some in an effort to establish their credentials. The subject that most inspired them was Spain and many IB members tried their hand at verse for the first time. Indeed, Sam Wild was the inspiration for several poems by fellow brigaders and, it is thought, by Nancy Cunard. Though Manchester did not produce any poets of note during the period, comrades explored poetry contemporary and otherwise. The Left Book Club ran poetry readings and created new readers, the *Daily Worker* and other Party publications reviewed poetry, with Randall Swingler as the *Worker*'s poetry editor. Just as there were growing political divisions at the time, so there was rupture in poetry. A new movement emerged, and eventually a new poetry establishment. The style was modernist rather than traditional, innovative and scholarly, but too opaque for some, and not written for the majority.

The pre-eminent literary group in Britain during the 1930s was a coterie of poets centred around W H Auden. The Auden Group, or the Auden Generation, included Christopher Isherwood, Stephen Spender and Edward Upward. Cecil Day-Lewis, Louis MacNeice, Auden and Spender were later described as the MacSpaunday poets; combined, they became more simply defined as the Thirties Poets. All were left-leaning, most becoming members of the Party or fellow travellers. It is doubtful that they were ever in the same room at once, but they were all artists who believed in publicly taking a stand, particularly over Spain.

At the centre of the wheel was Wystan Hugh Auden. Born in

York in 1907, he became a major figure in 20th century English literature, close behind W B Yeats and T S Eliot. He was once described as the "Kipling of the Left" though his political views, which changed later, cannot sum up his work. He never joined the Party, and though he went to Spain during the civil war, it is not established what his contribution was. The *Daily Worker* reported "Famous Poet [W H Auden] to Drive Ambulance in Spain", though there is no evidence that he ever did. It is claimed that he asked to be a stretcher bearer; had he taken on the job, he would have written about it, providing he had survived. Auden was in Spain for a few months in early 1937, broadcasting for the government radio station in Valencia. He wrote very little about the war but did hand over "a bundle" of poems to the Spanish Medical Aid Committee (SMAC) that were lost. On his return, he wrote a pamphlet length poem, *Spain*, that was sold for a shilling a go to raise money for the SMAC. It is the most well-known and oft-quoted poem from the conflict, though he later rejected it from his collected poems, describing it as dishonest. In *Inside the Whale*, Orwell described the poem as "one of the few decent things to have been written about the Spanish war". Auden's poetry is often distant, his style more cerebral than intuitive. Spender describes the pamphlet as "a bird's eye view of Spain… the element of personal experience and direct emotional response is rigorously excluded".[487]

Unlike Auden, Stephen Spender joined the Party in February 1937 and was possibly the most well-known poet to do so. There was an editorial fanfare in the *Daily Worker* for an episode that was to last a matter of weeks. Spender, who was 27 when he joined, was discovered as a poet by Eliot and as a potential recruit by Pollitt. At that point he had written a collection of short stories and a long poem, *Forward from Liberalism*, in praise of the Austrian socialist uprising in 1934, published by the Left Book Club (LBC). It proposed that the liberalism of the 1930s had to shift left in response to economic conditions and the rise of fascism. It was also critical of the Moscow show trials. Labelled as a book that sent undergraduates to Spain, decades later, Tony Benn described it as "one of the books that converted a generation".[488]

The Party actively recruited LBC authors and other intellectuals, a departure from its fiercely proletarian fixation of the 1920s and early 1930s. It was Randall Swingler who initially invited Spender to the *Daily Worker* offices and asked him to review poetry for the paper. Then Pollitt summoned Spender to the head office for a discussion, first reprimanding Spender for his criticism of the Soviet Union and then inviting him to join the International Brigades in Spain. Spender replied that he was no soldier, nor could he drive an ambulance or anything else, to which Pollitt is reputed to have said, the least he could do was to "go and get yourself killed to give the Party a Byron".[489] The remark has been cited as symptomatic of communist callousness but is possibly more characteristic of Pollitt's Mancunian humour. Pollitt then put another assignment to Spender. A Russian ship, the *Komsomol*, had been sunk in the Mediterranean by the Italian navy, and Moscow wanted to know where survivors were being held. Spender, who spoke Spanish, was asked to travel through Nationalist territory on a spying mission to find out. He travelled through Tangiers, Oran and Algiers and found the remainder of the Russian crew in Gibraltar. Had he been apprehended he may well have been shot, though what he determined could have been confirmed by telegram.

Spender returned to England in early February 1937 to be debriefed by Pollitt and to join the Party. On 19 February, the front page of the *Daily Worker* proclaimed "Spender for Spain". The poet was allowed almost half the editorial page to set out his reasons for joining, as well as a public recantation on his criticism of the first Moscow show trial, renouncing his own book.

> Sometime before my book had appeared, I had read the rest of the evidence, and I became convinced that there undoubtedly had been a gigantic plot against the Soviet Government and that the evidence was true. However, it was too late for me to alter my book.[490]

There is no doubt that *Daily Worker* editors liked to trumpet artists who gave their support to the Republic. Literary connections to IB volunteers, especially those killed, were emphasised. For example, in a list of 18 killed at the Battle of Teruel in February 1938, names and towns are mentioned, except in the case of Leslie Maugham of Kettering, who is described as the "great-nephew of Somerset Maugham".[491] Twenty-four-year-old Emmanuel Julius was killed advancing on a machine gun position during October 1936 and described as someone who "had written a number of poems, some of which were published".[492] Any writer or other kind of artist who spoke up for the Republic was given publicity. "Film Stars [Chaplin, Gable, Dietrich, Bette Davis, Joan Crawford] all back Spanish Republic." "Artists [Picasso, Heinrich Mann, Pablo Casals, Paul Robeson] to speak for Spain."[493] It was reported that 700 British writers and artists had petitioned the prime minister to restore the Spanish Government's right to buy arms. The Nationalists were portrayed as philistines and barbarians; after all they had murdered García Lorca.

If writers were useful publicity for the Republic's cause, some perceived the opposite to be the case. The young writer Julian Bell was the nephew of Virginia Woolf and had been friends with members of the Cambridge spy group. Though at one time a pacifist, he decided he wanted to fight for the Republic. His parents and his aunt tried to convince him otherwise, thus he agreed to volunteer as an ambulance driver rather than a soldier—a role, unbeknown to his family, that was equally as dangerous. Much of the driving had to be done at night, without headlights. In a letter to his brother Quentin, he gave as a reason for volunteering "the prestige one would gain in literature and even more, left politics".[494] In July 1937, during shelling in the Battle of Brunete, Bell was sheltering under his ambulance when a piece of shrapnel flew horizontally from the ground, embedding itself in his lung. He died a few days later; his last words were: "Well, I always wanted a mistress and a chance to go to war, and now I've had both."[495]

It is doubtful Spender got round to paying Party dues or attending his branch in west London. He was, however, applauded at a 7,000 strong LBC rally at the Albert Hall. "The transformation of Great Britain into a socialist state is imminent," announced Victor Gollancz.[496] Soon the Party requested Spender return to Spain to broadcast from the UGT-run radio station in Valencia as Auden had done.[497] Though Spender wrote for the *Daily Worker* for the best part of a year he was only a member of the Party for a matter of weeks. By February 1938, the Left Book Club was describing him as one of their former authors.

He wrote more poetry than most about the Spanish war and was enthused and moved by the poetry the conflict produced in English and Spanish. Spender's poems are not heroic in style and rarely about the casual heroism of others. They are personal, portraying his doubts and fears; the war is mentioned in an unexpected way, invading from elsewhere. His poetry is part informed by the fact that he wasn't a combatant and wasn't close to action, thus, some of it rests on abstractions. It's not hard to see why Spender would move away from the Party. What is more interesting is why he was attracted to it in the first place.

> I was driven on by a sense of social and personal guilt which made me feel firstly that I must take sides, secondly that I could purge myself of an abnormal individuality by co-operating with the workers' movement.[498]

His collaborator on *Poems for Spain*, John Lehmann, wrote of experiencing guilt in "ever smouldering fires" for not going to Spain. Cecil Day-Lewis wrote he "believed I ought to volunteer for it, but I lacked the courage to do so".[499] What Spender is referring to is the guilt borne merely of his social class. The Auden Generation members were socially privileged, a world away from the hungry 1930s. Many 1930s writers modified or changed their names to dissociate themselves from their class. Eric Blair became George Orwell and believed that to write about working-class people, you had to share their life, although as a teetotaller, he didn't frequent pubs. Critic William Empson claimed that Orwell also consciously changed his accent into a formalised cockney. Orwell didn't lack the courage or resolve to fight, though not as a communist of course, and in fact, became preoccupied with the Comintern's repression of the anarchist and POUM militias.

In 1937, the poet Nancy Cunard sent out a questionnaire to scores of writers on the Spanish Civil War issue. The result was *Left Review*'s *Authors Take Sides on the Spanish War*, a 10,000-word pamphlet of 148 contributions from the most renowned British writers of the decade. There is no entry in the pamphlet from Orwell. According to Nancy Cunard though, he did write a reply on the back of a questionnaire that she then forwarded on to poet Randall Swingler. It's a reply that reveals his antipathy for Auden and Spender and equates the conduct of communists with fascism.

> Will you please stop sending me this bloody rubbish. This is the second or third time I have had it. I am not one of your fashionable pansies like Auden and Spender. I was six months in Spain most of the time

fighting, I have a bullet-hole in me at present, and I am not going to write blah about defending democracy or gallant little anybody. Moreover, I know what is happening and has been happening on the Government side for months past, ie, that fascism is being riveted [sic] on the Spanish workers under the pretext of resisting fascism; also, that since May a reign of terror has been proceeding and all the jails and any place that will serve as a jail are crammed with prisoners who are not only imprisoned without trial but are half-starved, beaten and insulted. I dare say you know it too, though God knows anyone who could write the stuff overleaf would be fool enough to believe anything, even the war news in the *Daily Worker*. But the chances are that you—whoever you are who keep sending me this thing—have money and are well-informed; so no doubt you know something about the inner history of the war and have deliberately joined in the defence of "democracy" (ie capitalism) racket in order to aid in crushing the Spanish working class and thus indirectly defend your dirty little dividends.

By the way, tell your pansy friend Spender that I am preserving specimens of his war-heroics and that when the time comes when he squirms for shame at having written it, as the people who wrote the war-propaganda in the Great War are squirming now, I shall rub it in good and hard.[500]

Spain shaped allegiances and changed the course of literature amongst writers who saw themselves as part of the Left; no one more than in the case of Orwell and his later fiction.

Cheetham IB volunteer Ralph Cantor wrote in his diary for 13 April 1937: "Two American journalists accept poem for publication in United States."[501] The poetry of Battalion Commander Tom Wintringham and Clive Branson, also Party members, is anthologised alongside Spender and Auden. On the occasion of Sam Wild's 70th birthday John Shirle sent Sam two poems dedicated to the former Battalion Commander. It is uncertain whether Shirle fought in Spain but he recalls meeting Sam at the time in one of the poems.

Sam Wild

Dear Sam, you won't remember me
Long time ago you see
Nigh 40 years have passed
Since we last met
According to my memory.
And you, Sam Wild
With steady eyes unblinking
And tight grin, would
In the now old-fashioned words
Of those mixed days
Inspire in various ways
Democrats to take it on the chin
And then fight back
Against the odds
Despite the traitors and defeatists
Of that time
Many with power in the highest places.

But you and the original gallant few
Helped save our faces
Rescued British pride, and made
Through the British Battalion
Of the International Brigade
Many good people more aware
Of what would be in store
For all if there was war,
And how to combat and defeat
The Nazi fascist threat.[502]

John Shirle is possibly a pseudonym based on the John Shirle who was a leading figure in the Peasants' Revolt of 1381 alongside Wat Tyler, whom he compared to Sam in another of his poems. The poem reads as having been composed for Sam's birthday. In a later verse, the author refers to himself as being "on the active roll call of that time", by which he may mean that he fought in Spain or perhaps he was an anti-fascist activist. Though it appears that Shirle only met Sam briefly during the 1930s, he is nonetheless moved to dedicate a poem to him 40 years later. The experience of the civil war fused people, veterans in particular, together for the rest of their lives. After Franco's victory, people who had fought for or otherwise campaigned for the Spanish Republic from Britain were not publicly acclaimed as they are today; many were marginalised, even within the labour movement. Shirle writes of the IB rescuing "British pride", implying volunteers represented not just a political movement, but the nation, at a time when the political class shamed the country's reputation with its policy of non-intervention.

Ben Ainley's unpublished autobiography contains enough verse for a short publication, but it reads like he hadn't yet discovered the poetry of the 20th century. The communist-surrealist poet Roger Roughton was born in Bury, Greater Manchester. He edited *Contemporary Prose and Poetry*, which ran from 1936 to 1939, and was part of a London based group of surrealist poets led by David Gascoyne. Roughton took his own life in Dublin after news of the Nazi-Soviet Pact broke, though his half-sister, the novelist Deborah Moggach, believes it was because he had difficulties coming to terms with his sexuality.[503]

The years 1936-46 were a decade of commitment. Some writers found their voice and found acclaim through political commitment; others found their voice drowned out by the clamour. Some wore a mask to appeal to an audience; Stephen Spender and Auden disposed of theirs fairly quickly and publicly recanted. John Cornford and Randall Swingler were sincere and engaged in a flight from the privileges of their upbringing. Ewan MacColl's social class informed his work, but if his commanding officer was correct, he too wore a mask, and though he made much of his anti-fascism prior to the war, he was absent without leave when it came to the fighting in 1940. He did though, become influential in resurrecting the voice of working people through folk music. Poet Randall Swingler chose the front line and wrote from it, and his fate was to become almost unremembered.

*Comrades Come Rally*

## Chapter 18

# The Remains of Those Days

> "The fight became the determining factor: you learn more in struggle than when things are easy. We almost had it too easy. I know it's a Trotskyist point of view, but struggle does make you strong." Eric Jessop on war production

The defeat of the General Strike in 1926 and the Depression of the early 1930s drove socialists and trade unionists into retreat. Britain was governed by a national government from 1931, followed by a Conservative majority government, then a Conservative-led national government until 1945. Elsewhere in Europe, fascist parties were wrestling their way into dominance. By 1935 Adolf Hitler was rearming Germany and conscripting soldiers; the BUF was marching in Britain, as were the unemployed on hunger marches. Such was the severity of the Means Test, marchers gained weight because they ate better on the way to London than they did at home. While declining, unemployment was still above 15 percent, and many trade unionists were denied work.

Ten years later, in 1945, a 146-majority Labour government was elected with plans to nationalise the economy's commanding heights. Trade union membership had doubled, and the general secretary of the TGWU, Ernest Bevin, was Minister of Labour and National Service in Churchill's war cabinet. It was Bevin whom Churchill invited to join him on the balcony at Buckingham Palace on VE Day. Previously blacklisted shop stewards and the recently time-served became figures of authority on the shop floor. They also had the protection of full-time officials, some of whom were *Daily Worker* readers. The balance of forces had altered, and so had the broader atmosphere. During the 1930s, the spectre of the First World War and its aftermath haunted the horizon. At the end of the Second World War there was a widely held view that the state and working people's contribution to Britain's victory needed to be recognised and acted upon. The CPGB contributed to that political transformation in uncertain degrees.

During the two decades, individual communists had found themselves in contrasting circumstances—the Nazi-Soviet pact followed by Russia's victory in the east. But circumstances alone do not determine outcome; history does not happen of its own accord. People like Sam Wild and Hugh Scanlon turn up and shape events for historians. In Britain at this time, it is hard to think of another group of people, as equally committed, who worked so hard for social and political change. Volunteering in Spain not only risked one's life; if you were fortunate enough to survive, you would likely have been wounded, and on your return face unemployment, police harassment and the opprobrium of others. The lionising of IB veterans, with interest from academics, mainly arrived towards the end of veterans' lives in the late 1970s. Before then, they were controversial figures, pariahs to some, even within the labour movement. One wonders if the timing of their redemption is related to the demise of General Franco. Communists troubled the living stream. The street fights with Blackshirts earned them more respect in hindsight than they did at the time. They stood apart, not least in their allegiance to the Soviet Union. Many were remarkable individuals, natural leaders before they joined the Party and after they left, but, primarily, the Party made them so. They were drawn to it by pivotal times and influential books, the scaffolding from which membership was built. Comradeship and discipline helped them stand up to the foreman when others around them wouldn't.

Despite its ties to Moscow, the Party had a national consciousness alongside its class-based one. They sought to reclaim the idea of Britain for the left, looking to its pre-capitalist past and a modernist agenda. They spoke of a New Jerusalem and saw capitalism as the fall of man. The Party had its historians to make its case, led by Christopher Hill whose work on the English Civil War altered a route of enquiry for the next two generations.[504] Likewise, the trade union organisation constructed during these years endured to the end of the 1970s. The archetypal shop steward represented in the press and sitcoms would have read the *Morning Star*; he and tens of thousands of other readers played their part in bringing down the Heath government in 1974. If the archetype had a prototype, it was Hugh Scanlon, whose career was manufactured in Metro-Vicks. Scanlon left the Party quietly in 1954 but continued as the Broad Left's candidate for the presidency of the AEU with Manchester as his power base. Between 1968 and 1978, he and TGWU general secretary Jack Jones were regular visitors to Downing Street. In 1969 the two union leaders defeated Barbara Castle's "In Place of Strife" proposals to curb industrial action; two years later, they did the same to Edward Heath's Industrial Relations Act. Jones and Scanlon were said to be more influential on British prime minsters than American presidents and Russian general secretaries. They were both products of the two decisive decades of their youth. Ben Ainley said the young Scanlon had a habit of repeatedly pushing himself up onto his toes when addressing rallies and meetings. It may have been a subconscious reaction to his limited stature, or perhaps it was his enormous ambition, nurtured amongst his Mancunian comrades.

*Comrades Come Rally*

# Biographical notes post-1949

## Ben Ainley (1901-1984)
Ben was a teacher of 50 years' experience. On retirement, he became involved in Unity Arts, a plan to establish adult learning classes in art, cinema, theatre, music and literature groups. Ben founded and was first editor of *Voices*, a journal which published creative writing from working-class authors. It had a 12-year life, Ben dying shortly after its last issue.

## David Ainley (1909-1986)
After the Second World War David became secretary of the People's Press Printing Society from 1945 to 1972, the co-operative of readers that owned the *Morning Star*. He was also president of the London Co-operative Society, a member of the executive of the Co-operative Union and a central officer of the International Co-operative Alliance.

## Ted Ainley (1903-1968)
Ted was elected general secretary of the Association of Scientific Workers in 1949 but held it for only two years having to leave the post due to ill health. He worked in the West Middlesex Communist Party bookshop in 1952-53 and then for the central propaganda department at Party headquarters at King Street. He edited the Party's *Economic Bulletin* as well as *World News & Views* in 1957-62. He was secretary of the Party's cultural committee in 1960s.

## Frank Allaun (1913-2002)
Frank Allaun unsuccessfully contested Manchester Moss Side in 1951 for the Labour Party, then served as MP for Salford East from 1955-83. He helped to organise the first Aldermaston March in 1958 and was chair of the Labour Peace Fellowship. He was against British membership of the EEC. On standing

down as an MP he became vice president of CND. He was the first president of the Campaign for Labour Party Democracy in 1973 and wrote several books on nuclear weapons including *Stop the H-Bomb Race* (1959) and *The Wasted 30 Billions* (1975).

## Frances Dean (1917-1997)

Frances was elected vice-president of Manchester and Salford Trades Council in 1946, secretary in 1974 and then president in 1982. In the post-war era she was a member of Lancashire and then North West district leadership of the Party and a parliamentary candidate in Wythenshawe. She was a pioneer of pensioners' activism, helping found the journal *Grey Power*. She remained a lifelong communist.

## Vic Eddisford (1925-2021)

In 1949 Vic Eddisford was the first full-time secretary of Manchester and Salford YCL. He was also North West district secretary and national election agent for the Party. In 1968 he moved with his family to London to serve on the Party's national executive committee. In 1972 he returned to Manchester as North West district secretary. At the general election in 1967 he stood for Gorton in Manchester against Conservative candidate Winston Churchill Jnr, grandson of the former prime minister.

## Eddie Frow (1906-1997)

After the war Eddie continued as an AEU activist, never surviving long at factories where he worked. He supported many campaigns including the 40-hour week and Hugh Scanlon's efforts to become union president. In 1953 Eddie met Ruth Frow who joined the Party in 1945. They shared an interest in collecting books and the house they shared in Stretford soon overflowed with material. It was, according to Ruth during a visit by James Klugmann and a discussion regarding Khrushchev's revelations about Stalin, that Eddie and Ruth decided to pursue British labour movement history as an inspiration for future struggle. In 1961 Eddie was elected AEU Manchester district secretary whilst Ruth continued to teach. They also collected labour movement records, emblems, banners, badges, inscribed ceramics. Their house was part-archive, part-museum. They also wrote numerous WCML pamphlets and booklets. In 1987 Salford City Council provided Jubilee House, a former nurses' home, to accommodate what became the Working Class Movement Library.

*Biographical notes post-1949*

## Mick Jenkins (1904-1992)
After the Second World War Mick moved to the East Midlands to become the Party's district secretary. He wrote The General Strike of 1842 and several biographical pamphlets, including one on Frederick Engels in Manchester and another on George Brown, his comrade who was killed in Spain. He wrote many articles on the pre-war activities of the YCL and an unpublished memoir, *Prelude to Better Days*, now deposited in the WCML in Salford.

## Evelyn Taylor Jones (1913-1998)
Evelyn left the Communist Party to join the Labour Party, becoming ward secretary in Coventry and Solihull, where she was also CND secretary, taking part in the Aldermaston marches in the 1950s and 1960s. She became a justice of the peace and a juvenile court magistrate, although she was later removed from the bench by Lord Hailsham, then Lord Chancellor. She remained an active socialist all her life.

## Bernard McKenna (1916-2008)
In 1946 Bernard went through the forces' leaving programme for teacher training, eventually specialising in teaching educationally disadvantaged children. In the final stages of life, before he died aged 92, apparently he declared almost daily he was "buoyed by the thought that I have outlasted Franco".

## Benny Rothman (1911-2002)
Benny was a trade union activist at Metro-Vicks until he was victimised in 1951. Three thousand workers walked out on strike but failed to get him reinstated. He went on to work at Staveley Machine Tools of Broadheath, and became president of Altrincham Trades Council. He continued to campaign for access to the countryside, forming the Kinder Scout Advisory Committee in 1982, and the Rivington Pledge Committee in 1989. He led the campaign against the privatisation of water authority land, and took part in public enquiries on Ashton Moss, Kingswater Park and Davenport Green. He supported the efforts of Friends of the Earth, Greenpeace, Worldwide Fund for Nature and also fought against the motorway spoliation of the countryside at Twyford Down. In 1990 he was awarded the Special Award of Merit by the AEU, and in 1996 the Ramblers Association executive made him an honorary life member. He remained a lifelong communist.

## Hugh Scanlon (1913-2004)

From serving as AEU divisional organiser in Manchester, Hugh Scanlon was elected to the AEU national executive in 1963. Then, in 1968, he became union president. He left the Party in 1954 but remained associated with the Broad Left in the AEU. Along with Jack Jones he was the most powerful trade union leader of his generation and led resistance to successive governments' attempts to weaken the power of trade unions. When Edward Heath failed to form a coalition with the Liberals in 1974 and Labour formed a minority government, Scanlon and Jones acted as go-betweens for Labour, communicating the party's demands back and forth to Congress House. In 1977 he was prevented from becoming chairman of British Shipbuilders because MI5 advised he should not see documents marked "confidential". Two years earlier he was refused security clearance to join the British Gas Board. Like Frank Allaun, Scanlon was an outspoken opponent of Britain's membership of the EEC. He was elevated to the House of Lords as a life peer in 1979, taking the title Baron Scanlon of Davyhulme in the county of Greater Manchester.

## Henry Suss (1915-2007)

After the Second World War Henry returned to the clothing trade, becoming a Salford activist in the National Union of Tailors and Garment Workers. He was elected as a regional official of the union, serving on the national executive for 26 years. Henry stood unsuccessfully as a communist candidate for the Market Ward of Swinton and Pendlebury, Greater Manchester ten times before being elected as the first communist to the local council in May 1964. In 1967 he was returned for a second term but, because of boundary changes, his ward later disappeared and with it his seat. He remained a life-long communist and at the age of 87 he was on the 2003 anti-Iraq war demonstration.

## Bessie Wild (1911-1985)

In 1947 Bessie did a one-year emergency teacher training course then taught at Risley College of Education, Birley Street Secondary Modern School for Girls, Claremont Road Secondary Modern for Girls in Moss Side, Styal Women's Prison and North Cheshire FE College. She was an active member of the Party, as well as the National Union of Teachers and a director of Manchester and Salford Co-op. In 1977 Bessie turned down an OBE for services to education. She died in April 1985 aged 74.

*Biographical notes post-1949*

## Sam Wild (1908-1983)
Sam worked tirelessly for the interests of IB veterans right up until his death. He helped find them work, housed them, and raised money for them and their dependants. He also raised money for Republican prisoners in Franco's concentration camps in North Africa and elsewhere. After the war Sam worked as a steel erector and was a Construction Engineering Union shop steward. During the building of Barton bridge in 1959, four men died when several 50-ton girders collapsed. Sam led industrial action on the site for improved safety and successfully campaigned for compensation for the families. His former comrade Frank Allaun MP raised the matter in parliament. As a trade union activist, Sam was often out of work but he and Bessie remained politically active throughout their lives, attending anti-Vietnam War demonstrations and CND marches. In Easter 1966 he was International Brigade Association delegate to the German Democratic Republic's celebration of the 40th anniversary of the outbreak of the Spanish Civil War. In 1976 he and Bessie initiated an IB veterans' reunion and residential conference at Loughborough. A posthumous blue plaque appears on the former family home in Longsight.

*Comrades Come Rally*

# Bibliography

## Archives
CPGB online Archive
Imperial War Museum Sound Archives
Marx Memorial Library, London.
National Archives at Kew
Peoples' History Museum, Manchester
Tameside Archives, Ashton U Lyne.
Working Class Movement Library, Salford

## Recorded interviews
Norman Bates
Bessie Berry
Wilf Charles
Frances Dean
Vic Eddisford
Eddie Frow
Margaret Gadian
Eric Jessop
Maurice Levine
Mike Luft
Bernard McKenna
Joe Norman
Benny Rothman
Henry Suss
Hugh Scanlon
David Whitehead
Bill Whittaker
Sam Wild

## Telephone interviews
Louie Davies
Hilary Jones

Mike Luft
Dorothy Watts
Mike Wild

## Primary sources, documents

AEU Manchester District Committee, *Minute Books* 1939-1942. WCML

CPGB Lancashire and District, *Membership and Finances* 1936-1945. WCML

CPGB Lancashire and District, *Minutes of Metal Advisory Committee*, report to centre Nov 1942, WCML

David Ainley file. WCML PP/biogA/1/10

Fairey Aviation co. Erwood Park Works committee, *Minutes and Correspondence* 1941-44, WCML

Cantorovich, Ralph, *Diary* (Spanish Civil War) WCML

Ford Aero Engineering, *Aid to Russia Week*, programme of events. Manchester Central Ref. Library

Manchester and Salford Trades Council, *Minutes Book* 1941. WCML

Maurice Levine files, WCML

Metropolitan Metropolitan-Vickers Electrical Company, *Company Records 1939-1945*. Manchester Central Ref. Library, local history section

*Pollitt Papers* Peoples' History Museum, Manchester

Salford Women Citizens' Association, *Housing conditions St Matthias' Ward, Salford: a survey* (Manchester 1931).

## Memoirs

Ainley, Ted, unpublished memoir WCML Box PP/BIOGA/1/11

Jenkins, Mick, *Prelude to Better Days* (unpublished memoir) WCML

## Newspapers & Periodicals

*Daily Worker*

*Blackshirt*

*Volunteer For Liberty*

*New Propeller*

## Books and Pamphlets

Barry, Bernard, *From Manchester to Spain* (Manchester 2009)

Baxell, Richard, *Unlikely Warriors, The British in the Spanish Civil War and the Struggle Against Fascism* (London 2012)

Beckett, Francis, *Enemy Within, The Rise and Fall of the British Communist Party* (London 1995)

Beevor, Antony, *The Battle for Spain, The Spanish Civil War 1936-1939* (Wiedenfeld and Nicolson 2006)

Brendon, Piers, *The Dark Valley: a panorama of the 1930s* (London, 2000)

Bruce, George, *Second Front Now: The Road to D-Day* (London 1979)

Buchanan, Tom, *The Impact of the Spanish Civil War on Britain* (Sussex Academic Press, 2007)

Buchanan, Tom, *The Spanish Civil War and the British Labour Movement* (Cambridge 1991)

Calder, Angus, *The People's War* (London 2008)

Chapple, Dave, *Henry Suss and the Jewish Working Class of Manchester and Salford* (Somerset 2006)

Clifford, Alex, *The People's Army in the Spanish Civil War* (Yorkshire, Philadelphia 2020)

Cohen, Hilda, *Bagels with Babushka* (Manchester 1989)

Corkhill, David & Rawnsley, Stuart, *The Road to Spain* (Dunfermline 1981)

Croft, Andy, *The Years of Anger, The Life of Randall Swingler* (Abingdon 2020)

Croucher, Richard, *Engineers at War 1939-1945* (London 1982)

Cunningham, Valentine, editor, *The Penguin Book of Spanish Civil War Verse* (Middlesex 1980)

Figes, Orlando, *Revolutionary Russia 1891-1991* (London and New York 2014)

Frow, Edmund and Ruth, *The Battle of Bexley Square* (Salford 1994)

Frow, Edmund and Ruth, *The History of the Communist Party in Manchester 1920 -1926* (Salford 1979)

Frow, Ruth, *Edmund Frow, the making of an activist* (Talybont 1999)

Fussell, Paul, *Understanding and Behaviour in the Second World War* (New York, Oxford 1989)

Greenwood, Walter, *Love on the Dole* (London, 1993)

Gregory, Walter, *The Shallow Grave* (Nottingham 1996)

Harker, Ben, *Class Act, The Cultural and Political Life of Ewan MacColl* (London 2007)

Hitchens, Christopher, *Orwell's Victory* (London 2002)

Kladov, Ignatik, Fedorovich, *The People's Verdict. Krasnodar and Kharkiv Nazi Atrocity Trials* (London 1944)

Levine, Maurice, *From Cheetham to Cordova* (Manchester 1984)

Ewan MacColl, *Journeyman* (Manchester 1990)

Moorhouse, Roger, *The Devils' Alliance* (London 2014)

Morgan, Kevin, *Against War and Fascism – Ruptures and Continuities in British Communist Politics 1935-41* (Manchester 1989)

Morgan, Kevin, Cohen Gidon, and Flinn, Andrew, *Communists and British Society 1920-1991* (London, Sydney and Chicago 2007)

Orwell, George, *'Inside the Whale' The Collected Essays, Journalism and Letters of George Orwell. Vol 1. An Age Like This 1920 -1940* (Middlesex 1982)

Sutherland, John, *Stephen Spender: A Literary Life* (Oxford 2005)

Williams, Bill, *Jews and Other Foreigners: Manchester and the Rescue of the Victims of European Fascism 1933–40* (Manchester and New York 2011)

Williams, Bill, *Jewish Manchester: An Illustrated History* (Derby UK 2008)

## Journal articles

Allaun, Frank, 'Culture and Politics in the Hungry Thirties', *North West Labour History No. 17 1992/3*

Baldwin, M. Page. "Subject to Empire: Married Women and the British Nationality and Status of Aliens Act." Journal of British Studies, vol. 40, no. 4

Brian Brinkworth, 'On the planning of British aircraft production for the Second World War and reference to James

Connolly.' *Journal of Aeronautical History* 2018

Bambery, Chris, The Decline of the Western Communist Parties, *International Socialism* 2:49, Winter 1990, pp. 3–41

David Childs 'The British Communist Party and the War 1939-41: Old Slogans Revived.' *Journal of Contemporary History* 12 (1977)

Neil Barrett, A Bright Shining Star: The Communist Party and Anti-Fascist Activism in the 1930s, *Science & Society*, Vol. 61, No. 1

Baxell, Richard 'Myths of the International Brigades', *Bulletin of Spanish Studies: Hispanic Studies and Researches on Spain, Portugal and Latin America* (2014)

Casanova, Julián, Terror and Violence: The Dark Face of Spanish Anarchism. *International Labor and Working-Class History*, no. 67, 2005

Duncan Hallas A Soldier's Story, An interview by Clare Fermont & Chris Nineham, *Socialist Review* no. 186, May 1995

Gewirtz, Sharon, Antifascist Activity in Manchester's Jewish Community in the 1930s, *Manchester Region History Review* Spring/Summer 1990 Vol IV #1

Johnstone, Monty, 'The CPGB, the Comintern and the War, 1939-1941: Filling in the Blank Spots.' *Science and Society*, Spring 1997, Vol. 61, No. 1 Communism in Britain and the British Empire

McCulloch, Gary. 'Labour, the Left, and the British General Election of 1945.' *Journal of British Studies*, vol. 24, no. 4, 1985

Thorpe, Andrew 'The Membership of the Communist Party of Great Britain, 1920-1945', *The Historical Journal*, Vol. 43, No. 3 (Sep. 2000)

Thorpe, Andrew, 'Locking out the Communists: The Labour Party and the Communist Party, 1939–46,' *Twentieth Century British History*, Volume 25, Issue 2, June 2014.

## Theses and unpublished manuscripts

Richard Baxell, *The British Battalion of the International Brigades in the Spanish Civil War 1936-1939*. Thesis submitted for the Degree of Doctor of Philosophy in the University of London, London School of Economics and Political Science, 21 December 2001

Fishman, Nina, *The British CP and the Trade Unions, 1933-1945: The Dilemmas of Revolutionary Pragmatism.* PhD thesis UCL 1991

Mason, David, Unpublished biographical notes on his grandfather, Barnet Maransky

Livshin, Rosalyn D, *Non-Conformity in the Manchester Jewish Community: The Case of Political Radicalism 1889-1939.* Thesis submitted to the University of Manchester for the degree of Doctor of Philosophy in the Faculty of Humanities.

## Internet articles

manchesterjewishstudies.org/michael-wolf

*North West Labour History Society Journal* issue number: 18 (1993) nwlh.org.uk/?q=node/79

The Rise and Fall of the Jewish Labour Bund, *International Socialism*, Issue 135 (June 2012) isj.org.uk/the-rise-and-fall-of-the-jewish-labour-bund/#135englert21

socialhousinghistory.uk/wp/homes-fit-for-heroes

Leon Trotsky, 'Thermidor and Anti-Semitism' (February 1937) From *The New International*, Vol. VII No.4, May 1941. Transcribed for the Trotsky Internet Archive by Matt Siegfried in 1999. marxists.org/archive/trotsky/1937/02/therm.htm

## Websites

international-brigades.org.uk/the-volunteers

internationalbrigadesinspain.weebly.com/british-battalion.html

irelandscw.com/docs-3Deaths.htm

spartacus-educational.com/Wurmston.htm

richardbaxell.info/jarama/#_edn17

# Endnotes

*Introduction*

1 Francis Beckett, Enemy Within: The Rise and Fall of the British Communist Party (London 1995) p12

2 en.wikipedia.org/wiki/Communist_International

3 Francis Beckett, Enemy Within p13

4 Ruth Frow, Edmund Frow: The making of an activist (Talybont 1999) p30

5 Ted Ainley, unpublished memoir, WCML Box PP/BIOGA/1/11

6 Ted Ainley, p157

7 Andrew Thorpe 'The Membership of the Communist Party of Great Britain, 1920-1945', The Historical Journal, Vol 43, No. 3 (Sep. 2000), pp.777-800

8 David Ainley file at WCML PP/biogA/1/10

9 Interview with Margaret Gadian by the author WCML Salford

10 Interview Bessie Wild Tameside Archives

11 The Economic League was founded in 1919 to promote the interests of industrialists. It kept a blacklist of communist and left-wing organisations and individuals

12 International Brigade Memorial Trust roll of honour, at international-brigades.org.uk/the-volunteers

13 Kevin Morgan, Gidon Cohen, and Andrew Flinn, Communists and British Society 1920-1991 (London, Sydney and Chicago 2007) p49

14 Interview with Frances Dean by the author, WCML. From 1914 to 1922 The Herald was edited by George Lansbury and the paper was noted for its militant stance. From 1922 -29 it was the official organ of the TUC

15 Interview with Joe Norman, Imperial War Museum, reel one, see iwm.org.uk/collections/item/object/80000812

16 Interview with Eric Jessop by the author, WCML

| | |
|---|---|
| 17 | Interview with Margaret Gadian by the author, WCML |
| 18 | Andrew Thorpe 'The Membership of the Communist Party of Great Britain, 1920-1945', p785 |
| 19 | Bessie Wild interview Tameside Archives, Ashton U Lyne |

*Chapter 1*

| | |
|---|---|
| 22 | Frank Allaun, 'Culture and Politics in the Hungry Thirties', North West Labour History No. 17 1992/3 p42 |
| 23 | Ben Harker, Class Act, The Cultural and Political Life of Ewan MacColl, (London 2007) p26 |
| 24 | Harry McShane (7 May 1891 – 12 April 1988) was a Scottish socialist, involved in the Clyde Workers Committee and the anti-war movement during the First World War. His biography, No Mean Fighter was published in 1978 |
| 25 | Hyndman was the first author to popularise Marx's works in English. He set his ideas out in England for All in 1881. Hyndman developed a reputation as an authoritarian and failed to unite his party |
| 26 | Ben Harker, Class Act, The Cultural and Political Life of Ewan MacColl, (London 2007) p16 |
| 27 | Harker, p16 |
| 28 | Edmund and Ruth Frow, The History of the Communist Party in Manchester 1920 -1926 (Salford 1979) |
| 29 | Ruth Frow, Edmund Frow: The Making of an Activist, (Manchester 1999) p35 |
| 30 | Salford Women Citizens' Association, Housing conditions in the St Matthias' Ward, Salford: a survey, (Manchester 1931) Pamphlet available at Working Class Movement Library, (WCML) Salford |
| 31 | Ewan MacColl, Journeyman (Manchester 1990) p182 |
| 32 | Edmund and Ruth Frow, The Battle of Bexley Square, (Salford 1994) p12. Pamphlet available at WCML |
| 33 | MacColl, Journeyman, p195 |
| 34 | Edmund and Ruth Frow, The Battle of Battle Bexley Sq, p18 |
| 35 | Walter Greenwood, Love on the Dole (London, 1993) Kindle Edition, p199 |
| 36 | Greenwood, Love on the Dole, pp. 201-202 |
| 37 | Greenwood, Love on the Dole, pp. 204-205 |
| 38 | New Statesman 9 February 1935. "It was either dead before it was taken from the belly of the novel, or the two drama surgeons killed it as they were taking it out. |

There isn't a character in it worth a curse, and there isn't a thought in it worth remembering."
39 Clive Emsley, Hard Men: The English and Violence since 1750, (London, 2005) p141
40 Maurice Levine, From Cheetham to Cordova, (Manchester 1984) p22. A pamphlet
41 Wal Hannington, Unemployed Struggles 1919 -1936 (London 1977) p222. Hannington was a founding member of the Communist Party and national organiser of the National Unemployed Workers' Movement. He later became national organiser of the Amalgamated Engineering Union

*Chapter 2*
42 Daily Worker 23.2.1931
43 Daily Worker 2.3.1931
44 Interview with Benny Rothman by the author. WCML Salford TAPE/183
45 Ewan MacColl, Journeyman (Manchester 1990) p182
46 Interview with Benny Rothman by the author. WCML TAPE/183. Strachey himself suffered a very damaging nervous breakdown in the thirties which took him several years to recover from
47 Dorril, Stephen, Blackshirt: Sir Oswald Mosley and British Fascism Lume Books. Kindle Edition.p187
48 Dorril, Stephen, Blackshirt: Sir Oswald Mosley and British Fascism (pp. 212-213). Lume Books. Kindle Edition
49 Maurice Levine, From Cheetham to Cordova p26. Gresford colliery was situated in North Wales. A mining disaster at the colliery in 1934 resulted in 200 plus dead
50 A speech by Lloyd George the day after the armistice where according to the press he said there would be "homes fit for heroes". What he actually said was "Habitations fit for the heroes who have won the war" socialhousinghistory.uk/wp/homes-fit-for-heroes/
51 Hutt, Allen. The Condition of the Working Class in Britain, (London, 1933) cited in Neil Barrett, A Bright Shining Star: The Communist Party and Anti-Fascist Activism in the 1930s, Science & Society, Vol. 61, No.1, Communism in Britain and the British Empire (Spring, 1997), pp10-26
52 The dispute made the front page of the Blackshirt, the BUF's eight-page weekly paper launched in February 1933
53 manchesterjewishstudies.org/michael-wolf/

54     Recorded interview with Bessie Wild, Tameside Archives
55     Interview Maurice Levine WCML tape one
56     North West Labour History Society Journal issue number: 18 1993 nwlh.org.uk/?q=node/79
57     Maurice Levine interview WCML TAPE/078 reel one
58     The Blackshirt 18th March 1933
59     Daily Worker March 14th 1933
60     Manchester Guardian 16th October 1933
61     Dorril, Stephen . Blackshirt: Sir Oswald Mosley and British Fascism (p. 219). Lume Books. Kindle Edition
62     Manchester Guardian 1st October 1934
63     Hilda Cohen, Bagels with Babushka (Manchester 1989)
64     Maurice Levine interview WCML TAPE/078 reel one. Tommy Moran was a former miner and member of the Labour Party. He left Labour in 1933 to join the BUF and gained a reputation as a speaker at BUF events and before long was called to the national headquarters to help organise the BUF as a whole. Moran's wife Toni, a noted anti-semite, also became a BUF member and was a regular speaker in Manchester
65     Sharon Gewirtz, Antifascist Activity in Manchester's Jewish Community in the 1930s, Manchester Region History Review Spring/Summer 1990 Vol IV #1. p23
66     See Phil Piratin's memoir, Our Flag Stays Red, (London 2006). "A unique account of communist and anit-fascist activity in London' East End in the 1930s and 40s... the highlight of the book is its account of the events leading up to the famous 'Battle of Cable Street' in 1936
67     Maurice Levine interview, WCML TAPE/078 reel one
68     Interview with Mike Luft, author's personal collection
69     Maurice Levine interview, WCML TAPE/078 reel one
70     Neil Barrett, A Bright Shining Star: The Communist Party and Anti-Fascist Activism in the 1930s, Science & Society, Vol. 61, No. 1, Communism in Britain and the British Empire (Spring, 1997), p21
71     Maurice Levine interview, WCML TAPE/078 reel one
72     In 2006, the historian Stephen Dorril revealed in his book that the Nazis had donated about £50,000 to the BUF. Dorril, Stephen Blackshirt: Sir Oswald Mosley and British fascism. (London 2006)
73     Sharon Gewirtz, Antifascist Activity in Manchester's Jewish Community in the 1930s, Manchester Region

History Review Spring/Summer 1990 Vol IV number 1
74  Blackshirt February 1933 p1
75  Piers Brendon, The Dark Valley: a panorama of the 1930s. (London, 2000) p6
76  WH Auden Spain 1937

*Chapter 3*
77  For an account of the response of British journalists to the air raid see, Tom Buchanan, The Impact of the Spanish Civil War on Britain (Sussex Academic Press, 2007) p23
78  See in particular: Richard Baxell Unlikely Warriors, The British in the Spanish Civil War and the Struggle Against Fascism (London 2012) Giles Tremlett, The International Brigades, Fascism, Freedom and the Spanish Civil War, (London 2020). The most readable memoir for me is Walter Gregory's The Shallow Grave (Nottingham 1996)
79  Antony Beevor, The Battle for Spain, The Spanish Civil War 1936-39 (Wiedenfeld and Nicolson 2006), pp294-307
80  Beevor, The Battle for Spain, p178
81  Clem Beckett's story was dramatised by playwright Neil Gore in his play, Dare Devil Rides to Jarma, Townsend Productions 2016 townsendproductions.org.uk/shows/dare-devil-rides-to-jarama/
82  Christopher Caudwell was the pseudonym of Christopher St John Sprigg (20 October 1907 – 13 February 1937)
83  Interview Maurice Levine WCML reel 2, B side
84  The Bowes-Lyon family are an aristocratic Scots English family dating back to the eighteenth century. The Queen Mother was a member of the lineage
85  Maurice Levine interview WCML TAPE/078 reel one
86  Esmond Marcus David Romilly (10 June 1918 – 30 November 1941) was the nephew of Clementine Churchill, wife of Winston. He rebelled against his aristocratic background from the age of 15, declaring himself a communist, and abandoning his education at Wellington College to campaign against the public school system. He joined the IB at aged 18 and fought on the Madrid front
87  Romilly Esmond, Boadilla (London 2018) Kindle Edition, pp 17-20
88  Bernard Barry From Manchester to Spain (Manchester 2009) Pamphlet p17. Ralph Cantorovitch (1916-1937) left school at 14, joined the Jewish Lads Brigade and then

the YCL. He attempted to travel to Spain in September of 1936, but was initially refused permission by the Party

89 Interview Sam Wild, Tameside archives
90 David Mason, unpublished biographical notes on his father, Barnet Maransky
91 Interview with Sam Wild (TAPE/170) 28-Oct-74. Working Class Movement Library (WCML) Salford
92 Richard Baxell, Unlikely Warriors, The British in the Spanish Civil War and the Struggle Against Fascism, p273
93 Manchester and Salford district committee of the Party reported March 21st 1937. 'The membership of the Party in Manchester and Salford now stands at 405.' Most of the 200 Manchester volunteers had left for Spain by then and more than half of them were Party members
94 Interview with Benny Goldman by the author. (TAPE/032) WCML
95 Interview Bessie Wild Tameside Archives
96 Andrew Thorpe 'The Membership of the Communist Party of Great Britain, 1920-1945', The Historical Journal, Vol. 43, No. 3 (Sep. 2000), pp.777-800
97 Interview Benny Goldman, WCML
98 Angela Jackson, British Women and the Spanish Civil War, (Routledge 2003)
99 spartacus-educational.com/Wurmston.htm
100 Maurice Levine interview WCML TAPE/078 reel one
101 Goldman (WCML)
102 Interview with Joe Norman, Imperial War Museum, 1977, reel four iwm.org.uk/collections/item/object/80000812
103 Richard Baxell 'Myths of the International Brigades', Bulletin of Spanish Studies: Hispanic Studies and Researches on Spain, Portugal and Latin America, (2014) p23

*Chapter 4*
104 en.wikipedia.org/wiki/Asturian_miners%27_strike_ of_1934. A miners strike in Asturias in 2012 resulted in violent clashes between the police and miners. The miners occupied a mineshaft, blocked roads and a railway line
105 Health transition in Spain from 1900 to 1990 US National Library of Medicine National Institutes of Health ncbi.nlm.nih.gov/pubmed/8974757

| | |
|---|---|
| 106 | Antony Beevor, The Battle for Spain, The Spanish Civil War 1936-1939 (Wiedenfeld and Nicolson 2006) p6 |
| 107 | Julián Casanova, Terror and Violence: The Dark Face of Spanish Anarchism. International Labor and Working-Class History, no. 67, 2005, pp. 79–99. JSTOR jstor.org/stable/27672986 |
| 108 | Sushila Ramaswamy, Political Theory: Ideas and Concepts (PHI Learning 2015) p122 |
| 109 | Beevor, The Battle for Spain, The Spanish Civil War 1936-1939 p12 |
| 110 | Beevor, The Battle for Spain, The Spanish Civil War 1936-1939 p15 |
| 111 | Casanova, Terror and Violence: The Dark Face of Spanish Anarchism, p82 |
| 112 | Michael Schwab - courtroom speech after being sentenced to hang for the Haymarket bombing in Chicago, 1886. Schwab (1853-1887) was born in Mannheim, Germany. He worked as a bookbinder before emigrating to the United States in 1879 where he became a trade union organiser. He was sentenced to death which was commuted to a life sentence and released after six years. He denied any involvement in the bombing |
| 113 | Casanova, Terror and Violence: The Dark Face of Spanish Anarchism, p91 |

*Chapter 5*

| | |
|---|---|
| 114 | London communist Felicia Browne was reputedly the first British volunteer to fight for the Republic and the first to be killed. She was already on holiday in Spain at the time of Franco's rising and enlisted in the PSUC (Catalan Communist) Karl Marx militia. On 25 August 1936 Browne was killed in action on the Aragón front near Tardienta |
| 115 | Interview with Benny Goldman by the author (TAPE/032) WCML |
| 116 | Interview with Sam Wild (TAPE/170) 28-Oct-74. (WCML) |
| 117 | Interview with Joe Norman, Imperial War Museum, 1977, reel one iwm.org.uk/collections/item/object/80000812 |
| 118 | Interview Maurice Levine WCML TAPE/078 reel one |
| 119 | Interview Maurice Levine WCML TAPE/078 reel one |
| 120 | Interview Maurice Levine. WCML |
| 121 | Gurney, Jason, Crusade in Spain (London 1974) |
| 122 | Interview with Bernard McKenna (TAPE/200) WCML |

| | |
|---|---|
| 123 | Interview McKenna, WCML |
| 124 | Interview McKenna, WCML |
| 125 | Interview Goldman, WCML |
| 126 | Maurice Levine interview WCML TAPE/078 reel one |
| 127 | Interview Bernard McKenna, WCML |
| 128 | Interview Benny Goldman, WCML |
| 129 | Interview Sam Wild, WCML |
| 130 | Maurice Levine, Cheetham to Cordova: A Manchester Man of the Thirties (Manchester 1984) |
| 131 | Maurice Levine interview at WCML. Reel two side two |
| 132 | ML recorded interview |
| 133 | Goldman (WCML) |
| 134 | Maurice reel 2 |
| 135 | Richard Baxell's website richardbaxell.info/jarama/#_edn17 |
| 136 | international-brigades.org.uk/content/roll-honour |
| 137 | Wild (WCML). The man who rescued Sam was Jewish East Ender, David Crook, who whilst in Spain was recruited by the Russian secret police, NKVD. He was sent to China during the second Sino-Japanese War (1937-45) married and remained in China for the rest of his life, despite being imprisoned for five years during the Cultural Revolution |
| 138 | Interview Maurice Levine WCML reel 2 |
| 139 | Interview Maurice Levine reel 2 |
| 140 | Richard Baxell's website: richardbaxell.info/jarama/#_edn17 Reference is made to an interview with George Aitken available on the Imperial War Museum website: Interview with George Aitken, IWMSA 10357/3/1 |
| 141 | Interview Joe Norman, reel two, Imperial War Museum iwm.org.uk/collections/item/object/80000812 |
| 142 | Richard Baxell, Unlikely Warriors: The British in the Spanish Civil War and the Struggle Against Fascism, p163 |
| 143 | IBMT website. 'Jud' (Julius) Colman was a rifleman, with No 1 company of 14th Brigade and later the British Battalion of the 15th Brigade |
| 144 | Eugene Downing interview: extract on Maurice Ryan irelandscw.com/docs-3Deaths.htm |
| 145 | Richard Baxell Unlikely Warriors, The British in the Spanish Civil War and the Struggle Against Fascism (London 2012) p260 |

| | |
|---|---|
| 146 | Telephone interviews were conducted with Mike Wild throughout 2020 and 2021 due to COVID restrictions |
| 147 | Interview Joe Norman, IWM tape, reel three |
| 148 | Interview Sam Wild WCML |
| 149 | Daily Mail March 31st 1937 |
| 150 | internationalbrigadesinspain.weebly.com/british-battalion.html |
| 151 | The National Archives at Kew reference, KV-2-3512_89.jpg |
| 152 | Imperial War Museum interview IWMSA 809/6 cited on International Brigade Memorial Trust website |
| 153 | Interview Joe Norman, IWM, reel four |
| 154 | Interview Joe Norman, IWM, reel four |
| 155 | Alex Clifford The People's Army in the Spanish Civil War (Yorkshire, Philadelphia 2020) |
| 156 | Personal correspondence from Alex Clifford to author |
| 157 | Interview Maurice Levine WCML reel one |
| 158 | Bernard McKenna Interview (WCML) |
| 159 | Richard Baxell, 'Myths of the International Brigades', Bulletin of Spanish Studies: Hispanic Studies and Researches on Spain, Portugal and Latin America, (2014) p13 |
| 160 | Bernard McKenna (WCML) |
| 161 | Benny Goldman (WCML) |
| 162 | Bernard McKenna (WCML) |
| 163 | Interview Sam Wild, Tameside Archives |

*Chapter 6*

| | |
|---|---|
| 164 | The papers are in the Maurice Levine files at the WCML Salford. Spanish Civil War: International Brigaders - Maurice Levine (EVT/SPAIN/3/4) 1937-2000 |
| 165 | Beevor, The Battle for Spain, The Spanish Civil War 1936-1939 p344. "At the beginning of 1937 the Irish had nearly mutinied after the Lopera debacle, when they were prevented at the last moment from forming their own company" |
| 166 | international-brigades.org.uk George Nathan claimed Manchester volunteer Michael Browne was responsible for the death of Ralph Fox. See IWMSA 10356 interview with Walter Greenhalgh. Browne deserted after Lopera and was allegedly caught and executed. Regardless he never returned home |

| 167 | Richard Baxell, The British Battalion of the International Brigades in the Spanish Civil War 1936-1939 Thesis submitted for the degree of doctor of philosophy in the University of London, London School of Economics and Political Science, 21 December 2001, page 116 |
|---|---|
| 168 | Anthony Beevor The Battle for Spain, p220 |
| 169 | Hugh Thomas, The Spanish Civil War, 1st ed. (London 1961) p463 |
| 170 | Interview Maurice Levine, WCML |
| 171 | Richard Baxell, thesis p301 |
| 172 | Maurice Levine notes on Ralph Cantor's diary WCML US39 Spain Box 8 |
| 173 | Interview Sam Wild, Tameside Archives |
| 174 | Maurice Levine notes on Ralph Cantor's diary WCML US39 Spain Box 8 |
| 175 | Letters folder in Ralph Cantor box at WCML |
| 176 | Spanish Civil War: International Brigaders - Maurice Levine (EVT/SPAIN/3/4) 1937-2000 |
| 177 | Extract of a letter from George Brown to Mick Jenkins, 22 April, 1937. Maurice Levine file WCML |
| 178 | Mike Wild told me his father, Sam, "Worshipped Pollitt." |
| 179 | The International Memorial Trust record Dorothy Arnold as a Party member who arrived in Spain on 14.4.37. The letter was written on the 19.4.1937 and a note on the letter "27.4.37," presumably as received or read by Pollitt. From Pollitt papers PHM Manchester |
| 180 | Baldwin, M. Page. "Subject to Empire: Married Women and the British Nationality and Status of Aliens Act." Journal of British Studies, vol. 40, no. 4, 2001, pp. 522–556 jstor.org/stable/3070746. Accessed 28 Aug 2021 |
| 181 | Letter from Marion Teasdale to Harry Pollitt April 19th 1937. Pollitt Papers People's History Museum, Manchester |
| 182 | Letter from Evelyn Brown to Harry Pollitt. Pollitt Papers CPGB online Archive images 1- 3 |

*Chapter 7*

| 183 | C. Eby, Between the Bullet and the Lie: American Volunteers in the Spanish Civil War. (New York 1969) |
|---|---|
| 184 | Walter Gregory The Shallow Grave (Nottingham 1996) p144 |
| 185 | Interview with Bernard McKenna (TAPE/200) WCML |

| | |
|---|---|
| 186 | Richard Baxell, Unlikely Warriors: The British in the Spanish Civil War and the Struggle Against Fascism (Aurum Press. Kindle Edition) p352 |
| 187 | Interview with Joe Norman, Imperial War Museum, 1977, reel four |
| 188 | Norman, reel four |
| 189 | Norman, reel four |
| 190 | Norman, reel four |
| 191 | Norman, reel four |
| 192 | Interview with Norman Moss for London Illustrated News 1.10.1976 |
| 193 | Norman, reel four |
| 194 | Norman, reel four |
| 195 | international-brigades.org.uk/content/farewell |
| 196 | Interview with Bernard McKenna (TAPE/200) WCML |
| 197 | David Corkhill and Stuart J Rawnsley, The Road to Spain, (Dunfermline 1981) p24 |
| 198 | KV 2 - The Security Service: Personal (PF Series) Files File KV-2-3512-92 Samuel Wild National Archives. P92 |
| 199 | KV 2 - The Security Service: Personal (PF Series) Files File KV-2-3512-92 Samuel Wild National Archives, p42 |
| 200 | KV 2 - The Security Service: Personal (PF Series) Files File KV-2-3512-92 Samuel Wild National Archives, p25 |
| 201 | KV 2 - The Security Service: Personal (PF Series) Files File KV-2-3512-92 Samuel Wild National Archives, p26 |
| 202 | KV 2 - The Security Service: Personal (PF Series) Files File KV-2-3512-92 Samuel Wild National Archives, p27 |
| 203 | Interview with Sam Wild (TAPE/170) 28-Oct-74. Working Class Movement Library (WCML) Salford |
| 204 | Biographical notes from Mike Wild. I am grateful to Mike Wild for much correspondence and many hours of conversation over a period of 18 months |
| 205 | Giles Tremlett, The International Brigades, Fascism, Freedom and the Spanish Civil War, (London 2020) p216 |
| 206 | As battalion commander at the Battle of the Ebro, Sam was ordered by Brigade HQ to execute with Maurice Ryan who had fired his machine gun on his omen whilst drunk |
| 207 | Mike Wild, telephone interview, 26.3.2021 |

*Chapter 8*

| | |
|---|---|
| 208 | Jim Fyrth, The Signal was Spain (London and New York 1986) p21 |

| | |
|---|---|
| 209 | Joe Julius Heydecker, Johannes Leeb, The Nuremberg Trial: A History of Nazi Germany as Revealed Through the Testimony at Nuremberg, (Connecticut, 1975) p174 |
| 210 | Tom Buchanan, The Spanish Civil War and the British Labour Movement, (Cambridge 1991) p74 |
| 211 | Interview with Mike Luft 23.10.2019, personal collection. Communist Party and wider labour movement involvement was passed down the generations. Mike Luft's grandfather was George Staunton was a member of the British Socialist Party which merged with other groups to found the CPGB in 1921. George was the very first Manchester Communist Party organiser |
| 212 | Daily Worker November 26th, 1938 |
| 213 | Interview with Hugh Scanlon, WCML, Tape 125 July 1993 |
| 214 | Telephone interview with Mike Wild. Mike's father Sam, recounted the speech he made in Barcelona to him on a number of occasions |
| 215 | Bill Williams, Jews and other foreigners: Manchester and the rescue of the victims of European Fascism, 1933–40 (Manchester & New York 2011) Kindle Edition p104 |
| 216 | britishpathe.com/video/in-defense-of-madrid-sic-aka-spain |
| 217 | Williams, Bill. Jews and other foreigners: Manchester and the rescue of the victims of European Fascism, 1933–40 (Manchester & New York 2011) Kindle Edition p102 |
| 218 | Interview Bessie Wild Tameside archives |
| 219 | Ditto. Say what a communard |
| 220 | Interview with Henry Suss, personal collection Michael Crowley |
| 221 | Interview Henry Suss WCML Tape 203 |
| 222 | Picasso lived in Paris during the Nazi occupation of France. When his apartment was raided by the Gestapo, an officer pointed to a postcard of the mural Guernica and asked Picasso, 'Did you do that?' To which the artist replied, 'No you did.' openculture.com/2017/05/the-gestapo-points-to-guernica-and-asks-picasso-did-you-do-this.html |
| 223 | spartacus-educational.com/WhaldaneC.htm |
| 224 | Letter to Walter Citrine, Wounded and Dependants Aid Committee 22nd Nov 1937, Warwick Digital Collections, cdm21047.contentdm.oclc.org/digital/collection/scw/id/10510 |
| 225 | David Corkhill and Stuart Rawnsley, The Road to Spain (Dunfermline 1981) p13 |

226  Communist Party Manchester Area report 1938, WCML
227  Organisation Todt was a civil and military engineering organisation in Nazi Germany from 1933 to 1945, named for its founder, Fritz Todt, an engineer and senior Nazi
228  BH Philips, No Other Way, Major Sam Wild 1908-1983, p21. An unpublished account held by the Wild family, cited in Baxell, Richard. Unlikely Warriors: The British in the Spanish Civil War and the Struggle Against Fascism Kindle Edition p458
229  Manchester Guardian 1st June 1937, cited in Williams, Bill. Jews and other foreigners: Manchester and the rescue of the victims of European Fascism, 1933–40 Manchester University Press. Kindle Edition.p101
230  Salford City Reporter July 1937
231  From a column in the Manchester City News written by the editor, 11 March 1939. Cited in Williams, Bill. Jews and other foreigners: Manchester and the rescue of the victims of European Fascism, 1933–40 (Manchester University Press. Kindle Edition) p99
232  www2.bfi.org.uk/films-tv-people/4ce2b69c2a4b8 The title is a play on a 1921 American silent film, Orphans of the Storm, by DW Griffith, set during the French revolution which served as a warning about the rise of Bolshevism
233  Andrew Thorpe 'The Membership of the Communist Party of Great Britain, 1920-1945'p781

*Chapter 9*

234  Monty Johnstone 'The CPGB, the Comintern and the War, 1939-1941: Filling in the Blank Spots.' Science and Society, Spring 1997, Vol. 61, No. 1 Communism in Britain and the British Empire (spring, 1997), p 29
235  Daily Worker 7 October 1939 p2
236  Andrew Thorpe 'The Membership of the Communist Party of Great Britain, 1920-1945', The Historical Journal, Vol 43, No. 3 (Sep. 2000), p794
237  Kevin Morgan, Against War and Fascism – Ruptures and Continuities in British Communist politics 1935-41 (Manchester 1989) p 317. 'The fabric of the Party remained intact, if frayed at the edges'
238  Daily Worker 23 August 1939 p1
239  Morgan, Against War and Fascism – Ruptures and Continuities in British Communist politics 1935-41. p86
240  Daily Worker 4th September 1939

| | |
|---|---|
| 241 | Thompson, E. P. Beyond the Frontier, (Woodbridge, Suffolk, Merlin Press 1997) cited in Andy Croft, The Years of Anger, The Life of Randall Swingler. (Abingdon 2020) p107. A Croft adds in a footnote that Swingler's authorship was confirmed to him in a letter by Robert Conquest in 2008 |
| 242 | Daily Worker 4 September 1939 |
| 243 | Harry Pollitt, How to Win the War (London 1939) cited: spartacus-educational.com/TUpollitt.htm |
| 244 | John Mahon, Harry Pollitt, A Biography, (London 1976) cited in Monty Johnstone Science and Society p29 |
| 245 | Communist Party Online Archive Pollitt Papers, Outbreak of War, images 97-100 |
| 246 | Monty Johnstone 'The CPGB, the Comintern and the War, 1939-1941: Filling in the Blank Spots.' Science and Society, Spring 1997, Vol. 61, No. 1 Communism in Britain and the British Empire, (spring, 1997) p29 |
| 247 | Daily Worker 7 October 1939 p1 |
| 248 | Communist Party Online Archive, Pollitt Papers: Outbreak of War |
| 249 | Roger Moorhouse, The Devils' Alliance. (London 2014) Random House. Kindle Edition. p194 |
| 250 | Manchester Guardian 12 October 1939 |
| 251 | Interview with Wilf Charles, Working Class Movement Library, Tape 160B 1992 |
| 252 | Interview Wilf Charles, WCML |
| 253 | Interview Eddie Frow, personal collection Michael Crowley |
| 254 | Henry Suss interview WCML tape 203 |
| 255 | Interview Benny Rothman, personal collection Michael Crowley |
| 256 | Interview Frances Dean, personal collection M Crowley |
| 257 | Interview Hugh Scanlon WCML tape 125 |
| 258 | Interview Hugh Scanlon. WCML |
| 259 | Mick Jenkins Prelude to Better Days (Unpublished memoir) WCML p194 |
| 260 | Kevin Morgan, Harry Pollitt (Manchester 1993) p107 |
| 261 | Kevin Morgan, Harry Pollitt p109 |
| 262 | Interview Benny Rothman, WCML |
| 263 | Kevin Morgan Harry Pollitt p103 |
| 264 | G. Dimitrov, 'The Seventh World Congress of the Communist Interational' Selected Speeches and Articles |

| | |
|---|---|
| | (1951). Cited in Morgan Against War and Fascism p25 |
| 265 | Morgan, Against War and Fascism p25 |
| 266 | John Strachey What Are We to Do? (London 1938) p252 |
| 267 | Morgan Against War and Fascism p57 |
| 268 | Interview Henry Suss WCML |
| 269 | George Orwell 'Inside the Whale' The Collected Essays, Journalism and Letters of George Orwell Vol 1 An Age Like This 1920 -1940 (Middlesex 1982) p563 |
| 270 | Harry Pollitt, The Daily Worker (August, 1936) cited: spartacus-educational.com/TUpollitt.htm |
| 271 | Francis Beckett, Enemy Within: The Rise and Fall of the British Communist Party (London 1995) p73 |
| 272 | Orwell, 'Inside the Whale' p565 |
| 273 | Interview Hugh Scanlon WCML |

*Chapter 10*

| | |
|---|---|
| 274 | Interview with Bill Whittaker WCML TAPE/031 |
| 275 | Roger Moorhouse, The Devils' Alliance. (London 2014) Random House. Kindle Edition, location 2360 |
| 276 | Interview with Wilf Charles, WCML, Tape 160B 1992 |
| 277 | Andy Croft, The Years of Anger, The Life of Randall Swingler. (Abingdon 2020) p98 |
| 278 | Douglas Hyde, I Believed (Adelaide, 1950), p71. Cited in Moorhouse, Roger location 2386 |
| 279 | Interview with Wilf Charles WCML |
| 280 | Kevin Morgan, Against War and Fascism – Ruptures and Continuities in British Communist politics 1935-41 (Manchester 1989) p154 |
| 281 | Interview with Frances Dean, WCML TAPE/018 |
| 282 | Interview with Benny Rothman, WCML |
| 283 | Interview Hugh Scanlon WCML tape 125 |
| 284 | V Lenin, 'The War and Russian Social Democracy' Selected Works vol. 5. (1936) p130 cited in Kevin Morgan p106 |
| 285 | Interview Hugh Scanlon WCML |
| 286 | Interview Hugh Scanlon WCML |
| 287 | Richard Croucher Engineers at War 1939-1945 (London 1982). P114 |
| 288 | Interview Wild Charles WCML |
| 289 | Interview with Eric Jessop WCML TAPE/312 |

| | |
|---|---|
| 290 | Interview Margaret Gadian personal collection Michael Crowley |
| 291 | Interview Margaret Gadian |
| 292 | Interview Henry Suss WCML tape 203 |
| 293 | Sam's security file entry for 2.5.40 |
| 294 | Kevin Morgan p175 |
| 295 | Kevin Morgan 204 |
| 296 | Daily Mirror (13th January 1941) |
| 297 | Daily Worker (14th January 1941) |
| 298 | Interview Hugh Scanlon |
| 299 | David Childs 'The British Communist Party and the War 1939-41: Old Slogans Revived.' Journal of Contemporary History 12 (1977) pp237-253 |
| 300 | Roger Moorhouse The Devils' Alliance. (London 2014) Random House. Kindle Edition location 2447 |
| 301 | Minutes of the Manchester and Salford Trades Council 1941, WCML |
| 302 | Interview Frances Dean, WCML |
| 303 | Interview Eddie Frow, personal collection, author |

*Chapter 11*

| | |
|---|---|
| 304 | Orlando Figes Revolutionary Russia 1891-1991 (London and New York 2014) Chapter 15, War and Revolution |
| 305 | Adolf Hitler, Mein Kampf Chapter 14. Eastward Orientation versus Eastern Politics |
| 306 | Kay, Alex J. "Germany's Staatssekretäre, Mass Starvation and the Meeting of 2 May 1941." Journal of Contemporary History, vol. 41, no. 4, 2006, pp. 685–700. JSTOR jstor.org/stable/30036414. Accessed 18 May 2021 |
| 307 | Karel C Berkhoff, Harvest of Despair: Life and Death in Ukraine Under Nazi Rule. (Harvard 2004) |
| 308 | en.wikipedia.org/wiki/Hunger_Plan#cite_note-14 |
| 309 | Jürgen Förster The German Military's Image of Russia. Russia: War, Peace and Diplomacy (London 2005) |
| 310 | Christopher R Browning, The Origins of the Final Solution: The Evolution of Nazi Jewish Policy, September 1939-March 1942. (Nebraska 2007) |
| 311 | Ignatik Fedorovich Kladov, The People's Verdict. Krasnodar and Kharkiv Nazi Atrocity Trials, (London 1944) |
| 312 | Ignatik Fedorovich Kladov, The People's Verdict. Krasnodar and Kharkiv Nazi Atrocity Trials, p9 |

313  Ignatik Fedorovich Kladov, The People's Verdict. Krasnodar and Kharkiv Nazi Atrocity Trials, p53
314  Interview Wilf Charles WCML
315  Letter to Sam Wild, I Ashmore, et al. Personal collection Mike Wild
316  Interview Hugh Scanlon WCML
317  Harry Pollit tape, WCML

*Chapter 12*

318  Richard Croucher, Engineers at War, (London 1982) p144
319  New Propellor, February 1942, WCML
320  Interview Vic Eddisford, WCML
321  Interview Frances Dean, WCML
322  Dorothy Watts, telephone interview by the author, July 1993
323  How to Overcome Production Obstacles, a Communist Party internal document for local officials. (London February 1942) p26
324  AEU Journal, Nov. 1941 p256, cited Edmund Frow, Engineering Struggles (Salford 1982), p172
325  Frow, p172
326  Croucher, Engineers at War, p152
327  Frow, Engineering Struggles p178
328  Frow, Engineering Struggles p115
329  Nina Fishman, The British CP and the Trade Unions, 1933-1945: The Dilemmas of Revolutionary Pragmatism. PhD thesis UCL 1991, p256
330  Interview Hugh Scanlon, WCML
331  Interview Hugh Scanlon, WCML
332  Interview David Whitehead, personal collection author
333  Interview Vic Eddisford, WCML
334  Interview Eric Jessop, WCML
335  Interview Benny Rothman, WCML
336  Interview Vic Eddisford, WCML
337  Interview Benny Rothman, WCML
338  Interview Hugh Scanlon, WCML
339  Calder, The People's War, p395
340  Interview Eddie Frow, personal collection author
341  Richard Croucher, Engineers at War, p78

| | |
|---|---|
| 342 | Interview Benny Rothman, WCML |
| 343 | Interview Vic Eddisford, WCML |
| 344 | Interview Hugh Scanlon, WCML |
| 345 | Interview Vic Eddisford, WCML |
| 346 | Interview Margaret Gadian, WCML |
| 347 | Brian Brinkworth, 'On the planning of British aircraft production for the Second World War and reference to James Connolly.' Journal of Aeronautical History Paper No. 2018/09 pp274-277 |
| 348 | Brian Brinkworth, 'On the planning of British aircraft production for the Second World War and reference to James Connolly.' Pp274-277 |

*Chapter 13*

| | |
|---|---|
| 349 | jewishvirtuallibrary.org/churchill-broadcast-on-the-soviet-german-war-june-1941 |
| 350 | Winston Churchill The Grand Alliance, cited in George Bruce Second Front Now: The Road to D-Day (London 1979), p12 |
| 351 | George Bruce Second Front Now: The Road to D-Day, p15 |
| 352 | George Bruce Second Front Now: The Road to D-Day p16 |
| 353 | George Bruce, p16 |
| 354 | George Bruce, p18 |
| 355 | George Orwell, London Letter in Partisan Review (New York 1941) |
| 356 | George Bruce Second Front Now: The Road to D-Day p85 |
| 357 | Paul Fussell, Understanding and Behaviour in the Second World War (New York, Oxford 1989) p271. Fussell served in the US Infantry in WW2 and was wounded in France. A prolific writer, he wrote repeatedly about how and why war is mythologised |
| 358 | Interview with Eddie Frow, personal collection author |
| 359 | Interview Bill Whitaker, personal collection author |
| 360 | David Carlton, Churchill and the Two 'Evil Empires', p335. Transactions of the Royal Historical Society, vol. 11, 2001, pp. 331–351. JSTOR jstor.org/stable/3679427. Accessed 8 Nov 2020 |
| 361 | AJP Taylor, Churchill: Four Faces and the Man (London 1969), p36 |
| 362 | The Case for the Second Front: and the Arguments Against it, Communist Party of Great Britain 1942 WCML |

363 Interview Frances Dean WCML
364 Interview Hugh Scanlon WCML
365 Interview Benny Rothman WCML
366 Interview Hugh Scanlon, WCML
367 Interview Margaret Gadian WCML
368 R Palme Dutt, Britain in the World Front, (International 1943) p24
369 Interview Bill Whitaker WCML
370 Interview Margaret Gadian, WCML. Marcel Cachin was one of the founder members of the French Communist Party and the editor of L'Humanitie. He stood for the French presidency on four occasions
371 George Bruce, p22
372 Calder, The People's War, p298
373 Winston Churchill, speech at Lord Mayor's Luncheon, Mansion House following the victory at El Alamein North Africa, London, 10 November 1942 oxfordreference.com/view/10.1093/acref/9780191843730.001.0001/q-oro-ed5-00002969
374 Winston Churchill, Second World War vol. 4 (London 1951) cited oxfordreference.com/view/10.1093/acref/9780191843730.001.0001/q-oro-ed5-00002969
375 Calder p349
376 Winston Churchill: Broadcast on the Soviet-German War (22 June 1941), jewishvirtuallibrary.org/churchill-broadcast-on-the-soviet-german-war-june-1941
377 George Bruce p2
378 Interview Hugh Scanlon, WCML
379 Interview Vic Eddisford, WCML
380 How to Use the Services of Every Comrade in The Fight for The Second Front Communist Party leaflet (August 1942) WCML
381 Interview with Eric Jessop, WCML
382 Mike Wild, telephone interview 2.11.2020

*Chapter 14*
383 Mick Jenkins, Prelude to Better Days. Unpublished autobiography. WCML
384 Interview Eric Jessop, WCML
385 Interview Eric Jessop WCML
386 Interview Eric Jessop WCML

| | |
|---|---|
| 387 | Interview Frances Dean WCML |
| 388 | Interview Frances Dean WCML |
| 389 | Interview with Eric Jessop, WCML |
| 390 | Jenkins, p238 |
| 391 | Jenkins p238 |
| 392 | Jenkins, p240 |
| 393 | Interview Eric Jessop WCML |
| 394 | Interview Eric Jessop WCML. For more on David Ainley see: grahamstevenson.me.uk/2010/02/22/david-ainley/ |
| 395 | Fairey Aviation, Works Committee Correspondence, WCML |
| 396 | Fairey Aviation, Works Committee Correspondence, WCML |
| 397 | Jenkins, Prelude to Better Days, p245 |
| 398 | Fairey Aviation, Heaton Chapel Works Committee Minutes, WCML |
| 399 | Jenkins, Prelude to Better Days, p260 |
| 400 | Interview Jessop, WCML |
| 401 | Interview Vic Eddisford, WCML |
| 402 | Interview Vic Eddisford |
| 403 | Croucher, Engineers at War, p346 |
| 404 | Interview Vic Eddisford WCML |
| 405 | Interview Eric Jessop WCML |
| 406 | Richard Croucher, Engineers at War 1939-1945 (London 1982). P124 |
| 407 | Interview with Hugh Scanlon by the author. Copy at WCML |
| 408 | Dick Nettleton (1922-1993) was involved in political activity from age 14 when he joined the Labour League of Youth. He moved to join the Communist Party as a result of support for the International Brigades. He met his wife Alma during the Second World War when they were both involved in organising the apprentices' strike at Metro-Vicks in Manchester. Nettleton was a national organiser for YCL in the early 1950s. He became general secretary of CND in 1967 until 1973 |
| 409 | Duncan Hallas A Soldier's Story, An interview by Clare Fermont & Chris Nineham, Socialist Review no. 186, May 1995. Duncan Hallas (1925-2004) joined the YCL and then the Trotskyist Workers International League. He served in the infantry in WW2 in France, Belgium, Germany and then Egypt where he was sentenced to 3 months in a military prison for campaigning for the demobilisation of troops. Hallas was a founder member |

of the International Socialists, which became the Socialist Workers Party. He taught at the National Council of Labour Colleges and remained in the national leadership of the SWP for 27 years as an editor, writer and speaker
410 CPGB Lancashire District records WCML
411 Apprentice's Holiday, Diary of events up to Friday 29th March 1941, Lancashire District CPGB. WCML
412 Manchester Apprentice Committee Bulletin 1941. WCML
413 Apprentices' Holiday (April 5th 1941) CPGB Lancashire District document WCML

*Chapter 15*
414 en.wikipedia.org/wiki/Rape_during_the_occupation_of_Germany#:~:text=Antony%20Beevor%20describes%20it%20as,eight%20to%20eighty%20years%20old
415 Philip Gooden, Peter Lewis, Word at War. World War Two in 100 Phrases. (London 2014) page 212
416 Interview Hugh Scanlon, WCML
417 Interview Vic Eddisford, WCML
418 Interview Vic Eddisford WCML
419 Interview Benny Rothman by the author WCML
420 McCulloch, Gary. 'Labour, the Left, and the British General Election of 1945.' Journal of British Studies, vol. 24, no. 4, 1985, pp. 465–489. jstor.org/stable/175476. Accessed 10 Dec. 2020. P466
421 Maurice Levine, From Cheetham to Cordova (Manchester 1984) p52
422 Francis Beckett, Enemy Within: The Rise and Fall of the British Communist Party (London 1995) p104
423 Interview Hugh Scanlon WCML
424 Interview Wilf Charles by the author, WCML
425 McCulloch, p468
426 Thorpe, Andrew, 'Locking out the Communists: The Labour Party and the Communist Party, 1939–46,' Twentieth Century British History, Volume 25, Issue 2, June 2014, Pages 221 – 250 doi.org/10.1093/tcbh/hwt020 p239
427 McCulloch, 'Labour, the Left, and the British General Election of 1945.' p469
428 McCulloch, 'Labour, the Left, and the British General Election of 1945.' p469
429 marxists.org/history/etol/writers/bambery/1990/xx/cp-

decline.html#f9

430 marxists.org/history/etol/writers/bambery/1990/xx/cp-decline.html#f9

431 Interview Vic Eddisford, WCML

432 Interview Vic Eddisford, WCML

433 Maurice Levine, From Cheetham to Cordova (Manchester 1984) p54

*Chapter 16*

434 Rosalyn Livshin, Non-Conformity in the Manchester Jewish Community: The Case of Political Radicalism 1889-1938. A thesis submitted to the University of Manchester for Doctor of Philosophy in the Faculty of Humanities 2015 p108

435 Tony Cliff, Lenin (volume 1) marxists.architexturez.net/archive/cliff/works/1975/lenin1/chap02.htm

436 Sai Englert, 'The Rise and Fall of the Jewish Labour Bund', International Socialism, Issue: 135, June 2012, isj.org.uk/the-rise-and-fall-of-the-jewish-labour-bund/#135 englert21

437 Yiddish is the language of the Ashkenazim, (Germany) central and eastern European Jews and their descendants. Scholars believe Yiddish emerged in the 9th century, written in the Hebrew alphabet

438 Brossat, Alain. Revolutionary Yiddishland. (Verso) Kindle Edition location 3119

439 Brossat, Alain. Revolutionary Yiddishland. (Verso) Kindle Edition location 3146

440 Kevin Morgan, Gidon Cohen, Andrew Flinn, Communists and British Society 1920 – 1991 (London, Sydney, Chicago 2007) p189

441 Isaac Deutscher, Who is a Jew? From The Non-Jewish Jew and Other Essays, Tamara Deutscher, ed. (New York 1968) P51

442 Livshin, Non-Conformity in the Manchester Jewish Community, p106

443 Bill Williams, Jewish Manchester: An Illustrated History (Derby UK 2008) p137. Williams comments that many German Jews that arrived in the late 19th century returned home because of anti-German prejudice that arose during and after the First World War

444 Maurice Levine, From Cheetham to Cordova (Manchester 1984) p3

| | |
|---|---|
| 445 | Levine, p3 |
| 446 | Levine p6 |
| 447 | Liveshin, Non-Conformity in the Manchester Jewish Community p161 |
| 448 | Levine, p21 |
| 449 | Interview Frances Dean WCML |
| 450 | Mick Jenkins, Prelude, pp16-19, cited in Liveshin Non-Conformity in the Manchester Jewish Community, p115 |
| 451 | Interview Mike Luft by the author |
| 452 | Liveshin Non-Conformity in the Manchester Jewish Community, p149 |
| 453 | Bill William, Jewish Manchester: An Illustrated History, p139. Kindertransport/Children's transport. Children were placed in foster homes, hostels, schools and farms. Often, they were the only members of their families who survived the Holocaust. The British government waived all immigration requirements that were not within the ability of the British Jewish community to fulfil |
| 454 | Bill Williams, Jews and other foreigners: Manchester and the rescue of the victims of European Fascism, 1933–40 (Manchester University Press) Kindle Edition p194 |
| 455 | Williams, Bill. Jews and other foreigners: Manchester and the rescue of the victims of European Fascism, 1933–40 (Manchester University Press). Kindle Edition, p117 |
| 456 | Leon Trotsky, 'Thermidor and Anti-Semitism' (February 1937) From The New International, Vol. VII No.4, May 1941 Transcribed for the Trotsky Internet Archive by Matt Siegfried in 1999 marxists.org/archive/trotsky/1937/02/therm.htm |
| 457 | Rosalyn Livshin, Non-Conformity in the Manchester Jewish Community, p249. Livshin lists the 20 known Jewish individuals who went to Spain from Manchester and another six unconfirmed Manchester Jewish Volunteers |
| 458 | Giles Tremlett, The International Brigades, Fascism, Freedom and the Spanish Civil War, (London 2020) p182 |
| 459 | Interview Benny Rothman WCML |
| 460 | David Mason, unpublished biography of Bert Maskey |
| 461 | Thanks to Tony Fox for this table |
| 462 | David Mason |
| 463 | Maurice Levine From Cheetham to Cordova p47 |

| | |
|---|---|
| 464 | Maurice Levine From Cheetham to Cordova p49 |
| 465 | Liveshin, Non-Conformity in the Manchester Jewish Community p172 |

*Chapter 17*
| | |
|---|---|
| 466 | Samuels, Stuart. 'The Left Book Club', Journal of Contemporary History, vol. 1, no. 2, 1966, pp. 65–86. jstor.org/stable/259923. Accessed 18 June 2021 |
| 467 | Frank Allaun, 'Culture and Politics in the Hungary Thirties', Journal of the North West Labour History Group, issue 17 1992/3 p41 |
| 468 | Andy Croft ed. The Boys Round the Corner, essay in A Weapon in the Struggle, The Cultural History of the Communist Party in Britain, (London 1998) p146 |
| 469 | Jon Heddon, 'The Left Book Club in Manchester and Salford' Journal of the North West Labour History Group, issue 21, 1996/7 p58 |
| 470 | Frank Allaun, Journal of the North West Labour History Group, issue 17 1992/3 p42. According to Mike Wild, Frank Allaun made an unsuccessful proposal of marriage to Bessie in the mid-1930s |
| 471 | Interview with Bessie Wild, Tameside Archives, Ashton U Lyne, tape 450 |
| 472 | Telephone interview with Mike Wild, 20/06/20121 |
| 473 | Ruth Frow, Edmund Frow, The Making of An Activist (Talybont 1999) p58 |
| 474 | Browne was killed on 25 August 1936 on the Aragón front near Tardienta while part of a group attempting to dynamite a Nationalist munitions train. The party was ambushed, and Browne was shot dead assisting an injured Italian republican. She had initially travelled to Barcelona to watch the People's Olympiad: the Soviet response to the Olympic Games in Hitler's Berlin |
| 475 | Daily Worker 23 September 1936 |
| 476 | Mick Wallis, 'Heirs to the Pageant: Mass Spectacle and the Popular Front' in Andy Croft ed. A Weapon in the Struggle, The Cultural History of the Communist Party in Britain, (London 1998) p49 |
| 477 | Andy Croft, The Years of Anger, The Life of Randall Swingler. (Abingdon 2020) p100 |
| 478 | Mick Wallis, The Cultural History of the Communist Party in Britain, p64 |
| 479 | Howard Goorney and Ewan MacColl ed. Agit-Prop to |

        Theatre Workshop, Political Playscripts, 1930-1950, (Manchester 1986) pxxii
480    wcml.org.uk/maccoll/theatre/the-red-megaphones/
481    Ewan MacColl, Journeyman (Manchester and New York 1990) p209
482    Edward Braun, Meyerhold on Theatre (London and New York: Bloomsbury 2016) p205. Cited: culturematters.org.uk/index.php/arts/theatre/item/2705-spotlights-and-searchlights-theatre-and-the-russian-revolution
483    Raphael Samuel, Ewan MacColl and Stuart Cosgrove. Theatres of the Left, 1880-1935, Workers' Theatre Movements in Britain and America. (Oxon 1985) Cited: wcml.org.uk/maccoll/theatre/theatre-of-action/
484    Henry Suss quotes in this chapter: Dave Chapple, Henry Suss and the Jewish Working Class of Manchester and Salford, (Somerset 2006) pp75/76
485    wcml.org.uk/maccoll/theatre/theatre-union/
486    The National Archives reference KV 2/2175Mac
487    Left Review, III, No. 6 (July 1937) p361
488    John Sutherland, Stephen Spender: A Literary Life (Oxford 2005) p209
489    Sutherland, Stephen Spender: A Literary Life p209
490    Daily Worker 19th February 1937 p4
491    Daily Worker 8th February 1938 p2
492    Daily Worker 21st October 1936, p1
493    Valentine Cunningham editor, The Penguin Book of Spanish Civil War Verse (Middlesex 1980) p44
494    Valentine Cunningham editor, The Penguin Book of Spanish Civil War Verse, p39
495    Richard Baxell, Unlikely Warriors: The British in the Spanish Civil War and the Struggle Against Fascism, (London 2012) Aurum Press. Kindle Edition. p210
496    John Sutherland, Stephen Spender: A Literary Life, p212
497    The UGT was, and still is, a general workers' union affiliated to the Spanish Socialist Workers Party (PSOE)
498    Richard Crossman ed. The God That Failed, p272
499    Valentine Cunningham ed. The Penguin Book of Spanish Civil War Verse, p40
500    Andy Croft, The Years of Anger, The Life of Randall Swingler. (Abingdon 2020) p72. Nancy Cunard to Randall Swingler, undated letter, August 1937; Orwell's reply (written on the back of the questionnaire) was dated 6th

|     | August Croft offered it to the New Statesman (18th March 1994), and was denounced in the letters' pages over the following weeks as a 'Stalinist,' while the Orwell estate threatened to sue him for breach of copyright |
| --- | --- |
| 501 | Ralph Cantorovich Diary WCML |
| 502 | Thanks to Mike Wild for permission to republish the poem, which was among his father's papers |
| 503 | theguardian.com/lifeandstyle/2009/jan/24/family-dementia-death-deborah-moggach |

*Chapter 18*
| 504 | Hill attempted to join the International Brigade but was rejected. In 1946, he and other Marxist historians formed the Communist Party Historians Group. He left the Party in 1957. His books include Puritanism and Revolution (1958), Intellectual Origins of the English Revolution (1965 and revised in 1996), The Century of Revolution (1961), Anti-Christ in 17th-century England (1971), The World Turned Upside Down (1972) |
| --- | --- |

*Index*

# Index

Abraham Lincoln Brigade  104
AEU    21, 37, 40, 48, 63, 156, 188, 193, 194, 195, 205, 208, 209, 214, 216, 232, 236, 237, 238, 239, 241, 247, 249, 250, 253, 254, 255, 256, 262, 271, 296, 319, 322, 323, 324
Ainley  26, 27, 29, 30, 32, 33, 35, 69, 240, 242, 278, 280, 281, 295, 297, 301, 315, 319, 321
Aircraft manufacture  205
Albacete  18, 96, 98, 101, 102, 110, 118, 125, 135
Allaun, Frank  36, 45, 278, 279, 290, 295, 297, 298, 321, 324, 325
Anarchism/Anarchists  89, 90, 113/148, 268
Anti-semitism  285, 286
Appeasement  84, 258
Apprentices' Strike March 1941  248
Armstrong, Alec  49, 50, 52, 57, 99, 106, 118, 194, 290, 305, 307
Attlee, Clement  19, 27, 104, 144, 154, 163, 258, 262, 264, 266, 270, 271, 281, 294, 297
Auden, WH  301, 308, 309, 311, 312, 313, 315

Basque  161, 163, 164, 165, 166, 284
Battle Of Britain  18, 177, 192, 197, 205, 215
Battle Of Brunete  36, 39, 79, 108, 111, 112, 117, 127, 145, 157, 311
Beckett, Clem 77, 95, 118
Bernard Mckenna  39, 83, 99, 100, 101, 112, 113, 114, 139, 140, 141, 145, 287, 323
Berry, Bessie 159
Bevan, Aneurin  56, 229, 262, 295
Bevin, Ernest 254, 259, 317
Bexley Square  49, 52, 57
Blackshirts  10, 29, 55, 58, 59, 60, 64, 67, 68, 69, 70, 71, 73, 80, 81, 95, 136, 154, 170, 278, 281, 282, 289, 292, 318
Bolsheviks  84, 188, 224, 231, 275, 276, 304, 305
Brown, George 32, 41, 118, 133, 134, 136, 157, 287, 323
Browne, Felicia 300
BUF  29, 58, 59, 60, 61, 62, 64, 65, 66, 69, 70, 71, 73, 282, 317

Bukharin 180
Bush, Alan 301, 302

Catalonia 76, 87, 88, 90, 93, 114
Cantor, Ralph 32, 36, 69, 72, 79, 83, 117, 118, 119, 121, 122, 124, 125, 127, 129, 132, 134, 287, 290, 313
Caudwell, Christopher 76, 77
Challenge Club 17, 30, 35, 36, 40, 68, 69, 73, 79, 80, 158, 166, 280, 282, 290, 291, 295
Chamberlain, Neville 100
Cheetham 7, 17, 29, 30, 33, 35, 36, 37, 38, 39, 40, 41, 56, 61, 62, 63, 66, 67, 68, 69, 70, 72, 79, 80, 98, 117, 124, 125, 127, 129, 133, 154, 155, 158, 159, 166, 176, 190, 236, 237, 271, 277, 278, 279, 280, 281, 282, 285, 286, 288, 289, 290, 291, 292, 295, 305, 313
Churchill, Lady 230
Churchill, Winston 78, 322
Class Against Class 26, 27, 95, 282
Clyne sisters 278, 292
CNT 21, 75, 90, 91, 93
Cold War 19, 269, 270, 302
Colman, Jud 37, 108, 127, 278, 279, 287
Comintern 21, 24, 25, 26, 27, 29, 37, 41, 76, 95, 98, 147, 169, 170, 173, 176, 178, 180, 231, 266, 268, 269, 282, 312
Cornford, John 33, 76, 95, 103, 131, 315
Copeman, Fred 108, 122, 145, 159

D-Day 19, 219, 220
Dean, Frances 30, 37, 176, 187, 189, 195, 207, 225, 238, 239, 240, 280, 322
Delasalle, Gaston 103, 104, 119
Dieppe 223
Dimitrov, Georgi 173

Ebro 83, 95, 108, 109, 111, 114, 144, 160
Economic League 28, 48

Factory branches 27, 231, 234, 244, 245, 246, 248, 261, 271
Faireys 27, 235, 236, 237, 239, 241, 242, 243, 244
Fox, Ralph 103, 118, 119, 120, 131
Franco, Francisco 18, 87, 93
Frow, Eddie 9, 10, 15, 26, 28, 29, 37, 47, 49, 50, 51, 53, 128, 176, 195, 223, 231, 296, 298, 301, 303, 322

Gadian, Margaret 10, 28, 31, 37, 190, 215, 227, 228

*Index*

General Strike of 1926  9, 27, 29, 38, 51, 157, 210, 265, 317, 323
Greenwood, Walter 43, 49, 50, 51, 53
Goldman, Benny 38, 81, 82, 83, 96, 100, 102, 105, 114, 118, 124, 287
Gollancz, Victor 126, 185, 279, 294, 311
Guernica  75, 161, 164, 268

Hallas  252
Holocaust  264, 283

Jarama  36, 39, 52, 77, 78, 81, 83, 84, 101, 102, 104, 105, 106, 107,
       108, 109, 110, 111, 114, 122, 123, 136, 143, 144, 146, 149,
       150, 157, 290, 307
Jeans, Arnold  36, 76, 78
Jenkins, Mick  32, 33, 38, 99, 132, 133, 177, 178, 236, 240, 242, 243,
       244, 278, 280, 286, 323
Jessop, Eric 31, 38, 189, 211, 233, 235, 237, 238, 240, 241, 242, 243,
       244, 246, 257, 281, 317
Joint production committees  265

Kinder Trespass  302
Krasnodar  200
Kristallnacht  283

Labour Party  21, 23, 26, 27, 31, 36, 45, 46, 51, 55, 56, 62, 71, 84, 136,
       144, 153, 154, 155, 156, 158, 159, 188, 195, 246, 261, 262,
       263, 264, 266, 267, 289, 291, 294, 297, 321, 322, 323
Lee, Fred 262, 263
Lenin  24, 25, 30, 35, 38, 40, 48, 91, 92, 188, 274
Lenin School  30, 35, 38, 40
Levine, Maurice 32, 39, 52, 59, 63, 64, 67, 68, 69, 70, 72, 75, 77, 78, 83,
       97, 101, 103, 104, 105, 107, 112, 117, 118, 122, 123, 124, 127,
       129, 132, 133, 134, 145, 162, 263, 271, 277, 279, 280, 281,
       286, 287, 289, 290
Lopera  103, 104, 117, 118, 119, 120, 130

MacColl, Ewan 10, 33, 41, 50, 52, 57, 160, 293, 302, 305, 315
Madrid  11, 18, 88, 92, 93, 104, 105, 107, 112, 124, 127, 130, 150, 155,
       158, 177
Madrigueras  102, 103, 105
Mann, Tom 9, 47, 196, 301
Maskey, Albert 39
Maurice Ryan  108, 149
Means Test  17, 29, 31, 43, 46, 49, 51, 52, 258, 317
Metro-Vicks  27, 37, 40, 70, 84, 156, 177, 181, 187, 188, 193, 195, 206,
       207, 210, 211, 212, 213, 214, 226, 231, 244, 245, 248, 249,

250, 251, 252, 253, 255, 256, 262, 264, 265, 281, 286, 319, 323
Miller, Jimmie  43, 45, 49, 50, 52, 302
Mitford  55, 73
Morrison, Herbert 73, 194, 266
Mosley, Oswald 45, 55, 56, 58, 65, 66, 96
Murphy, JT 24, 26, 27
Mussolini, Benito 17, 58

Nazi-Soviet pact  174, 178, 185, 191, 279, 297, 318
Night Of The Long Knives  71
Norman, Joe 30, 40, 83, 84, 97, 108, 109, 110, 111, 112, 139, 140, 141, 142, 145, 149

Orwell, George 75, 76, 163, 294, 312

Pollitt, Harry 24, 71, 76, 97, 127, 135, 136, 146, 159, 169, 172, 173, 175, 176, 177, 180, 183, 196, 202, 215, 223, 225, 227, 245, 264, 267, 289, 301, 306
Popular front strategy  25, 178, 246
POUM  75, 76, 312

Red Army  19, 110, 112, 149, 185, 198, 199, 219, 224, 226, 227, 230, 232, 241, 257
Red Megaphones  44, 49, 303, 304
Rothman, Benny 10, 33, 40, 56, 57, 62, 64, 70, 72, 81, 157, 176, 177, 187, 211, 213, 226, 262, 278, 281, 286, 323

Scanlon, Hugh 40, 81, 156, 158, 176, 181, 188, 193, 202, 210, 212, 214, 226, 227, 231, 247, 249, 253, 255, 261, 262, 264, 318, 319, 322, 324
Show trials  18, 173, 180, 279, 309
Soviet Union  21, 25, 38, 57, 85, 102, 145, 147, 148, 154, 158, 159, 169, 170, 171, 172, 173, 174, 176, 177, 179, 180, 184, 185, 187, 192, 193, 196, 197, 198, 201, 208, 212, 219, 221, 222, 224, 225, 229, 230, 233, 243, 244, 249, 268, 269, 279, 285, 289, 294, 297, 304, 310, 318
Spanish Medical Aid Committee  82, 155, 309
Spender, Stephen 33, 76, 126, 308, 309, 315
Stalin  18, 25, 26, 33, 48, 95, 120, 170, 173, 174, 180, 181, 197, 198, 216, 219, 220, 221, 222, 224, 225, 229, 230, 231, 232, 233, 262, 266, 268, 269, 270, 271, 273, 279, 285, 322
Stalingrad  19, 230
Strachey  56, 57, 66, 179, 185, 294, 295, 297
Suss, Henry 41, 159, 160, 176, 179, 190, 305, 324
Swingler, Randall 7, 33, 171, 186, 301, 308, 309, 312, 315

*Index*

Taylor, Evelyn 29, 41, 63, 64, 136, 323
Textiles 36, 45, 61
Trotsky 26, 173, 180, 285

Valencia 78, 84, 93, 104, 105, 107, 118, 177, 309, 311
VE Day 19, 317
Shammah, Vic 99, 118, 278, 286

Wild, Bessie 28, 32, 41, 62, 81, 153, 158, 297, 324
Wild, Sam 7, 33, 42, 79, 80, 81, 83, 96, 101, 102, 106, 108, 109, 110, 111, 114, 124, 145, 146, 147, 148, 149, 150, 151, 157, 159, 163, 186, 191, 196, 201, 202, 233, 288, 289, 307, 308, 313, 314, 318, 325

YCL 7, 21, 26, 27, 30, 35, 36, 37, 38, 39, 40, 41, 67, 68, 69, 70, 72, 76, 77, 80, 98, 108, 133, 158, 166, 187, 195, 237, 248, 249, 250, 253, 255, 278, 279, 280, 281, 282, 286, 288, 290, 303, 305, 322, 323